The UML Profile for Framework Architectures

The Addison-Wesley Object Technology Series

Grady Booch, Ivar Jacobson, and James Rumbaugh, Series Editors

For more information check out the series web site [http://www.aw.com/cseng/otseries/].

Armour/Miller, *Advanced Use Case Modeling, Volume 1*

Atkinson, *Component-based Product line Engineering with UML*

Binder, *Testing Object-Oriented Systems: Models, Patterns, and Tools*

Blakley, *CORBA Security: An Introduction to Safe Computing with Objects*

Booch, *Object Solutions: Managing the Object-Oriented Project*

Booch, *Object-Oriented Analysis and Design with Applications, Second Edition*

Booch/Rumbaugh/Jacobson, *The Unified Modeling Language User Guide*

Box, *Essential COM*

Box/Brown/Ewald/Sells, *Effective COM: 50 Ways to Improve Your COM and MTS-based Applications*

Cockburn, *Surviving Object-Oriented Projects: A Manager's Guide*

Collins, *Designing Object-Oriented User Interfaces*

Conallen, *Building Web Applications with UML*

D'Souza/Wills, *Objects, Components, and Frameworks with UML-The Catalysis Approach*

Douglass, *Doing Hard Time: Developing Real-Time Systems with UML: Objects, Frameworks, and Patterns*

Douglass, *Real-Time UML, Second edition: Developing Efficient Objects for Embedded Systems*

Fowler, *Analysis Patterns: Reusable Object Models*

Fowler/Beck/Brant/Opdyke/Roberts, *Refactoring: Improving the Design of Existing Code*

Fowler/Scott, *UML Distilled. Second Edition: A Brief Guide to the Standard Object Modeling Language*

Gomaa, *Designing Concurrent, Distributed, and Real-Time Applications with UML*

Gorton, *Enterprise Transaction Processing Systems: Putting the CORBA OTS, Encina++ and Orbix OTM to Work*

Heinekiens, *Building Scalable Database Applications: Object-Oriented Design, Architectures, and Implementations*

Hofmeister/Nord/Dilip, *Applied Software Architecture*

Jacobson/Booch/Rumbaugh, *The Unified Software Development Process*

Jacobson/Christerson/Jonsson/Overgaard, *Object-Oriented Software Engineering: A Use Case Driven Approach*

Jacobson/Ericsson/Jacobson, *The Object Advantage: Business Process Reengineering with Object Technology*

Jacobson/Griss/Jonsson, *Software Reuse: Architecture, Process and Organization for Business Success*

Jordan, *C++ Object Databases: Programming with the ODMG Standard*

Kruchten, *The Rational Unified Process, An Introduction, Second Edition*

Lau, *The Art of Objects: Object-Oriented Design and Architecture*

Leffingwell/Widrig, *Managing Software Requirements: A Unified Approach*

Marshall, *Enterprise Modeling with UML: Designing Successful Software through Business Analysis*

Mowbray/Ruh, *Inside CORBA: Distributed Object Standards and Applications*

Oestereich, *Developing Software with UML: Object-Oriented Analysis and Design in Practice*

Page-Jones, *Fundamentals of Object-Oriented Design in UML*

Pohl, *Object-Oriented Programming Using C++, Second Edition*

Pooley/Stevens, *Using UML: Software Engineering with Objects and Components*

Quatrani, *Visual Modeling with Rational Rose 2000 and UML*

Rector/Sells, *ATL Internals*

Reed, *Developing Applications with Visual Basic and UML*

Rosenberg/Scott, *Use Case Driven Object Modeling with UML: A Practical Approach*

Royce, *Software Project Management: A Unified Framework*

Ruh/Herron/Klinker, *IIOP Complete: Understanding CORBA and Middleware Interoperability*

Rumbaugh/Jacobson/Booch, *The Unified Modeling Language Reference Manual*

Schneider/Winters, *Applying Use Cases: A Practical Guide*

Shan/Earle, *Enterprise Computing with Objects: From Client/Server Environments to the Internet*

Warmer/Kleppe, *The Object Constraint Language: Precise Modeling with UML*

White, *Software Configuration Management Strategies and Rational ClearCase: A Practical Introduction*

Component Software Series

Clements Szyperski, Series Editor

Allen, *Realizing eBusiness with Components*

Cheesman/Daniel, *UML Components: A Simple Process for Specifying Component-Based Software*

The UML Profile for Framework Architectures

Marcus Fontoura
Wolfgang Pree
Bernhard Rumpe

An imprint of **Pearson Education**

Boston • San Francisco • New York • Toronto • Montreal • London • Munich •
Paris • Madrid • Cape Town • Sydney • Tokyo • Singapore • Mexico City

PEARSON EDUCATION LIMITED

Head Office:
Edinburgh Gate
Harlow CM20 2JE
Tel: +44 (0)1279 623623
Fax: +44 (0)1279 431059

London Office:
128 Long Acre,
London WC2E 9AN
Tel: +44 (0)20 7447 2000
Fax: +44 (0)20 7240 5771

Web site: www.aw.com/cseng

First published in Great Britain in 2002

© Pearson Education Limited 2002

The rights of Marcus Fontoura, Wolfgang Pree, and Bernhard Rumpe to be identified as Authors of this Work have been asserted by them in accordance with the Copyright, Designs and Patents Act 1988.

ISBN 0-201-67518-8

British Library Cataloguing in Publication Data
A CIP catalogue record for this book is available from the British Library.

Library of Congress Cataloging in Publication Data
Applied for.

All rights reserved; no part of this publication may be reproduced, stored in a retrieval system, or transmitted in any form or by any means, electronic, mechanical, photocopying, recording, or otherwise without either the prior written permission of the Publishers or a licence permitting restricted copying in the United Kingdom issued by the Copyright Licensing Agency Ltd, 90 Tottenham Court Road, London W1P 0LP.

The programs in this book have been included for their instructional value. The publisher does not offer any warranties or representations in respect of their fitness for a particular purpose, nor does the publisher accept any liability for any loss or damage (other than personal injury or death) arising from their use.

Many of the designations used by manufacturers and sellers to distinguish their products are claimed as trademarks. Pearson Education Limited has made every attempt to supply trademark information about manufacturers and the products mentioned in this book.

10 9 8 7 6 5 4 3 2 1

Typeset by Pantek Arts Ltd, Maidstone, Kent
Printed and bound by Biddles Ltd of Guildford and King's Lynn

The Publishers' policy is to use paper manufactured from sustainable forests.

Table of contents

Preface   x

Part I: The UML-F profile   1

Chapter 1: Why a UML profile for frameworks?   3

1.1 UML profiles   3
1.2 Object-oriented frameworks–extensibility is the key   5
    1.2.1 White-box components of frameworks   7
    1.2.2 Black-box components of frameworks   8
1.3 Pros and cons of frameworks   9
    1.3.1 UML-F as a means of supporting framework
           development and adaptation   10
1.4 Goals for the UML-F profile   11

Chapter 2: UML essentials for framework documentation   13

2.1 UML overview   14
2.2 Class diagrams   15
2.3 Object diagrams   19
    2.3.1 Object diagram example   19
    2.3.2 Exemplar nature of object diagrams   21
2.4 Sequence diagrams   22
    2.4.1 Sequence diagram example   23
    2.4.2 Considerations about collaboration diagrams   24
2.5 Summary   26

Chapter 3: Basic elements of the UML-F profile   27

3.1   UML-F as a profile   28
    3.1.1   Properties of the UML-F profile   28
3.2   UML-F tags – standard UML tagged values and stereotypes unified   31
    3.2.1   Stereotypes   31
    3.2.2   Tagged values   33
    3.2.3   UML-F tags for describing properties   34
3.3   Standard UML tags for framework documentation   35
3.4   UML-F presentation tags   38
    3.4.1   Completeness and abstraction   38
    3.4.2   Flat and hierarchical representation of classes and expanded class views   41
    3.4.3   UML-F extensions of the object diagram notation   44
    3.4.4   Tags for sequence diagrams   45
3.5   UML-F framework tags   51
    3.5.1   Framework and application classes   52
    3.5.2   Overview of adaptation tags   53
    3.5.3   Method adaptation tags   54
    3.5.4   Tags in the context of classes and interfaces   57
    3.5.5   Tags in the context of generalization   59
3.6   The UML-F mechanism for defining new tags   63
3.7   Summary   65

Chapter 4: UML-F tags for framework construction principles and patterns   67

4.1   Unification principle – adaptation by inheritance   68
    4.1.1   UML-F template and hook tags   72
    4.1.2   UML-F tags for the Unification construction principle   77
4.2   Separation principle – adaptation through composition   79
    4.2.1   Compositional adaptation with predefined black-box components   80
    4.2.2   Extending a set of black-box components at runtime   81
    4.2.3   UML-F tags for the Separation construction principle   83
4.3   Terminology and concept excursion: abstract classes, abstract coupling, Java interfaces   87
    4.3.1   Abstract classes and abstract coupling   87
    4.3.2   Java interfaces   88

		Hooks as name designators of pattern catalog entries	91
4.4			
	4.4.1	GoF patterns with a template–hook unification	92
	4.4.2	GoF patterns with a template–hook separation	93
	4.4.3	GoF patterns with recursive template–hook combinations	94
4.5		UML-F tags for framework patterns	95
	4.5.1	UML-F tags for the Factory Method pattern	97
	4.5.2	UML-F tags for the Strategy pattern	99
	4.5.3	UML-F tags for the Composite pattern	103
	4.5.4	UML-F tags for a domain-specific pattern	107
	4.5.5	UML-F tags for non-framework GoF patterns?	110
4.6		How essential framework construction principles scale	110
	4.6.1	Finding a balance between template and hook methods	111
4.7		Summary	112

Chapter 5: Framework adaptations of UML-F pattern annotations — 113

5.1	Cookbooks for framework adaptation	113
5.2	A sample cookbook recipe	116
5.3	Recipe for adapting the Unification construction principle	119
5.4	Recipe for adapting the Separation constuction principle	120
5.5	Recipe for adapting the Composite pattern	121
5.6	Automating the adaptation of UML-F pattern annotations	123
5.7	Summary	123

Part II: UML-F @ work — 125

Chapter 6: UML-F based documentation and adaptation of the JUnit testing framework — 127

6.1		An overview of JUnit	127
	6.1.1	Test cases	129
	6.1.2	Test suites	130
	6.1.3	Reporting the test results	132
6.2		Recipe for defining new tests	134
	6.2.1	Recipe for creating automated tests in JUnit	135
	6.2.2	Cookbook recipe for the definition of a test case	137
	6.2.3	Definition of several test cases in one source code file	140

6.3	Organizing test cases into test suites	144
	6.3.1 A cookbook recipe for composing a test suite	144
	6.3.2 Adaptation of a sample test suite	146
6.4	Reporting test results	147
6.5	Summary	149

Chapter 7: Hints and guidelines for the framework development and adaptation process — 151

7.1	The cluster cycle process model of framework development and adaptation	152
7.2	Defining the key abstractions as an initial step	156
7.3	Class families, class teams, and subsystems	157
7.4	Identification of a framework's variation points	160
	7.4.1 Variation point driven framework development	160
	7.4.2 Definition of a specific object model	162
	7.4.3 Variation point identification	162
	7.4.4 Framework (re)design	163
	7.4.5 Framework usage	163
7.5	The AOCS framework: a case study	163
	7.5.1 Controller functionality	165
	7.5.2 The telemetry functionality	170
7.6	The AOCS manager pattern	173
7.7	Framelets as an aid to framework design	176
7.8	eXtreme Design (XD), with implementation cases	181
	7.8.1 Implementation cases as a vehicle for framework specification	183
	7.8.2 Implementation cases to cookbook recipes	184
7.9	Framework adaptions through cookbook recipes, adaptation cases, and adaptation reports	186
	7.9.1 Adaptation cases	187
	7.9.2 Adaptation reports	193
7.10	Summary	196
7.11	UML-F outlook	196

Appendix A: UML-F tag quick reference — 197

A.1	Tag notations	197
A.2	Presentation tags	198
	A2.1 Completeness and hierarchy tags	198
	A2.2 Enhanced graphical inheritance indicators	198
	A2.3 Sequence diagram tags	199
A.3	Basic framework modeling tags	200
A.4	Essential tags for the framework construction principles	200
	A4.1 Template and hook tags	200
	A4.2 Tags for the Unification and Separation construction principles	201
	A.4.3 Tags for Composite, Decorator, and Chain of Responsiblility	201
A.5	Framework pattern tags	202

Appendix B: UML-F tags for the GoF framework patterns — 203

B.1	Factory Method pattern tags	204
B.2	Template Method pattern tags	205
B.3	Abstract Factory pattern tags	206
B.4	Bridge pattern tags	208
B.5	Builder pattern tags	209
B.6	Command pattern tags	210
B.7	Interpreter pattern tags	212
B.8	Observer pattern tags	213
B.9	Prototype pattern tags	214
B.10	State pattern tags	216
B.11	Strategy pattern tags	217
B.12	Composite pattern tags	218
B.13	Decorator pattern tags	219
B.14	Chain of Responsibility pattern tags	220

Bibliography — 221

Index — 225

Preface

The Unified Modeling Language (UML) community has started to define so-called 'profiles' in order to better suit the needs of specific domains or settings. For example, a profile for embedded systems should refine notational elements that represent real-time constraints. Another one for electronic business might take the typical software architecture of such systems, and thus its principal domain-specific entities, into consideration to come up with a UML notation tailored for that purpose.

Object and component frameworks represent a special breed of object-oriented systems – they are extensible semi-finished pieces of software. Completing the semi-finished software leads to different software pieces, typically specific applications, that share the same core. Though frameworks have been developed for a wide range of domains, they use common construction principles. For example, many of the design patterns written up by Gamma et al. (1995) rely on the framework construction principles.

The aim of the UML profile for framework architectures is the definition of a UML subset, enriched with a few UML-compliant extensions, which allows the annotation of such artefacts. Thus, the resulting profile that we call UML-F does not correspond to a specific domain, but to framework technology. Though profiles might be standardized in the future, sound proposals from various communities will get the process of defining and standardizing UML profiles started. In that sense, this book sets the stage for the UML profile for framework architectures.

The book is structured under two parts.

Part I: The UML-F profile

The first chapter promotes the UML-F profile as an essential means of describing framework architectures and summarizes framework-related terminology. The following chapters cover the UML subset on which UML-F is based, and the notational elements of UML-F that support framework modeling and annotation. This includes a mechanism to define sets of related tags for essential construction principles and design patterns.

Part II: UML-F@work

This part illustrates how UML-F is applied in the context of the sample framework JUnit. Considerations on the methodological implications of UML-F and a selection of practical hints and guidelines intended to assist in the design, development, and adaptation of frameworks complete this part.

The UML-F web site (http://www.UML-F.net) provides additional material, such as the source code of the examples discussed in the book, additional examples, research papers, and UML-F presentations.

Acknowledgments

Many people helped and advised us in the course of writing this book. Rebecca Wirfs-Brock carefully reviewed the manuscript. Her detailed hints and suggestions led to significant improvements. We would also like to thank Alan Wills and Mohamed Fayad for their helpful comments on an early version of the manuscript.

Timothy Brown, a computer science graduate from Washington University in St. Louis, not only corrected the English but also provided many useful ideas. Timothy Brown and Alessandro Pasetti co-authored Chapter 7. Several other colleagues helped us by reviewing parts of the manuscript and providing helpful feedback, including Lothar Schmitz, Heinrich Hussmann, Birgit Demuth, and Ljiljana Döhring. Thanks also go to the students of Wolfgang Pree's software architecture course at the University of California, Berkeley in the Fall semester 2000.

We thank Carlos Lucena, Edward Hermann Haeusler, Sergio Carvalho, Julio Leite (all at Pontifícia Universidade Católica–PUC, Rio de Janeiro); Donald Cowan, Paulo Alencar (at the University of Waterloo); and Marcos Borges at the Federal University of Rio de Janeiro. They made excellent comments on and contributions to a previous version of this work (Fontoura, 1999).

Special thanks go to Andrew Appel (Princeton University), and to Thomas K. Truong, Norm Pass, and Anant Jhingran (IBM Almaden Research Center, San Jose, CA) for their support regarding this work.

Finally, it was a pleasure to cooperate with the people from Addison-Wesley: Alison Birtwell, J. Carter Shanklin, Katherin Ekstrom, Claudia Orrell, and the copy editor Derek Atkins.

This work was partially funded by Nokia and the Bayerisches Staatsministerium für Wissenschaft, Forschung und Kunst under the Habilitation-Förderpreis Programm, by the Bayerische Forschungsstiftung under the FORSOFT research consortium, and the Bundesministerium für Bildung und Forschung (BMBF) under the Virtual Software Engineering Competence Center (ViSEK).

Traces of the book's history

The book was initiated by Marus Fontoura when Wolfgang and Marcus met in Rio in July 1999. A month later Bernhard joined the team. Besides the truly distributed writing (Princeton, NJ; Constance, Germany; Munich, Germany; San Jose, CA; Berkeley, CA), the authors worked on the book during a sailing trip in the Caribbean in Spring 2000. The final proof-reading was accomplished on a lake near Salzburg in August 2001, exactly two years after Bernhard and Wolfgang met there for their initial discussions.

PART I

The UML-F profile

This part presents the notational elements that comprise the UML-F profile. Chapter 1 points out what a profile is and why the development and adaptation of framework architectures requires one.

The UML presentation in Chapter 2 follows a trend in the UML community. As UML has become quite complex, development teams often use subsets for modeling systems. This chapter summarizes a UML subset that has proven useful in several framework projects and thus forms the basis of UML-F. That UML subset stresses class, object, and sequence diagrams.

Chapter 3 discusses the extension mechanism that UML-F relies on. The tag concept is defined as a unification and improvement of the UML extension mechanisms tagged values and stereotypes. This chapter also presents the basic UML-F tags used for framework modeling.

Chapter 4 builds on the basic tags in Chapter 3. It defines the tags for the framework construction principles, and discusses how to define tags for modeling and annotating design patterns.

Chapter 5 describes how UML-F tags and adaptation cookbooks can be used together to support a framework user in the adaptation process. It presents recipes for some of the framework construction principles discussed in Chapter 4.

Chapter 1

Why a UML profile for frameworks?

Over the past decade, object technology has gained widespread use in software development. The Java programming language and its associated products have significantly contributed to the broad acceptance of the object-oriented paradigm. Overall, three essential concepts comprise object technology: information hiding, inheritance/polymorphism, and dynamic binding. The mixing ratio of these ingredients defines the flavors of object technology. Object-based systems stress information hiding. Object-oriented systems add inheritance and dynamic binding. Object-oriented frameworks form a special breed of object-oriented systems with extensibility as a key characteristic. This chapter first describes what a UML profile is. It goes on to outline the characteristics of object-oriented frameworks. These characteristics provide more concise means for describing such artifacts necessary than provided by standard UML.

1.1 UML profiles

UML is a large and regrettably complex language. Still, there are many requests to represent additional features explicitly that cannot be described conveniently with UML in its current version. Therefore, UML provides mechanisms, in particular *stereotypes* and *tagged values*, that allow extensions. These extensions may be defined and grouped in so-called *profiles*. UML-F represents such a profile, with a focus on framework description. We define a UML profile as an extension of the UML standard language with specific elements. A profile provides new notational elements and usually specializes the semantics of some elements. It may also restrict the use of UML elements.

UML is intended to cover a wide variety of application domains. It is not even restricted to describing software, but offers concepts to describe hardware as well as real-word requirements. Apparently these different domains require different modeling elements. Therefore, it became clear quite early on that UML was not going to become a single language fitting all purposes, despite all the efforts to unify its syntax, semantics, and usage. Instead, UML is a *family of languages* with one common core. This core is defined in the UML standard documents produced by the Object Management Group (OMG, 2001).

The UML family of languages consists of individual members that extend, adapt, restrict, and/or modify the meaning of UML elements. The UML-F variant presented in this book is such a member. For a systematic introduction of new family members, UML provides a *profile mechanism*. A profile describes a modification of the UML standard. Such a profile may target a specific application domain – the UML-RT real-time profile (Powel Douglass, 2000) is a prominent example. Other profiles provide tool-specific extensions. For example, these might shape the UML so that it is better suited for modeling web-based systems: a Java profile would restrict the UML to single class inheritance; a JavaBean subprofile should additionally provide notational elements to mark classes that comply with JavaBean requirements. We suggest that you have a look at OMG's web sites to understand the current efforts in defining profiles.

Profiles usually build a hierarchy. Figure 1.1 shows a sample profile structure. Such profiles form the basis of tool-specific extensions, as well as project-specific extensions to already given profiles. The current challenge of the UML standardization process is to define a standard meaning for the important and widely used concepts. Only a few extensions should be project- or tool-specific. From Figure 1.1 it can be inferred that some profiles will be as standardized as UML itself is. UML-RT is the primary profile in that direction. A further layer of profiles may be available publicly for some time before it becomes an OMG standardized profile. Other profiles may only be used within companies, or even within projects. Project-specific profiles may be built on more general profiles, sometimes only adding a few stereotypes or specializing the meaning of object serialization. The UML-F profile is intended to be used publicly and is designed to be a general profile toolsmith which project-specific profiles can be based on.

A paper by Cook et al. (1999) describes the profiling mechanism in further detail and also an extension of it, called *prefaces*.

Chapter 1 Why a UML profile for frameworks?

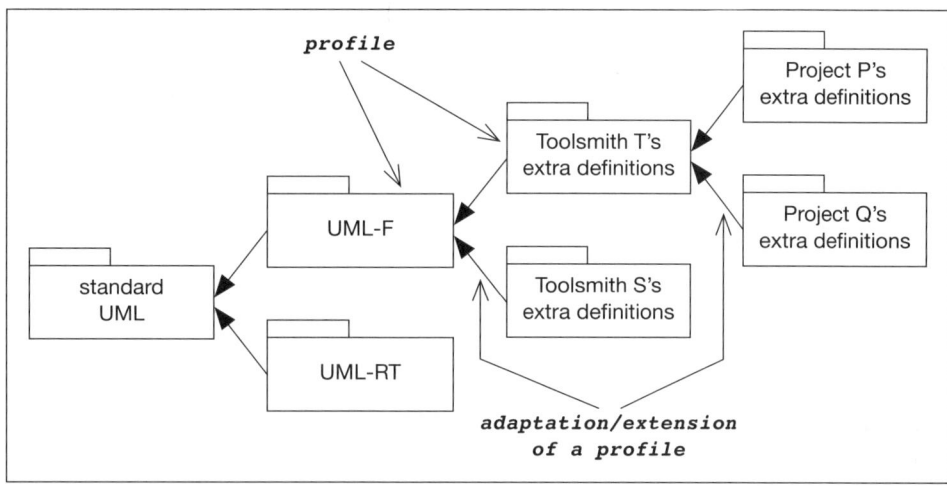

Figure 1.1 Sample hierarchy of profiles illustrated as a UML package diagram

1.2 Object-oriented frameworks—extensibility is the key

The UML-F profile focuses on object-oriented frameworks for which we define the relevant terminology in this section. What are frameworks? Instead of having to assemble systems using single Lego-like building blocks, object-oriented frameworks are prefabricated extensible sets of classes/components[1]. For example, think of a universal kitchen device into which one can plug in a certain part and use it as shaker. Another part converts the device to a meat grinder. This multipurpose device illustrates the characteristics of an object-oriented framework. It consists of several separate components such as an electric motor, a driving axle, a power plug, a switch, and a casing – all of which are assembled as a unit that offers a well-defined extension interface. An adaptation of the framework simply requires a compatible plug-in. Any future extension part compliant with the interface can be plugged into the framework. Contrast this with the effort involved in building the device from Lego-like single components. This involves selecting the appropriate components and assembling them without explicitly defining an extension interface. In other words, frameworks significantly improve reuse, as not only code is reused but also architecture design.

---

[1] The term 'component-ware' has become the vogue in the software engineering community but there are many different uses of the term 'component'. We define 'component' as a piece of software with a programming interface, deployable as unit (Pree and Templ, 2000). For a discussion of component standards we refer you to Szyperski (1998).

In general, a software framework is a piece of software that is extensible through the *call-back style* of programming (Pree and Templ, 2000). Frameworks built with conventional languages rely on function or procedure parameters. In order to modify the behavior of object-oriented frameworks, programmers apply inheritance to override dynamically bound methods in subclasses of framework classes. Note that from this point of view the Java interface construct is a similar concept that provides a conceptually analogous extension mechanism. Such method (re)definitions are analogous to providing specific procedures or functions in conventional programming – in both cases the application architecture resides in the framework.

Figure 1.2(b) illustrates the call-back style of programming. Structured programming languages, such as Pascal, provide procedures and functions as building blocks. Figure 1.2 (a) shows an application that invokes several small library routines. Contrast this with Figure 1.2(b) where the library contains a framework that is extended by passing specific procedures or functions as parameters to the framework. The framework calls them back.

Object-oriented frameworks usually consist of a collection of components with predefined collaborations between them and extension interfaces. We call the points of predefined extensions *hot spots* (Pree, 1995) or *variation points*. Figure 1.3 shows these framework characteristics in a schematic runtime snap shot (not UML) with the two variation points in gray. An adaptation of the framework plugs in specific objects instead of these placeholders. The arrows connecting method interfaces express the interaction between the concrete and abstract components. The box around the preassembled objects expresses that this ensemble can be viewed as one parameterizable component.

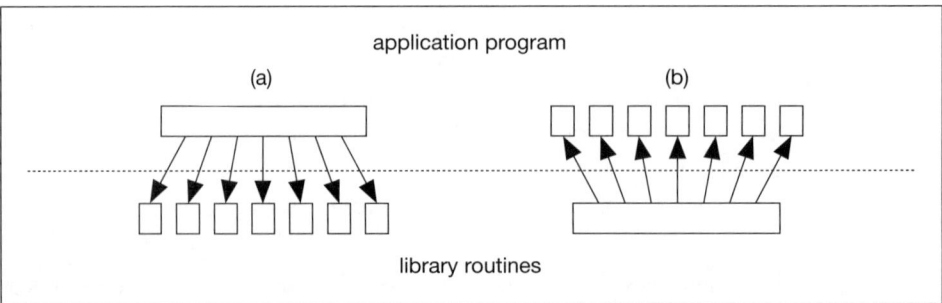

Figure 1.2   Structured (a) and call-back (b) style of programming

Chapter 1 Why a UML profile for frameworks?

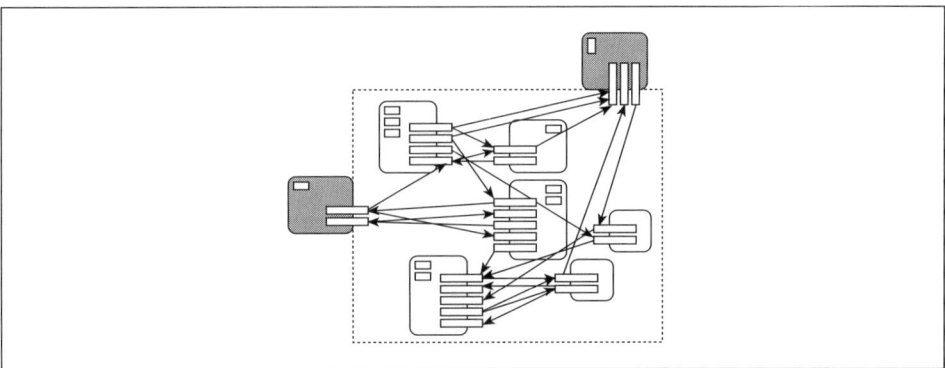

Figure 1.3 Schematic runtime snapshot of a framework with two variation points

A framework deserves the attribute well-designed if it offers the domain-specific variation points to achieve the desired flexibility via adaptation. Well-designed frameworks also predefine most of the overall architecture – that is, the composition and interaction of its components. Applications built on top of a framework reuse not only source code but also architecture design, which we consider to be an important characteristic of a framework.

1.2.1 White-box components of frameworks

Frameworks differ from ordinary class libraries since they predefine an architecture that models the interaction between several components. Nevertheless, the classes of a framework form a class hierarchy that does not differ from a class hierarchy of single components. It just might have more high-level abstract classes and/or interfaces.

White-box components of frameworks are incomplete classes – that is, classes that contain methods without meaningful default implementations. Class Promotion in the sample framework class hierarchy depicted in Figure 1.4 illustrates this characteristic. Let us assume that the framework supports the building of web-based shopping applications. A subclass of Promotion defines the rules for a customer receiving certain benefits such as discounts or gift certificates. A method box with a diagonal line represents an abstract method.[2] Class Promotion has one abstract method that has to be overridden in a subclass.

---

[2] This notation is introduced in Chapter 3.

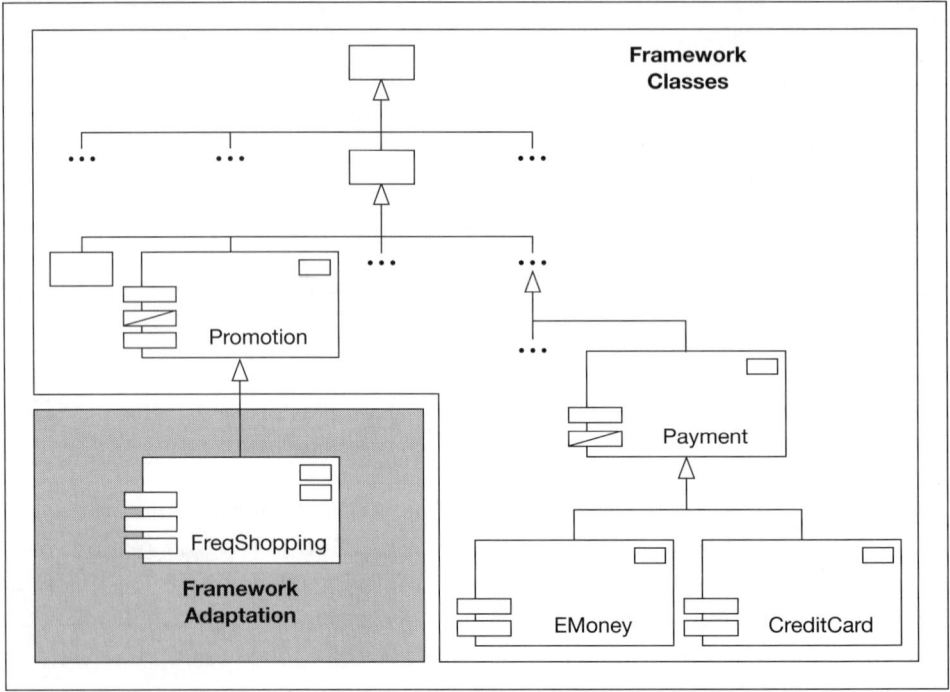

Figure 1.4 Sample framework class hierarchy

Programmers adapt the framework by overriding methods called out from other methods in the framework. The need to override methods implies that programmers have to understand the framework's design and implementation, at least to a certain degree. That makes the documentation of variation points crucial to the success of a framework.

1.2.2 Black-box components of frameworks

Black-box components are ready-made components for framework adaptations. Modifications are accomplished by composition and parameter definitions, not by conventional programming.

The framework class hierarchy in Figure 1.4 currently offers two subclasses of the abstract class Payment, EMoney and CreditCard, that provide default implementations of Payment's abstract method. Supposing that the framework components interact as depicted in Figure 1.5(a), an adaptation plugs in instances

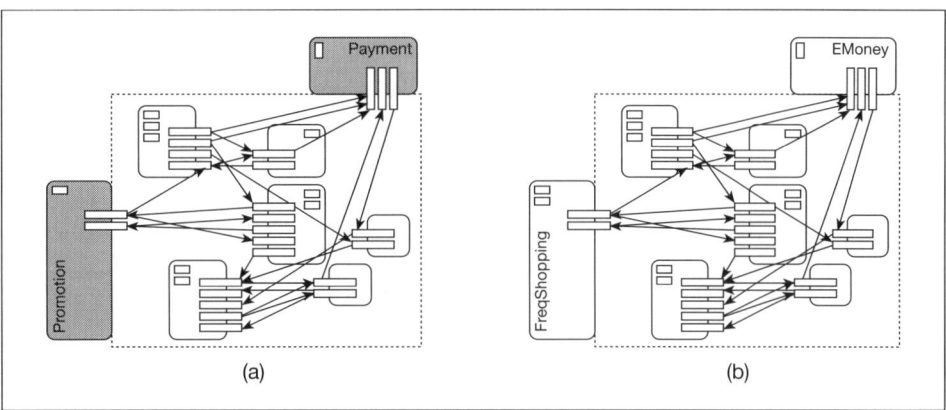

Figure 1.5 Framework (a) before, and (b) after specialization by composition

of classes FreqShopping and EMoney – see Figure 1.5(b). In the case of class Payment, the framework provides the appropriate ready-to-use subclasses; in the case of class Promotion appropriate subclasses must be created first. As the classes EMoney and CreditCard can be used as they are, they represent black-box components.

This example illustrates that frameworks typically neither provide just white-box nor just black-box components. If the framework is heavily reused, numerous adaptations will suggest which black-box defaults could be offered instead of just providing a white-box interface. So frameworks are likely to offer more and more black-box components as they mature.

1.3 Pros and cons of frameworks

Frameworks offer several advantages. Besides the fact that reuse of architecture design amounts to a standardization of the application structure, adapting a framework to produce specific applications implies a significant reduction in the size of the source code that has to be written by the application programmer. Mature frameworks allow a reduction of up to 90% (Weinand et al., 1989; Fayad et al., 1999a, b, c) compared to software written with the support of a conventional function library.

More good news is that framework-centered software development is not restricted to specific domains, such as graphic user interfaces (GUIs). Actually, frameworks are well-suited to almost any commercial or technical domain. To name just a few: process control systems, and commercial systems such as web-based software, reservation systems, and banking software.

The bad news is that framework development requires an extraordinary amount of development effort. The costs of developing a framework are significantly higher than the costs of developing a specific application. If similar applications already exist, they have to be studied carefully to come up with an appropriate generic semi-finished system – the framework for the particular domain. Adaptations of the resulting framework lead to an iterative redesign. So frameworks represent a long-term investment that pays off only if similar applications are developed again and again in a given domain.

Framework development and reuse is currently at odds with the project culture that tries to optimize the development of specific software solutions as opposed to generic ones. As this book focuses on the technical aspects of framework development, we refer to the discussion of organizational issues by Goldberg and Rubin (1995). Nevertheless, selected hints and guidelines taken from several framework projects can support the framework development and adaptation process. Chapter 7 completes the book by presenting hints and guidelines that have proved to be useful in practice and that are relevant to the UML-F profile.

1.3.1 UML-F as means of supporting framework development and adaptation

It takes a considerable effort to learn and understand a framework. The application developer can neither use a black-box nor white-box framework without knowing the basics of the functionality and interactions that the framework provides. This makes it essential to not only provide a high quality framework, but also a straightforward way to learn it. Standard UML does not offer notational elements tailored for that purpose. The extensions summarized as UML-F profile support framework development and adaptation. The UML-F profile focuses on pinpointing a framework's variation points.

So-called 'cookbooks' document frameworks and support their adaptations. They contain a set of recipes that provide step-by-step guidelines for typical adaptations together with sample source code. Chapter 5 discusses how cookbooks can benefit from the UML-F profile.

1.4 Goals of the UML-F profile

The intention of the UML profile for framework architectures is the definition of a UML subset, enriched with a few UML-compliant extensions, allowing the annotation of such artifacts. Thus, the resulting profile that we call UML-F does not correspond to a specific domain, but to framework technology. The UML-F profile presented in the book pursues the following goals.

- UML-F provides the notational elements to precisely annotate and document well-known design patterns. There currently exists only rather limited UML support for that purpose.
- UML-F is itself in the spirit of frameworks – straightforward extensibility is the key to providing a suitable means for documenting any framework pattern, including those that are produced in the future.
- UML-F comprises a lean, mnemonic set of notational elements.
- UML-F is built on the UML standard – that is, the extensions should be defined on the basis of existing UML extension mechanisms.
- The notational elements are adequate for integration in UML tool environments. For example, tools should be able to create hyperlinks between annotated framework patterns and the corresponding online pattern documentation.

More profiles will be standardized by OMG in the future, sound proposals from various communities will get the process of defining and standardizing UML profiles started. In that sense, this book sets the stage for the UML profile for framework architectures.

Chapter 2

UML essentials for framework documentation

A number of object-oriented modeling languages, such as those described by Rumbaugh et al. (1994), Coleman et al. (1994), Booch (1994), and Jacobson (1993), were defined in the early 1990s. In a determined and difficult effort, some of the best features of these modeling techniques have been merged into the UML published by OMG.[1] Furthermore, many CASE[2] tool vendors have adopted the UML as their standard notation.

This chapter presents the notational elements of UML diagrams that will be used throughout the book: class, object, and sequence diagrams. We don't discuss all the features of these diagrams but focus on the features that are of particular interest for framework development and adaptation. Thus, this chapter is not meant as yet another introduction to UML; instead, it focuses on a subset of UML notational elements that have proven useful for framework development and adaptation. Usually, this set of notational elements suffices to model frameworks. This does not mean that the other UML elements might not be used. In particular, package diagrams are helpful in the context of UML tools for structuring a class model into subsystems, and thus into subdiagrams. For a detailed and complete overview of UML, you are referred to the technical recommendation published by OMG (2001), or the books of D'Souza and Wills (1998), Booch et al. (1998), and Rumbaugh et al. (1998). A number of detailed and sophisticated technical and methodical issues is

---

[1] The UML 1.4 standard is currently (September 2001) a final draft and is mainly a consolidation of its predecessor, UML specification 1.3.

[2] CASE is an acronym for Computer Aided Software Engineering. Its basic idea is to use sophisticated tools to assist the development process. So far, many CASE tools have used their own notations.

dealt with in the UML conference series published by Bézivin and Muller (1999), France and Rumpe (1999), and Evans et al. (2000).

2.1 UML overview

Nowadays, software systems, like organisms, are far too complex to be described by a single blueprint. Instead, a number of descriptions are necessary so that each can focus on a different aspect of a system. Similar to the architecture of a building, the core structure of a software system is the foundation around which all other aspects are built. Whereas a building is a static artifact, software systems mainly derive their value from their behavior. To further complicate the situation, the structure of a software system is not a concrete, touchable thing, which makes its behavior even more difficult to describe and grasp.

The various notations provided by UML are each designed to focus on individual aspects of a software system. The static structure of a piece of software is described by the most important part of UML, the *class diagram*. A class diagram gives an overview of the whole system – it captures the structure and relationships between the components. Object diagrams are closely related to class diagrams. They are a useful and important technique to describe snapshots of a system.

UML provides several notations to describe different aspects of behavior. *Sequence diagrams* are among the most prominent, for they capture interactions between objects. They describe how several objects interact with each other through sending and receiving messages. They normally do not consider the state of participating objects.

Collaboration diagrams provide almost the same information, but in a different way. In our experience, collaboration diagrams often turn out to be harder to read than sequence diagrams – it is more difficult to understand the overall message flow. Additionally, collaboration diagrams are more difficult to manipulate, e.g. through adding new participating objects, filtering irrelevant messages, or combining two diagrams. Thus, collaboration diagrams are not used in this book, and we do not follow the line of UML documentation that suggests using these diagrams specifically for pattern presentation.

Statechart diagrams describe the life cycle of single objects: Statecharts[3] combine information about an object's state, including information about its behavior.

---

[3] First defined by David Harel (Harel, 1987).

Other kinds of diagrams focus on workflow (*activity diagrams*), on the software components and their physical distribution over several computers or nodes (*component diagrams* and *deployment diagrams*), and on describing how users perceive the system (*use case diagrams*). None of these types of diagram is used in this book.

Although UML is a complex language offering a number of notations for various aspects of a software system, these notations are not necessarily tightly coupled. This is a problem, because it makes the consistent and systematic use of several notations within a development process more difficult. But it is also an opportunity, as it allows a focus on a subset of UML. As with natural languages, it is not necessary to understand and speak the entire UML language perfectly in order to communicate. Instead, a UML subset (or a UML profile) may focus on the essentials of the context in which it is used. In this book, the focus is on the description of the relevant aspects of a framework. We identify subsets of class, object, and sequence diagrams as our basic language. These diagrams cover the structure on a general level (class diagram) as well as on an instance level (object diagram), and the intended interactions between objects (sequence diagram). The following sections introduce the relevant features of these diagrams.

2.2 Class diagrams

Class diagrams are the most important notation for object modeling. A class diagram serves several important purposes:

- a class diagram gives an overview of the type structure of a system;
- associations and generalizations shown in a class diagram describe structural relationships among classes;
- class diagrams contribute to the description of the system architecture, since components are implemented by (sets of) classes;
- several other kinds of UML diagrams, such as sequence and object diagrams, are based on class diagrams;
- a class diagram describes the set of possible states of the overall system and therefore acts as a constraint on the possible states of the system;
- attaching notes that contain constraints or implementation bodies to elements of class diagrams allows us to describe behavior to some extent – notes can also be used to describe additional information, such as the last date of change, the review status, etc.

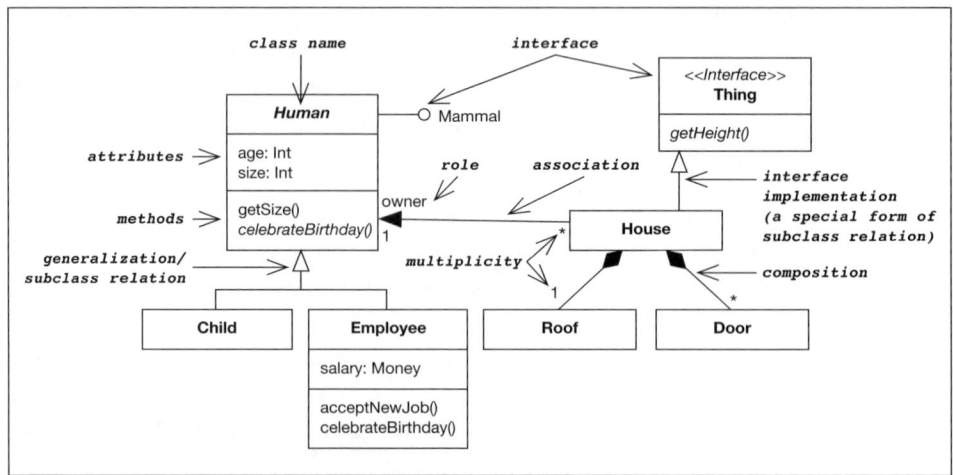

Figure 2.1 A sample class diagram

Figure 2.1 shows a sample UML class diagram that contains all the elements provided by the UML standard. The diagram consists of six *classes* (namely Human, Child, Employee, House, Roof, and Door) and two *interfaces* (Mammal and Thing). The interfaces are presented in different shapes. Thing is drawn as a class with the so-called stereotype «interface» on it, whereas Mammal is drawn as a small circle without any indication of an interface method.

Class House *implements* the Thing interface. Classes Child and Employee are *subclasses* of Human – a *generalization relation* is shown in the form of an unfilled triangular arrowhead. Generalization is a relationship between a subclass and a superclass. Compared to Java, where a subclass may have only one direct superclass, the UML standard allows classes to inherit from as many superclasses as desired. In Java, however, each class may implement an arbitrary number of interfaces. This is sufficient to allow general type hierarchies, but avoids technical involvement when inheriting the same attribute or method several times along different paths.

Furthermore, the implementation relationship between classes and interfaces and the generalization relation between classes are quite similar. Both are therefore visualized in the same way through triangles with a solid line.[4] An abstract class is drawn with a class name in italics, such as class *Human*.

Chapter 2 UML essentials for framework documentation

The unnamed *association* between the classes Human and House represents ownership. It has one *role* and two *multiplicity identifiers* attached to it. The role name 'owner' can be used to navigate from an object of class House to the corresponding Human object (its owner). A solid arrow shows the navigability of the association in this direction. Multiplicity 1 describes that there is exactly one such object. Note that associations may have quite a number of different realizations, but in many cases it is a good choice to use an attribute[5] as the implementation choice. Multiplicity * in the other direction indicates that many objects of class House may belong to one Human object. However, as there is no arrow associated with it, it is unclear whether navigation in the direction described is possible.[6]

Classes and interfaces do have signatures. An interface signature consists of methods, while a class signature consists of methods and attributes. Each method is described through its name, argument types, and return type. An attribute signature consists of name and type. The UML calls the methods *operations* – we use the terms 'method' and 'operation' interchangeably in the rest of this book.[7]

The class diagram in Figure 2.1 omits method and attribute signature lists for most classes; only the classes Human and Employee, and the interface Thing carry a signature. As class Employee *inherits* from class Human, it automatically inherits its signature, which it extends by the newly defined attribute salary and method acceptNewJob(). In an analogous way, class House inherits the signature of interface Thing and therefore has to provide an implementation of method *getHeight()*. Abstract methods are denoted in italics, as exemplified by *celebrateBirthday()* in class Human.

House objects are composed of objects of classes Roof and Door. Each House object consists of exactly one Roof object (multiplicity 1) and an unspecified number of Door objects (multiplicity *). There are a number of different flavors of object

---

[4] The UML standard 1.4 proposes the use of a dashed line for interface implementation, but that distinction from inheritance is not necessary because it is clear already from the context of the line. We suggest this simplification in UML-F to show that, from a conceptual viewpoint, interfaces and classes are just variants of each other (with different restrictions on their capability).

[5] 'Attribute' is the UML jargon for instance variable. In this book, both are used synonymously.

[6] We will later develop a concept that allows us to distinguish between the lack of information (e.g. through omission) and the explicit decision to not have the navigation available. This concept is generalized for many circumstances and nicely extends the UML standard.

[7] In general, the concept of operations embraces the notion of method implementation. In particular, operations identified in early development phases don't necessarily become methods in the implementation stage.

composition. A weak form, namely *aggregation*, is represented through an unfilled diamond.[8] Aggregation has a number of different interpretations, with some of them almost identical to normal associations. Thus, one recommendation is not to use this weak form at all. The strong form, namely *composition* (represented by a black diamond), is characterized by coincident lifetimes and unshared composed objects. This means that the composed elements do not live longer than the composition itself, and that each composed element belongs to, at most, one composition. In this example, it means that whenever a house is destroyed, the corresponding roof and doors must also be destroyed, and that each door and roof belong only to one house. For a detailed discussion, we refer to Henderson-Sellers and Barbier (1999).

Attributes and methods are given in two compartments within a class rectangle. Figure 2.2 shows how to represent these elements together with their visibility. Visibility marker '+' denotes public attributes or methods. It corresponds to Java's public language construct, allowing access from any other object. Private access is marked by '–'. It corresponds to Java's 'private' language construct, allowing access only within the scope of that object. Finally, visibility marker '#' expresses that a class and its subclasses may access this element. In C++ this is called 'protected', whereas in Java the same concept was originally called 'private protected'.[9]

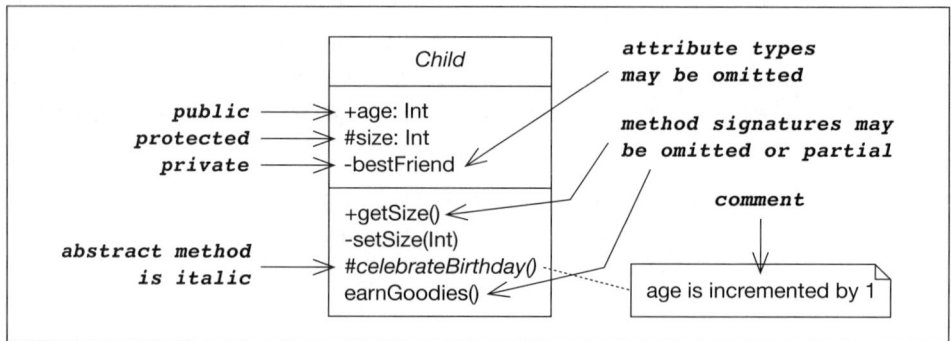

Figure 2.2 The notational elements of a class

---

[8] Unfilled diamonds, and therefore aggregation, are not shown or used anywhere in this book. Unfilled diamonds are also called 'white' diamonds. By analogy, 'black' diamonds are the same as filled diamonds.

[9] Java no longer supports the accessibility modifier 'private protected'. Java's protected accessibility modifier is about as close as you can get, but it is not quite the same since it allows classes in the same package to access the attribute or method, whether or not they are subclasses. Thus, we recommend clarification of the meaning of '#' for each specific project, or its omission from use altogether. The UML standard does not fully determine its meaning.

Figure 2.2 also contains a *comment* in a rectangle with a dog's ear. Comments can contain informal explanations (such as the one above), pseudocode, such as age+=1, or properties specified in the Object Constraint Language (OCL), such as age=age@pre+1. OCL is part of the UML standard. It is a textual supplement that allows formal specification of conditions. For a complete description of OCL, we refer to Warmer and Kleppe (1999).

2.3 Object diagrams

UML object diagrams are closely related to class diagrams. Because both deal with the structure and the data of the system, object diagrams are often not treated as a stand-alone notation but as a variant of class diagrams. Object diagrams are a useful and important technique for describing snapshots of a system – indeed, important enough to regard and introduce this kind of diagram as a notation on its own. Object diagrams are useful for conveying certain kinds of information that class diagrams cannot. Object diagrams contain objects and, thus, describe a system on an instance level that might occur at runtime. A set of object diagrams can describe variants of *object structures* to the very same class diagram. A single object diagram thus describes an *actual* object structure, whereas a single class diagram describes a *set of potential* object structures.

2.3.1 Object diagram example

The object diagram in Figure 2.3 shows one sample object structure. It is consistent with the class diagram in Figure 2.1. Objects, like classes, are drawn as rectangles. However, for a clear distinction from classes, the names of objects are underlined. A name consists of two parts – an object name, and its class name. For example, mary:Child is an object of class Child with the name 'mary'. Note that the object name must neither be confused with a variable referring to an object nor with the object identity; although in the implementation, these object names are often mapped to variable names. The object name in an object diagram is used to identify the object within the diagram. In a running system, the very same diagram structure may occur several times, thus allowing several objects to take the role of 'mary' – 'mary' can be regarded as a *prototypical* object describing a *role*.

The object name is optional and may be used to refer to that object in the explaining text. Object names in the diagram are primarily used to distinguish instances of the same class, since one diagram may contain an arbitrary number of objects of the same class. The class name can also be left out, provided that the

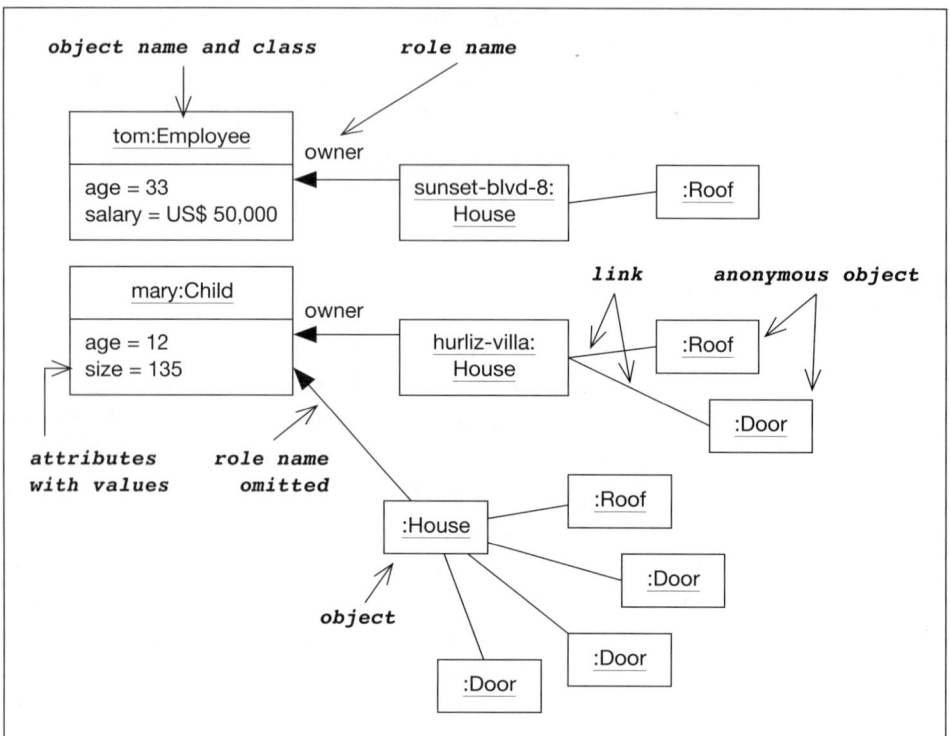

Figure 2.3 A sample object diagram

class of the object is clear from the context in which it is presented. Each rectangle in a diagram stands for a unique object, even if the objects are not distinguished by explicit names. Objects that are not given explicit names are called *anonymous* objects.

In order to clarify a certain *snapshot* the object attributes may show concrete *values*. Although subclass structures are not shown in object diagrams, the inherited attributes can be mentioned explicitly (e.g. attribute 'age' in Figure 2.3). Methods are usually not shown in an object diagram.

In the same way as an object is an instance of a class, a *link* is an instance of an association. According to the association in the class diagram in Figure 2.1, each House object has exactly one link to a Human object, namely its owner. In the opposite direction, Human (and therefore also Employee and Child) objects may have an arbitrary number of links. The given association has an arrow from class House to Human, thus allowing navigation starting from houses. This is reflected by the link carrying an arrow in that direction. Although links in standard UML are bidirectional in nature, an implementation might only allow navigation in one direction.

In this example, the role name 'owner' can be added to a link. A role name can be used in an object diagram to clarify which association a link represents. Alternatively, if an association name is given, it may also be attached to its links.

Object diagrams reflect the composition of House objects consisting of exactly one Roof object, and an arbitrary number of Door objects – composition is realized by means of links to the aggregated objects. As the class diagram in Figure 2.1 does not contain navigation arrows for the composition relationships, the object diagram also does not show navigation arrows. If desired and inferable from the context of a link, the diagram may also drop association and role names.

2.3.2 Exemplar nature of object diagrams

During runtime, a system may dynamically change its structure. New objects are created, and others become obsolete and are eventually removed from the system by garbage collection. Of course, the linkage between objects changes. An object diagram only shows a snapshot of the system. A snapshot is a partial view of the system because it does not usually show all objects and links. Furthermore, it shows the structure of the system only at a particular point in time. Figure 2.4, for example, represents another object diagram consistent with the class diagram in Figure 2.1.

Object diagrams are therefore of exemplar nature. Several of them may complement the information conveyed by a class diagram, because the latter

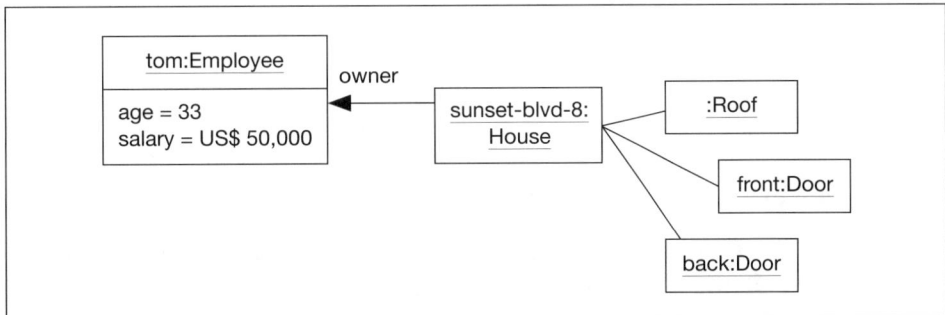

Figure 2.4   Another sample object diagram

describes all the potential snapshots. A class diagram is a constraint on snapshots in the sense that each snapshot of a system actually has to conform to the class diagram. An object diagram, instead, is useful to exemplify a particular situation, e.g. during the initialization phase, before or after a particular operation, or an erroneous state. Also, object diagrams can be used to describe the structure of a composite object or a desired object structure – and they are especially useful in describing standard situations within a framework, or in describing how objects of newly added classes integrate with existing framework objects.

Several object diagrams may coexist to exemplify different situations. In the case that explicit names are given, it is even possible to specify overlapping object structures – for example, in Figures 2.3 and 2.4 employee Tom owns sunset-blvd-8. It is important to keep in mind that an additional textual explanation may be needed to clarify which situation is described with these diagrams. Both may, for example, describe different situations in the life of Tom, e.g. before and after winning the lottery.

The situation captured by an object diagram does not necessarily occur while the system is running – it might happen that the described object composition never occurs. On the other hand, an object structure may also occur more than once – it may repeatedly occur at different points in time, or may occur several times in the same system snapshot. One of the most prominent uses for object diagrams is to describe an object structure that is created initially and that statically holds for the whole system's execution, or until its objects are deleted.

Object diagrams give a developer a useful clue about the structure of the framework to be used. Object diagrams are particularly useful in explaining framework architectures. In complex situations, or when association multiplicity of more than 1 is involved, the diagrammatic depiction of several distinct objects of the same class allows the illustration of situations that cannot be described well using class diagrams alone. Thus, object diagrams become a useful tool for the discussion of framework construction principles later in the book. Many pattern descriptions also use object diagrams to exemplify the object structures on which they operate.

2.4 Sequence diagrams

As David Harel has eloquently stated: "While bridges and other architectural buildings are there *to be*, software systems are there *to do*." Thus, it is inevitable that behavioral notations are needed in addition to structural notations. In order to describe the overall behavior of a system, it is useful to look at the interactions among its components, and its interactions with the environment. Sequence diagrams present interactions in two dimensions. At the top level, the *involved objects* are shown. From top to bottom, the order of the method calls between the objects is shown according to a *timeline*. A sequence diagram tells a story about a system. The story describes a certain aspect of the running system – namely a number of collaborating objects and how they interact in a particular situation.

2.4.1 Sequence diagram example

The sequence diagram in Figure 2.5 presents an interaction between one Bank object with the name db and two Account objects with the names a and c. The diagram shows how these objects interact in order to transfer an amount, m, between the two accounts. A transfer(m,a,c) message is issued by the environment – possibly by some user interface component. The message activates the corresponding method in the Bank object, leading to three more calls. One of these calls is *object recursive* – the log_transfer() method is invoked on Bank itself.[10]

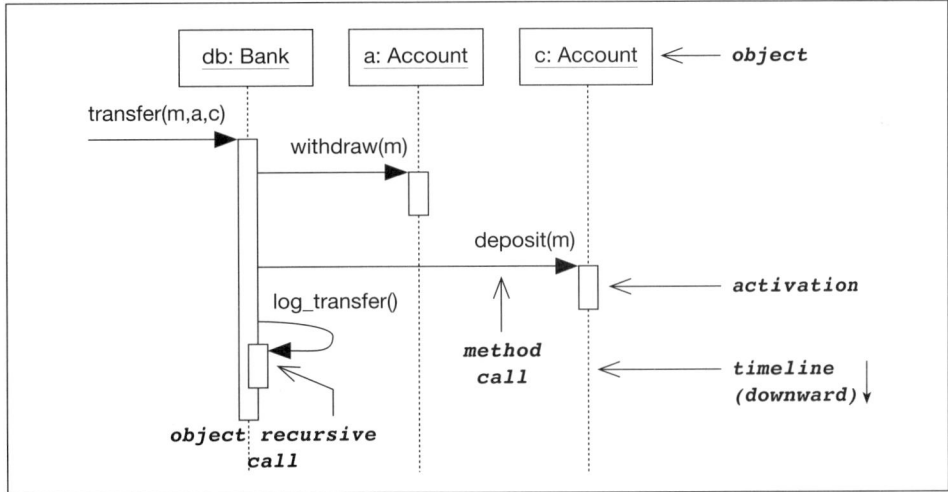

Figure 2.5   A sample sequence diagram

---

[10] A call of another method of the same object is not recursive in the sense of the classical definition, but it is object recursive. Such calling structures employ special power as a large number of design patterns are based on them. But a recursive calling structure also needs careful programming because the object state may exhibit temporal inconsistency during activation. The calling object and the calling method must be robust with regard to changes in the called methods.

The duration of a method can be shown by using an *activation box*. However, we use the timeline only qualitatively, which means the actual length of an activation box or distance between two method calls does not give any quantitative measure about execution time duration. The objects in the sequence diagram use the same naming conventions as in object diagrams.

In a system that applies information hiding, an attribute is normally only changed by the object owning that attribute. Thus, method calls are the important interactions between objects. Method calls often have return values. If it is relevant to show a return value in a diagram, a dashed arrow can be used. It also happens that an object is created dynamically during an interaction sequence. Both object creation and return values can be described in a sequence diagram, as shown in Figure 2.6. In this figure, activations are omitted. Instead, two return arrows are shown carrying the account number of the newly created Account object. This object is not drawn at the top level in the diagram in order to indicate that it is created as a reaction to the Bank object's open_account request.

2.4.2 Considerations about collaboration diagrams

UML provides an alternative way to present interaction sequences, namely collaboration diagrams. These diagrams exhibit information similar to sequence diagrams, but present it in a different form. Instead of showing a timeline, a

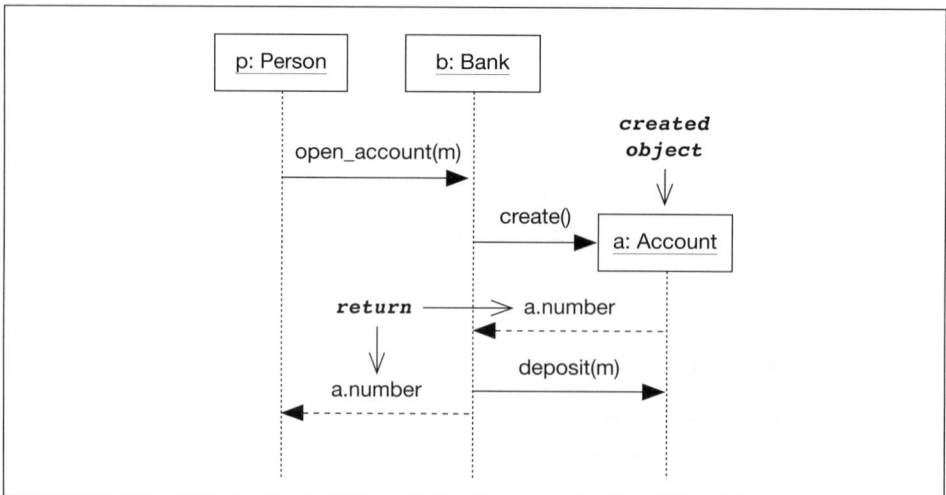

Figure 2.6   Return parameters and object creation in sequence diagrams

numbering of the interactions between the collaborating objects is used. Thus, collaboration diagrams can use two dimensions to arrange objects, instead of only the horizontal axis as in sequence diagrams. Collaboration diagrams are thus similar to object diagrams in layout and intuition.

In practice, following the time axis of sequence diagrams is often a more intuitive way to grasp the interactions than following the numbered arrows of collaboration diagrams.

UML also provides concepts to describe aspects of design patterns, by using collaboration diagrams. Figure 2.7 is taken directly from the UML standard document. It demonstrates the application of the Observer design pattern (Gamma et. al., 1995) to two respective classes. It uses constraints in a comment to describe structural invariants between participating classes. The ellipse denotes a pattern, and lines serve as connections to participating classes. However, given the generally high density of design patterns in a framework, such a representation could quickly clutter a framework class diagram. Another drawback is that it does not show which attributes or methods actually participate in a design pattern. The following chapters address this problem, introducing a significantly enhanced design pattern annotation as the core of the UML-F profile. The collaboration diagram based notation still represents an alternative and is suitable, for example, when the details of a pattern are irrelevant.

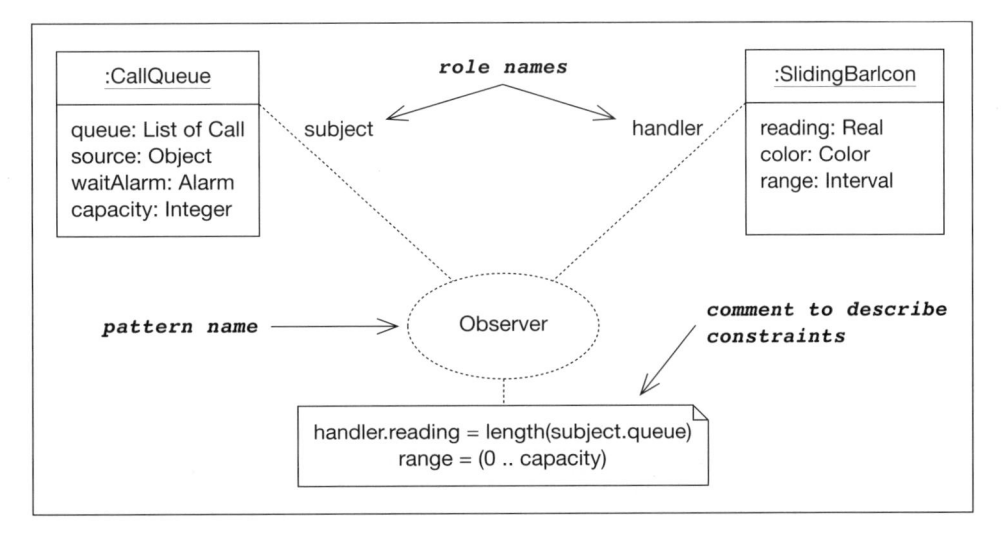

Figure 2.7   UML suggestion for pattern description

2.5 Summary

Now we are equipped with a subset of notational elements available from the UML standard. Some diagrams from the UML standard are omitted, and a number of concepts in the presented diagrams are not discussed, but we have suggested further reading in the introductory paragraphs of this chapter.

The next chapter discusses the necessary extensions to suit the needs of framework development better.

Chapter 3

Basic elements of the UML-F profile

Chapter 2 introduced a subset of UML that helps framework developers to document their products. However, framework developers want to describe more than the mere architecture and interaction patterns of a framework. They want to describe their intentions behind the architecture. The UML-F profile is designed for this purpose. The UML-F profile uses the UML 1.4 standard extension mechanisms – in particular, *stereotypes* and *tagged values* – to define these extensions.

Firstly, the profile mechanism is explained. Then the UML extension mechanism for defining profiles by unifying the concepts of tagged values and stereotypes are enhanced to what we call *tags*. A number of basic tags from the UML standard have proven useful for framework documentation. These tags are discussed and a UML extension as a set of UML-F tags that specifically support framework design and adaptation is provided. Finally, we present a mechanism that allows the definition of new tags.

In the tradition of UML, the methodical issues and the syntactic/semantic issues are presented separately. This chapter focuses on language elements, their representation, and their meaning. In succeeding chapters – and in particular in the case studies – numerous examples illustrate where and how to apply the UML-F set of language extensions.

3.1 UML-F as a profile

The UML standard provides a number of concepts to extend the language. So-called stereotypes and tagged values are a kind of UML hook concept and form the principal means of specializing or extending the meaning of particular UML elements. Section 3.2 provides a unified enhancement of these two techniques, the enhancement being used to define the UML-F profile.

UML offers another concept for extensions, namely *constraints*. If used in their full capacity, constraints have a complexity of their own and are not directly useful to our approach. In order to keep UML-F simple, we do not base it on constraints. However, a few simple constraints of standard UML are introduced as tags in UML-F.

3.1.1 Properties of the UML-F profile

First, UML-F identifies a subset of UML, namely a lightweight UML, that suffices for framework development and adaptation (see Chapter 2). This does not mean that the rest of UML should not be used. Instead it helps the framework developer to identify a subset of UML that allows the modelling of the important features of a framework.

Second, UML-F provides additional mechanisms for describing frameworks. For that purpose, UML-F adapts standard UML. Furthermore, UML-F profile targets the design and implementation of software systems. It does not focus on requirements engineering or on distribution issues – this is the main reason why a number of diagrams from UML are left out in UML-F.

A number of standard UML concepts get a more specific meaning. In particular:

- in UML-F all classes are implementation classes – in standard UML, classes can also denote real-world concepts that do not necessarily appear in an implementation;
- method calls are the primary form of considered interaction between objects;
- the composition of objects is based on associations with an additional dependency on the lifetimes of the associated objects.

The underspecification principle is applied consistently. This means that whenever some information is not present in the model, then drawing default conclusions of what the implementation will be is not allowed. For example, a missing navigation arrow just means that it is not known if navigation in that direction is possible. If a specification is complete, then it has to be explicitly marked as complete.

The underspecification principle is an important concept for a modeling language. It allows the modeling of desired features, and the omission of details that are not yet well understood by the developer. As a framework is designed for a *set* of systems with a large variety of functionality and behavior, the principle of underspecification is particularly useful for framework description. Because of its executable nature, a programming language alone cannot be used for this purpose. For example, a programming language cannot be used to describe the range of intended behaviors of a method that can be redefined in subclasses. A default implementation that is provided only shows one possible behavior, but cannot serve as a constraint on a whole behavioral spectrum. The underspecification principle applied in the context of UML is a more appropriate tool. For example, sequence diagrams with alternatives, iterations, etc. are suited for this purpose.

The described semantic specialization of UML as used in this book has already been presented in Chapter 2, and will again be apparent in the following chapters. All further adaptations of a class or its objects should be marked explicitly by appropriate tags. These tags constitute the extension part of the UML-F profile. They mainly serve the following purposes:

- some tags describe what is visible in a model representation in print or on the screen – these tags express, for example, whether the information presented is complete or incomplete;
- some tags reveal additional information about the class or object it is attached to – this can be information about the signature, behavior, interaction paths, or functionality;
- a third category of UML-F tags allows the framework developer to express his or her intention underlying a class, interface or method – this is particularly useful when the class or interface does not provide an implementation but provides a signature that is to be implemented by other classes.

Because the tags that comprise the UML-F profile partially depend on each other, they are arranged in several layers (see Figure 3.1). In the upper layers, where essential construction principles and patterns are described, usually a set of related tags (tag set) is defined for each concept. All these layers of tags are used by the framework developer to document the intended use of certain framework concepts for the application developer. These tags, therefore, give guidance to the application developer through the framework adaptation process. Furthermore, they give guidance for the enhancement of a framework, as they also allow co-developers to document their intentions. It is important to keep in mind that the framework developers are the masters of the framework – hence they change the framework and its decorating tags, and the application developers may not.

Four layers of tags are essential for the UML-F profile:

- *presentation* tags deal with the presentation of a model and can be used independently of a framework definition;
- *basic modeling* tags describe basic properties, such as adaptation flexibility, but do not reveal further information about the intention of the developer;
- tags for the *essential construction principles* are grouped into sets of related tags – such tags deal with roles of objects that participate in an essential construction principle;
- tags for *catalog patterns* and new *domain-specific patterns* are finally built on the essential construction principles – new domain-specific patterns can be introduced by using the UML-F tag introduction mechanism.

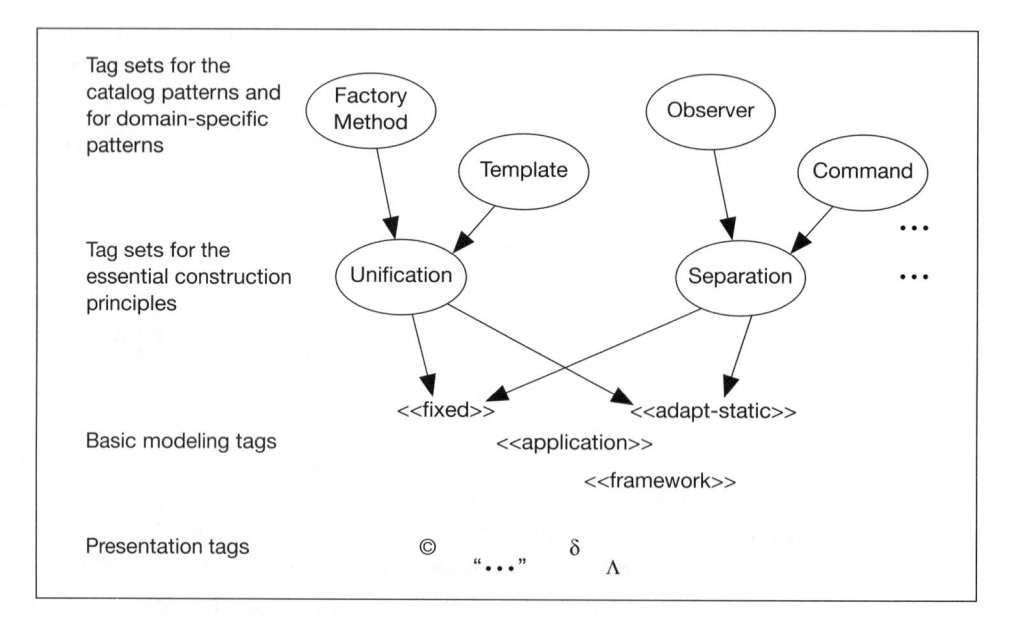

Figure 3.1 Categorization of UML-F tags according to abstraction levels

3.2 UML-F tags – standard UML tagged values and stereotypes unified

If UML did not provide built-in extension mechanisms, then it would be necessary to include countless additional concepts to the core UML in order to satisfy various requirements imposed on UML. This would result in a UML even more complex than the current standard, which might well render it useless in practice.

Let us roughly compare UML, which is a software modeling language assisted by computer tools, with an ordinary programming language. An ordinary programming language defines a small set of core concepts, and libraries provide additional functionality. The most important feature of a programming language is the ability for a programmer to extend its vocabulary, and therefore its expressiveness, through the introduction of new names for methods, classes, functions, modules, and so on. In an analogous way, UML supports vocabulary extension through the introduction of new modeling elements, such as specific classes, associations, and methods. These elements can be regarded as *first class elements*. In addition, UML provides two extension mechanisms – stereotypes and tagged values – for describing specific properties of these elements. However, these two kinds of extensions are *second class elements*, because they apply on a 'meta' level. They do not represent phenomena of the system directly, but constrain or describe phenomena of the UML model.[1]

UML-F provides an enhanced mechanism that unifies stereotypes and tagged values: the UML-F tag. The standard UML stereotype and tagged value mechanisms are discussed first.

3.2.1 Stereotypes

Figure 3.2 shows a standard use of UML stereotypes and tagged values attached to a class. Stereotypes are normally written enclosed in guillemets.[2]

The stereotype «ActionListener» attached to class AccountWindow in Figure 3.2 denotes that this class implements the ActionListener interface, as provided by the

---

[1] Meta-modeling is comparable to the meta-programming (or reflective programming) that is provided by some programming languages such as Java. Although UML meta-modeling is a powerful concept and has great appeal for some purposes, it has a number of inherent problems and should be avoided. Therefore, we don't go into a discussion on meta-modeling in this book.

[2] Tools sometimes provide specific styles of representation for stereotypes. For example, icons may be used.

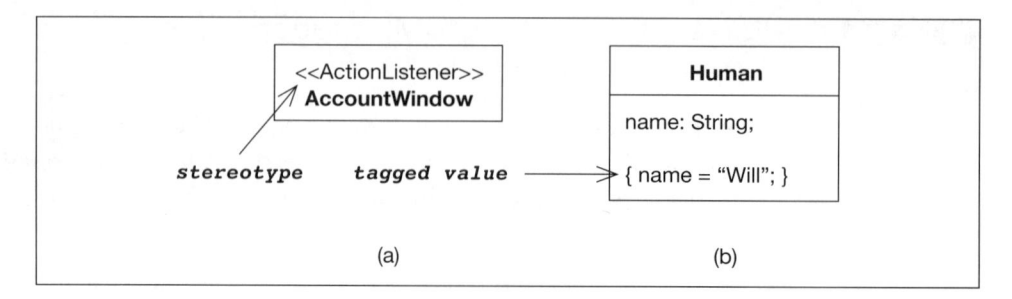

Figure 3.2 Stereotype (a) in comparison to tagged value (b)

Java Swing library. This stereotype acts as a shortcut for a representation with an implementation relationship from the interface ActionListener to the class AccountWindow.

Stereotypes can be used for several purposes. A stereotype is often used to classify (mark) model elements in order to impose certain additional properties or constraints on these model elements. The property or constraint is defined informally, because UML itself does not provide a language mechanism to introduce a stereotype explicitly and bind a certain property to it.[3] In the UML 1.4 standard, a technique based on tables is proposed to introduce new stereotypes. This technique is further elaborated in Section 3.6.

Some of the uses of stereotypes are as follows:

- A stereotype deals with the properties of the piece of software, for example a class, that the stereotype model element annotates. For example, stereotype «ActionListener» expresses that an interface ActionListener is implemented.
- The stereotype may deal with the representation of a model in a view. UML-F introduces the marker '©' that can be regarded as a stereotype whose intention is to express that a set of elements is shown completely in the model.
- A stereotype can also describe a certain constraint. For example, «persistent» may express that instances of a class are storable, without prescribing how that property is implemented.

---

[3] The use of OCL on the meta level (this is, on the abstract syntax of UML represented by a meta-model) is an attempt in that direction.

- A stereotype can also describe a methodological relationship between two modeling elements. For example, an association that is refined through an association class can have a «refine» connection to this class.
- A stereotype can express an intention of the modeler that any user of a model element should understand. For example, a class can be marked as «adapt-static» to indicate that it is a good candidate to be extended and adapted by subclasses.
- Finally, a stereotype can describe the role of a class in a collaboration pattern. This allows a compact description of the participants of particular patterns.

There is certainly overlap between these various uses of stereotypes. Furthermore, the above classification of stereotypes is probably not exhaustive as future applications of the stereotype mechanism cannot be foreseen.

3.2.2 Tagged values

Tagged values represent another UML extension mechanism. A tagged value is a pair consisting of two elements – a name and a value. As with stereotypes, tagged values can be attached to any modeling element. They can describe certain properties, such as:

- an initial value of an attribute, as in Figure 3.2(b)
- the name of the creator of a class
- the version number or the date of its last change
- a string value containing a comment or a constraint on the model element
- a policy for storage or transmission over a network
- an icon for graphical representation in a case tool.

Tagged values are written in brackets in the form {tag-name = value} and are attached to model elements. Although it could be useful to build an explicit system of types on the tagged values, this has not yet been incorporated into standard UML. Even though nothing is said in the UML standard, it is a reasonable assumption within the UML-F profile that tagged values are typed – for example, numbers identify the versions of a system: {version=2.0}; and strings represent names: {created-by = "Tom"}

3.2.3 UML-F tags for describing properties

The usage of tagged values and stereotypes is quite similar. Indeed, the border between the mechanisms is not sharp and sometimes confusion arises as to which concept to use. Since stereotypes do not have values, tagged values in general provide more descriptive power. To overcome this restriction, the UML standard suggests attaching tagged values to stereotypes as well. Unfortunately that further complicates the use of these extension mechanisms. This gives us enough reason to adapt the usage of stereotypes and regard them as a restricted form of tagged values of type Boolean. In particular, the stereotype «stereotype-name» is regarded as a shortcut for the Boolean tagged value {stereotype-name = True}.

The standard UML also offers a shorthand for Boolean tagged values if the value is True: {tagged-value-name}.

In the rest of this book, a stereotype is treated as a synonym for a tagged value (or *tag* for short), and for a Boolean tag it is equivalent to write:

- «name»
- «name = True»
- {name}
- {name = True}.

A tag with a value of a type different from Boolean – for example, a version number – may be written in the equivalent forms:

- «name = value»
- {name = value}.

With this enhancement and unification of UML's extension mechanisms, it is now possible to attach any number of tags to a model element.[4] Of course, not all combinations of tags are allowed and tools should therefore detect inconsistent use of tags.

---

[4] We expect future versions of UML to adopt this unification of stereotypes and tagged values.

To further enhance the expressiveness of tags, UML-F allows combining tags in the form of enumerated lists, for example «name1=value1; name2=value2», provided that they are applied to the same model element. In addition, UML-F introduces another shortcut. If the type of the tag is a string, then «name» is a shortcut for attaching a tag with an empty string: «name=""». This allows us to apply a tag of type string omitting the string if it is not of interest in a certain situation. As strings are often used as values, we also find it convenient to write «name:value» instead of «name="value"», and «name1,name2:value» as a shortcut for attaching the same string value to several tags: «name1="value"; name2="value"». Figure 3.3 illustrates the use of UML-F tags.

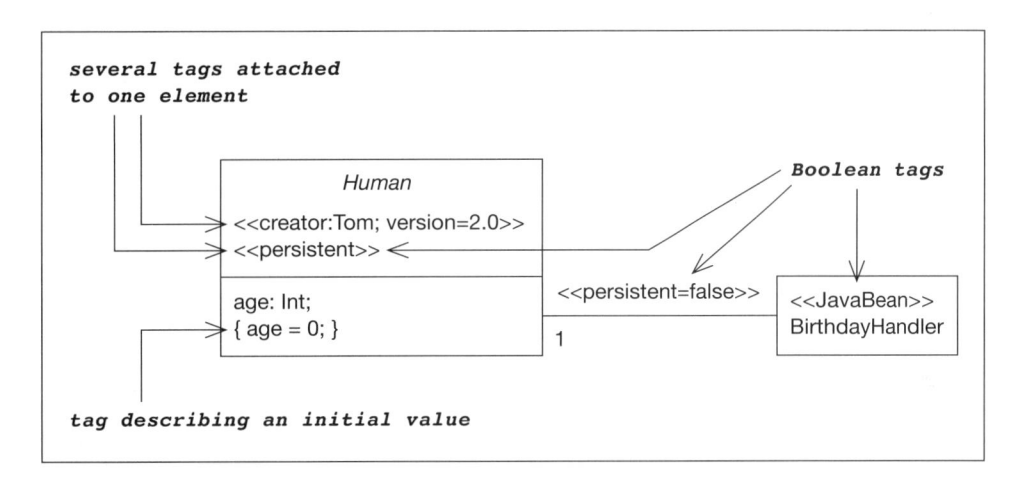

Figure 3.3   Sample UML-F tags

3.3 Standard UML tags for framework documentation

UML version 1.3 lists 47 stereotypes and seven tagged values (OMG, 2001). UML 1.4 considerably increased these numbers, but only a few of them are useful for framework documentation. Table 3.1 provides an overview.

Tag name	Applies to	Value type	Description
«implicit»	Association	Boolean	The association has no direct implementation, but may be of conceptual use only. For example, it may be derived from a combination of other associations (such as grandfather from father).
«global»	Association	Boolean	A global variable is used to implement the association.
«local»	Association	Boolean	A local variable within a method is used. The association is therefore temporary.
«parameter»	Association	Boolean	The association is temporarily established through a method parameter (similar to a local variable).
«implementationClass»	Class	Boolean	The class is implemented in a programming language.
«type»	Class	Boolean	The class is used to specify a domain of instances together with their operation signatures

Table 3.1 UML standard tags

The «implicit» tag states that the association to which it is attached is not implemented through a standard technique, such as links from one class to another. The association may be of conceptual use or defined for modeling purposes only, without a counterpart in the implementation. Often, such an association can be derived through the combination of others. A common example is the association to all (and not only the direct) descendant parts in a part–whole hierarchy. In this case, derived associations help us to clarify the diagrams but do not exist explicitly in an implementation. They are thus marked as «implicit». In Figure 3.4, a comment provides additional information about how the association is derived from other modeling elements.

In several cases, an association may be realized through a global variable («global») that allows all objects to navigate to the desired object. The stereotype «local» is used to indicate that this is not a permanent association, but that association links only exist temporarily in a local variable during a method call. In similar fashion, the stereotype «parameter» describes a temporary association that is established through the parameter of a method call.

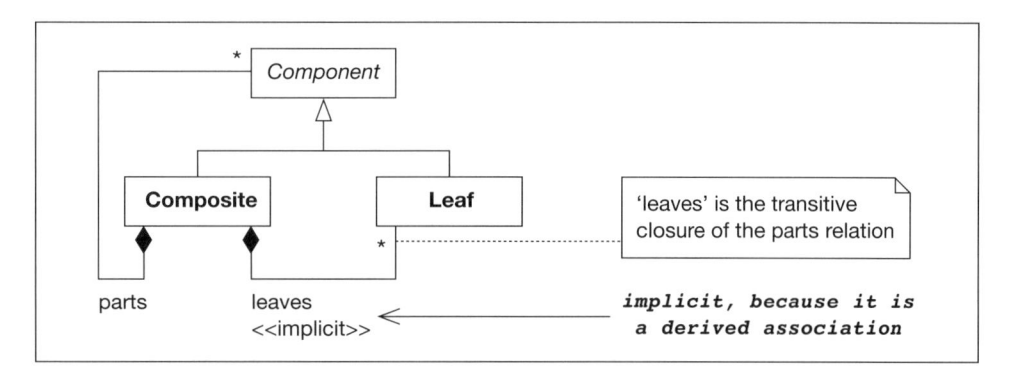

Figure 3.4 A derived implicit association

UML diagrams are applied in a wide variety of areas. During business analysis, a class can represent a real-world concept, and during design it may represent a high-level design concept. It sometimes happens that these classes do not have a counterpart in the actual implementation. Therefore, it is useful to discriminate the classes through appropriate tags. In the context of framework documentation, the implementation-level tags «implementationClass» and «type» are of particular interest. The former identifies classes that actually provide implementations. If a heterogeneous system implementation in different programming languages is necessary, this tag might be extended with values to denote the programming language in which a class is implemented. The «type» tag is used to explicitly mark certain classes as data types. A type corresponds to an abstract Java class or, more accurately, to a Java interface.

As mentioned above, standard UML offers a number of additional stereotypes, tagged values, and constraints – but, in our experience, those listed in Table 3.1 are the ones that have turned out to be the most useful for describing frameworks. The standard UML constraints of 'complete', 'incomplete', 'disjoint', and 'overlapping' that apply to generalizations may also be of use. Through further enhancement of the UML-F tag concept below, these constraints are presented as tags in Table 3.2.[5]

Other standard UML stereotypes and tags become useful if their implementation or meaning is slightly modified. One example is the stereotype «framework», which in standard UML is applied to packages only. There, it expresses that the contents of a

---

[5] Often, stereotypes impose constraints on the elements to which they are attached. The boundary between standard UML constraints and stereotypes is not sharp. Therefore, UML-F treats these constraints also as tags.

Tag name	Applies to	Value type	Description
«complete»	Generalization	Boolean	No new subclasses may be added. This also holds for already existing subclasses.
«incomplete»	Generalization	Boolean	New subclasses may be added during design time.
«disjoint»	Generalization	Boolean	Subclasses may not inherit from more than one direct superclass in the hierarchy (single inheritance is essential in Java and C# class hierarchies).
«overlapping»	Generalization	Boolean	Subclasses may inherit from several superclasses in the hierarchy directly.

Table 3.2 UML tags for generalization

package do not belong to any specific application but to a framework. Section 3.5 extends this stereotype to classes, and complements it with the «application» tag.

3.4 UML-F presentation tags

The basic UML-F tags introduced in the following sections deal only with the visual representation of elements – they do not define any properties of the annotated modeling elements.

3.4.1 Completeness and abstraction

Frameworks tend to have large numbers of classes and interfaces. A complete class diagram that shows all classes and interfaces, as well as their relationships, can easily become incomprehensible and overloaded. Thus, class diagrams usually show only the relevant aspects. In other words, a diagram normally presents information about the existence of elements in a system. However, typically there are other elements that have been omitted in a particular view. Two class diagrams that show the same class with different attributes are not to be considered inconsistent since they might just highlight different aspects of the system structure. In general, the structural part of the architecture of a framework can be captured by one class diagram (or a small number of them) that shows only the essential classes of the framework. The subclasses of a larger class hierarchy, auxiliary classes, and parts of aggregated classes may be omitted in these architectural descriptions.

Chapter 3 Basic elements of the UML-F profile 39

As visibility, multiplicity, and role names are attachments to other class diagram elements, their omission is obvious – missing types for attributes and methods can also be detected. However, omitted classes, interfaces, associations, attributes, and methods are not as readily apparent. Standard UML provides the ellipsis ('…') to mark omissions of attributes and methods. However, we also find it useful to be able to mark elements as complete. Therefore, we propose the UML-F tag '©' to mark completeness and the tag '…' to explicitly mark incompleteness.[6] In accordance with standard UML, the '…' tag is the default. This means that class diagrams and all their elements are considered incomplete unless explicitly marked as complete via use of '©'.

Figure 3.5 shows three representations of class Human. The first is complete, whereas the second omits an attribute and the third omits the attribute compartment as well as the method compartment. We can mark the attribute and the method sections as complete and incomplete independently of each other. Each of the sections may be empty and still be marked as complete, denoting that there are no entries required.

To clarify the use of these markers, let us distinguish three levels of models: the system itself, the UML model of the system, and the diagrammatic *representation* of that model on the screen, on paper, or on a white board. The latter representation

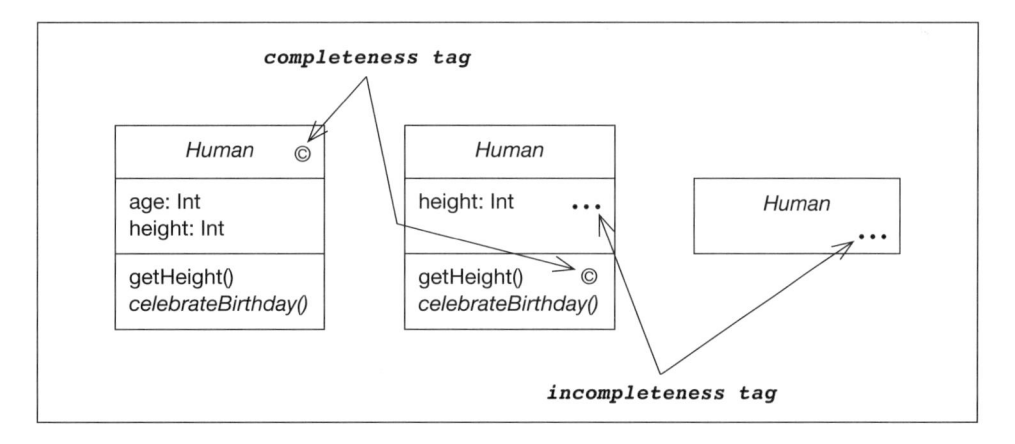

Figure 3.5   Three representations of the same class

---

[6] The proposed marker '©' and the further application of marker '…' extend standard UML. They have been used successfully by the authors for many years. Neither is framework-specific and can therefore be used independently of the rest of UML-F for any kind of UML modeling.

is often also called a *view*. The two markers '©' and '…' provide information about the relationship between the view (for example, on a screen) and the UML model we are working on. This is in contrast to most of the other UML-F tags which express information about the relationship between the model and the system.

These markers are necessary to allow the description of a system using incomplete views. Thus we call '©' and '…' *presentation markers* as they are used for presentation purposes. They do not indicate, for example, whether or not a class is extensible. Furthermore, it may be the case that a superclass is shown completely, whereas its subclasses may have only incomplete attribute or method lists.

Table 3.3 summarizes the semantics of the completeness tags. Formally, both markers can be seen as graphical shortcuts for a Boolean tag «complete», denoting «complete=True» and «complete=False».

Tag form	Applies to	Description
©	Class	The graphical representation of the class contains a complete list of all attributes and methods.
©	Interface	The graphical representation of the interface contains all methods and constants of the interface.
©	Attribute list	The list of attributes is complete.
©	Method list	The list of methods is complete.
©	Object	Analogous to class.
©	Set of links belonging to an association or composition	The object diagram shows all links of that association/composition.
©	Generalization	The generalization shows all existing direct subclasses.
©	Association	All information about this association is listed in the diagram.
…	Class, interface, attribute list, method list, generalization, association	Inverse of ©: the graphical representation may be incomplete (but may also be complete – we simply don't know).

Table 3.3 UML-F completeness tags

3.4.2 Flat and hierarchical representation of classes and expanded class views

This section introduces a notation for a graphical representation of hierarchical and flat views of classes. This is particularly useful in the context of framework representations. Thus, we incorporate it as a UML-F extension to the UML standard. We regard this notation as an extension of the visual representation of a class. It allows us to denote quite intuitively the signature of a class, namely its public and non-public methods. Furthermore, one class may have several different representations. One view might show the class in its *hierarchical* context; another shows all inherited methods and attributes in a *flat* form.

In this UML-F extension, a small box represents a method or attribute graphically. If the method or attribute is protected or private, the small box is drawn completely inside the class boundary; if it is a public method or attribute, the corresponding box crosses the border of the class, denoting that it is accessible from outside (see Figure 3.6).

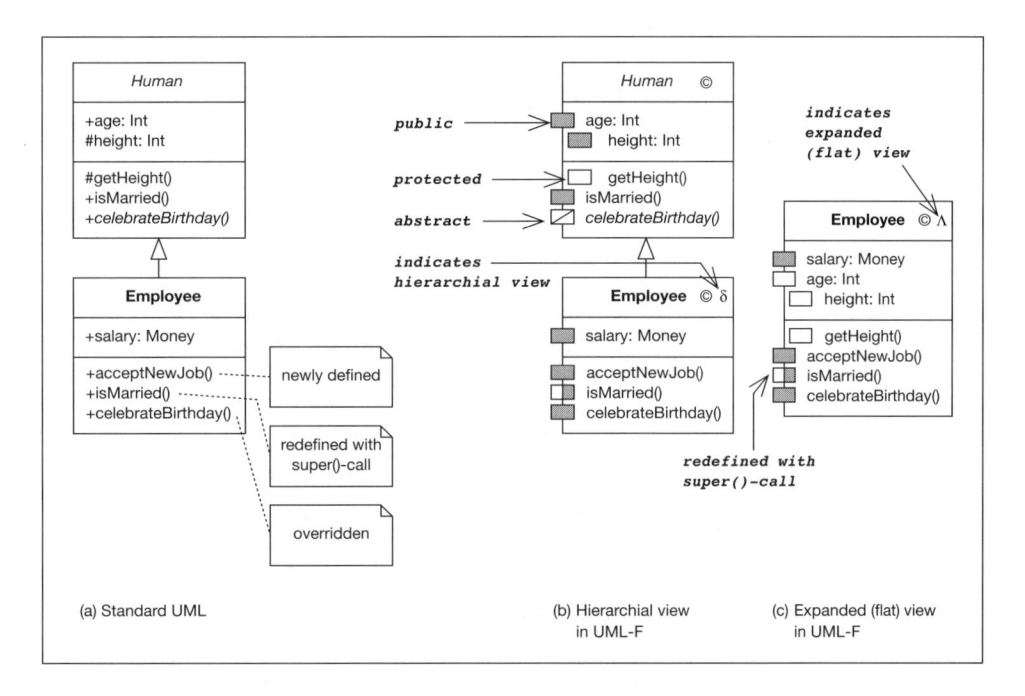

Figure 3.6   Hierarchical (a and b) and flat (c) representation of class Employee

UML-F introduces the class marker 'δ' as a tag that denotes a hierarchical view, which shows only the difference between a class and its direct superclass.[7] For expanded lists of attributes and methods, UML-F provides the symbol 'Λ'.[8] As a default, we assume that classes are represented hierarchically ('δ'), where only the differences from the particular superclass(es) are shown. This is consistent with the UML standard presentation of classes. Figure 3.6 demonstrates several variants of representing class Employee: Figure 3.6(a) shows the standard UML representation, and Figures 3.6(b) and (c) apply the UML-F extensions in a hierarchical and flat context respectively.

In addition, UML-F introduces a graphically more enhanced representation for individual methods. UML-F allows the representation of methods with a gray or unfilled rectangles to show whether a particular method has been (re-)defined.

- ▢ An unfilled rectangle expresses that the method is inherited and not redefined – such as method getHeight() in class Employee. In superclasses we use this marker if it is irrelevant whether a method is newly defined or inherited.
- ▣ A gray rectangle indicates that the method is either newly defined, or is inherited but completely redefined (methods acceptNewJob() and celebrateBirthday() demonstrate this).
- ◩ A half-gray/half-unfilled rectangle denotes that the method is redefined but uses the inherited method through a super()-call (e.g. method isMarried() in class Employee). Thus the inherited code is augmented by new code pieces.
- ◨ A rectangle with a diagonal line indicates that the method is abstract and needs to be overridden in subclasses.

The unfilled and the gray rectangles, marking inheritance ▢ and a new definition ▣, apply to attributes as well. As attributes are neither abstract nor overridden, the other two markers do not apply to instance variables.

In the expanded version of a class representation ('Λ'), one cannot see in which class a method was actually defined. If desired, we may therefore augment the method name with a class path, e.g. Human.getHeight() in Java format, or Human::getHeight() in C++ style. The proposed markers are sufficient to denote the situations for the object structures presented in this book. However, tools that are capable of roundtrip engineering could offer additional features, such as

---

[7] Hence the Greek lower case letter delta (δ) for difference.

[8] The Greek upper case letter lambda (Λ) denotes a list, but its iconic shape also resembles the inheritance hierarchy where the listed methods come from.

subcompartments of the instance variable or method sections indicating in which class it is defined (see Figure 3.7(a)).

Another variant would be to stack the markers from superclasses behind the direct marker. Figure 3.7(b) shows the markers from superclass Human right behind the direct markers of the class.

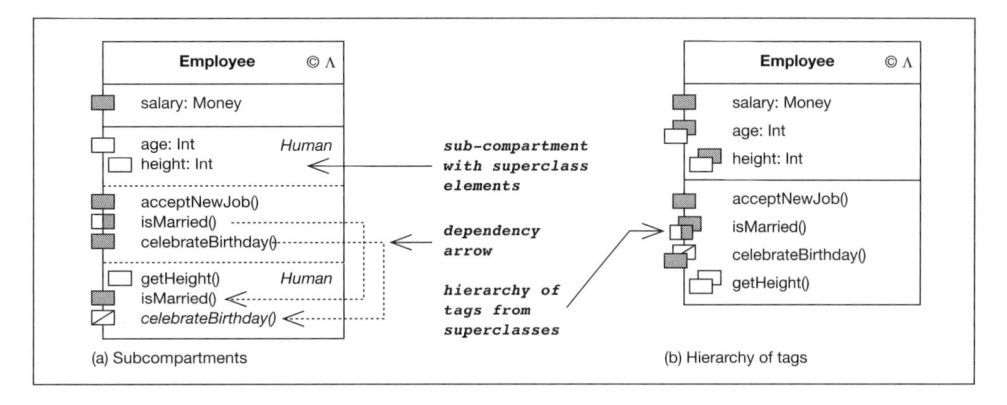

Figure 3.7 Alternatives to extend markers for more details on the hierarchy

To summarize the UML-F class (hierarchy) presentation tags, UML-F introduces two tags, 'δ' and 'Λ', to denote hierarchical and flat representations of classes and objects, as well as unfilled and gray rectangles to denote overriding and inheriting of methods. Table 3.4 summarizes the use of the tags.

Tag	Applies to	Description
δ	Class, interface	The graphical representation of the class only lists attributes and methods that are introduced or redefined in that class, but not the inherited properties. This is the *difference* between this class and its superclass.
Λ	Class, interface	The graphical representation of the class lists inherited methods and attributes as well as newly introduced or refined methods and attributes.

Table 3.4 UML-F tags for flat and hierarchical representations

The application of the two tags 'δ' and 'Λ' is orthogonal to applying the completeness tags '...' and '©'.

Four inheritance indicators apply to methods and attributes. They are represented by unfilled and gray rectangles to express the overriding and inheriting of methods. Table 3.5 summarizes these tags.

Tag	Applies to	Description
▭	Method, attribute	A method implementation is inherited and not overridden or newly defined, and an attribute is inherited or newly defined.
▬	Method, attribute	A method is newly defined or overridden. The class provides the complete code for the method. An attribute is newly defined.
▭▬	Method	The method is overridden, but the superclass method is called (for example, through a super()-call in Java).
◿	Method	The method is abstract and has to be overridden in subclasses.

Table 3.5 UML-F inheritance indicators

All the tags introduced here can also be represented in UML standard form by using the Boolean tag «expanded» with the value false for 'δ' and true for 'Λ'. The inheritance indicator symbols can be represented in the same way by a textual tag «inherited».

3.4.3 UML-F extensions of the object diagram notation

Just like class diagrams, object diagrams can represent abstractions of actual object structures in the system. Therefore, the markers '©' and '...' are useful for characterizing their completeness or incompleteness. An object state is defined by the attributes of its class, including not only the directly given attributes but also the inherited ones. Therefore, the flat and hierarchical representations indicated by the markers 'Λ' and 'δ' for classes apply equally well to attributes in object diagrams.

Figure 3.8 shows an object diagram extended by UML-F markers. These markers are mostly carried over from class diagrams in a straightforward way. However, completeness and incompleteness markers are also used to describe whether the set of given links is complete. Marker '©' on the two links called owner of the Mary object indicates that all links belonging to that association and concerning the Mary object are shown. The incompleteness marker '...' instead denotes that her

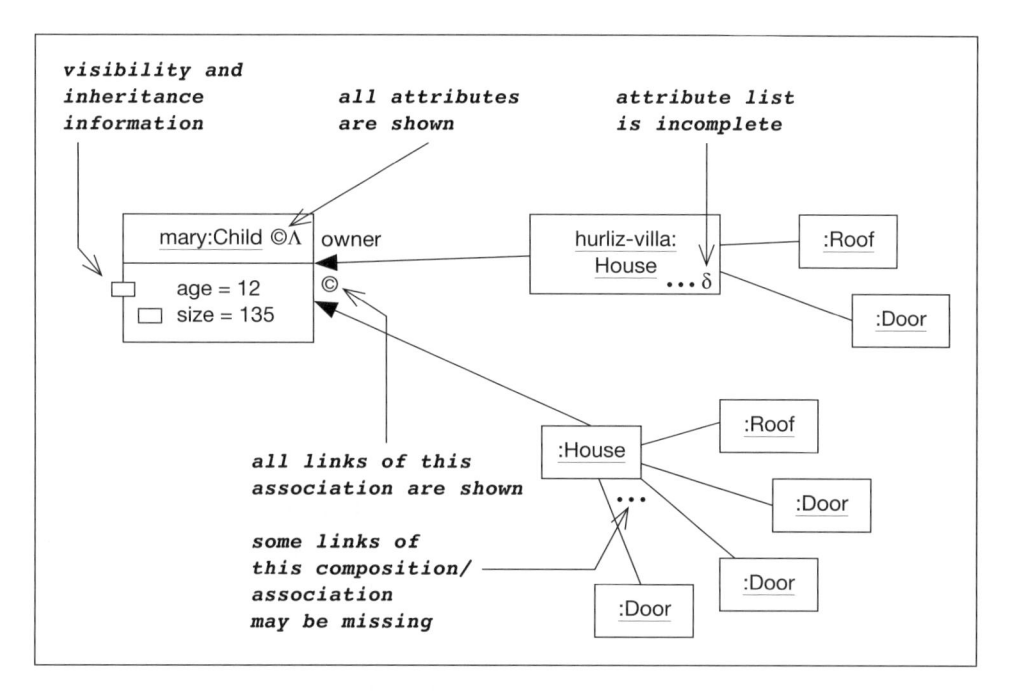

Figure 3.8 Sample object diagram with UML-F extensions

second house (the anonymous one) has at least three doors, but may have more. Omitted markers mean incompleteness by default.

The following sections introduce a number of concepts that allow additional markings of classes, associations, and the composition relationship for different purposes. As a rule of thumb, these concepts are also useful in the context of object diagrams as well. They apply to an object if they apply to an object's class. The same holds true for links and their respective associations or composition relationships.

3.4.4 Tags for sequence diagrams

Sequence diagrams are an intuitive and appealing means of describing desired interaction sequences. However, they have some drawbacks. Like object diagrams, they denote objects that may not actually exist, since the system can have a completely different structure at runtime. Even if the objects exist as described in the sequence diagram, the denoted interaction may still not occur at runtime. There may be alternative paths of interaction, for example in order to handle an error or because of a different configuration of the participating objects.

Furthermore, the interaction behavior of an object often depends on its attribute values. For example, Boolean values may govern whether a certain interaction does or does not happen. Finally, the sequence diagram may describe the reaction of the system to an action that will never occur, such as a specific user input.

Due to the exemplary nature of a sequence diagram, the described interaction may occur many times, repeatedly involving the same objects or involving different object structures each time. In recursive object structures, it may even happen that the interaction is stacked. In concurrent systems, different threads may exhibit the same interaction sequence in parallel.

The examples above corroborate that UML sequence diagrams are necessarily incomplete because a sequence diagram can neither capture all objects of a system, nor cover the complete lifetime of the system in all its details and all its branches. Instead, it focuses on a subset of the existing objects, during an interval in time, and on one branch only. Furthermore, it disregards irrelevant messages within this time interval, even though these messages are sent or received by one of the objects depicted in the diagram. A sequence diagram tells a story that stresses certain aspects, but removes irrelevant details. Sequence diagrams are an abstraction of actually occurring sequences of method invocations. Thus, producing appropriate sequence diagrams often requires a solid understanding of the overall behavior.

As we have already described, the reaction of a method invocation can depend on the current state of the objects and the environment. To describe variable behavior, the current UML standard provides control techniques to overcome the limited expressiveness of such exemplary sequence diagrams. Among others, these control techniques cover:

- guards
- repetition
- alternatives
- optional method calls
- referencing.

Many of these techniques closely resemble the control structures of programming languages (see Table 3.6).

Sequence diagram construct	Corresponding programming construct	Explanation
Repetition	While-do constructs	A message (or a sequence of messages) occurs repeatedly.
Alternative with or without guard	If-then-else and case constructs	Two (or more) variants of interactions exist.
Optional part	Guarded command: if Test then X	A message (or message sequence) may be omitted.
Referencing	Method invocation	If the diagram becomes too complex, then a subdiagram can be used to describe a subinteraction in the same way that operations can be decomposed within subroutines.

Table 3.6 Control structures in sequence diagrams

However, some subtle differences exist. In a program – being a *constructive* executable description – the while-do constructs must describe their termination conditions, and alternatives must be guarded by an if-then-else condition. A sequence diagram instead is a *descriptive* constraint on the possible behavior of the system. This is an analogy to class diagrams that are constraints on possible object structures. Therefore, sequence diagrams may, for example, describe repetitions that define no explicit termination condition.

A *guard*, as defined in standard UML, is denoted as a condition in square brackets, such as [m < 0] in Figure 3.9. A guard discriminates alternatives. Only if a guard condition is true does the guarded interaction occur. Using a guard does not necessarily specify what happens if the guard is not satisfied. In particular, another behavior, possibly specified by another sequence diagram, may occur.

Guards are particularly useful in combination with *alternatives*, when two guards cover all possibilities. Alternatives allow the description of different paths of interaction. They can describe two different reactions to a method invocation that can occur. Alternatives can, but need not, have a guard attached in order to discriminate which alternative will be taken. If the guards are missing, or they overlap, it is left to the implementer to choose which variant the system should follow. The UML standard way of describing alternatives within a single sequence diagram becomes awkward to read and understand easily. Thus, UML-F offers another way of describing alternatives in combination with referencing that

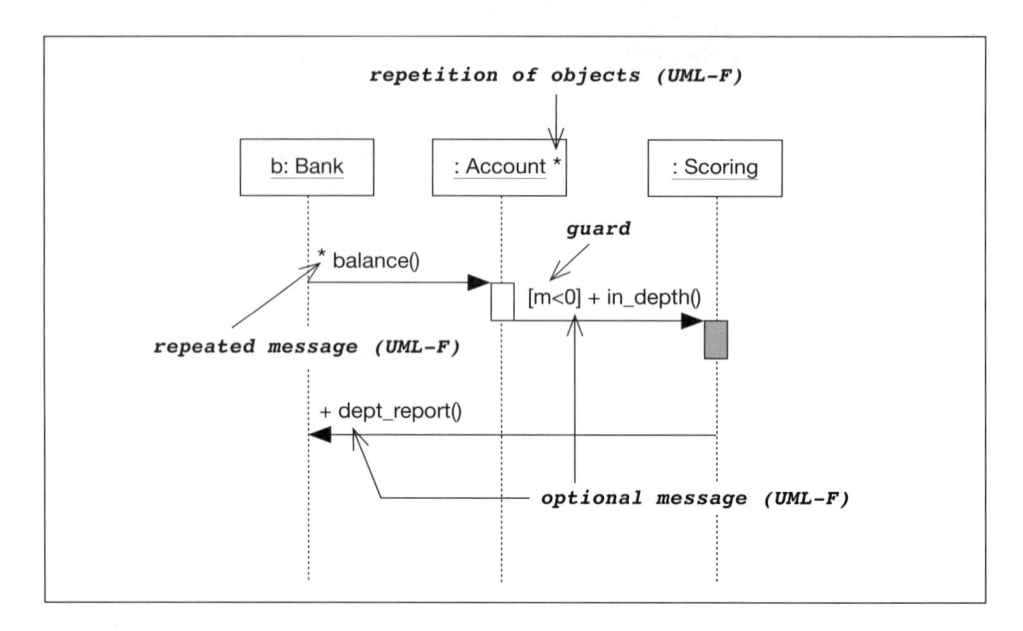

Figure 3.9 Repetition, guards, and optional messages

allows the structuring of sequence diagrams in a crisper and clearer manner (see Figure 3.10).[9]

Optional parts describe whether a certain method invocation happens at all. If, for example, an observer gets the notice from its observable that the values have changed, the observer may fetch the new values. However, if the observer is an element of a GUI and is currently not visible on the screen, the fetch method call might be omitted or deferred. In UML-F, a '+' sign is used to describe that a message is optional. For example, the in_dept() method in Figure 3.9 is optional and the guard specifies when it is issued. The method dept_report(), sent from the Scoring department to the Bank, is also optional but the specification of an associated condition is left open.

If a certain single or compound interaction occurs repeatedly within a sequence diagram, the *repetition* mechanism is used. To denote repeated messages, UML-F introduces the '*' sign.[10] An interval such as (2–5), used instead of '*', may constrain the minimum and maximum number of repetitions. For example, a pin

---

[9] The UML-F solution to presenting alternatives in sequence diagrams is not an additional concept but just a different form of presentation.

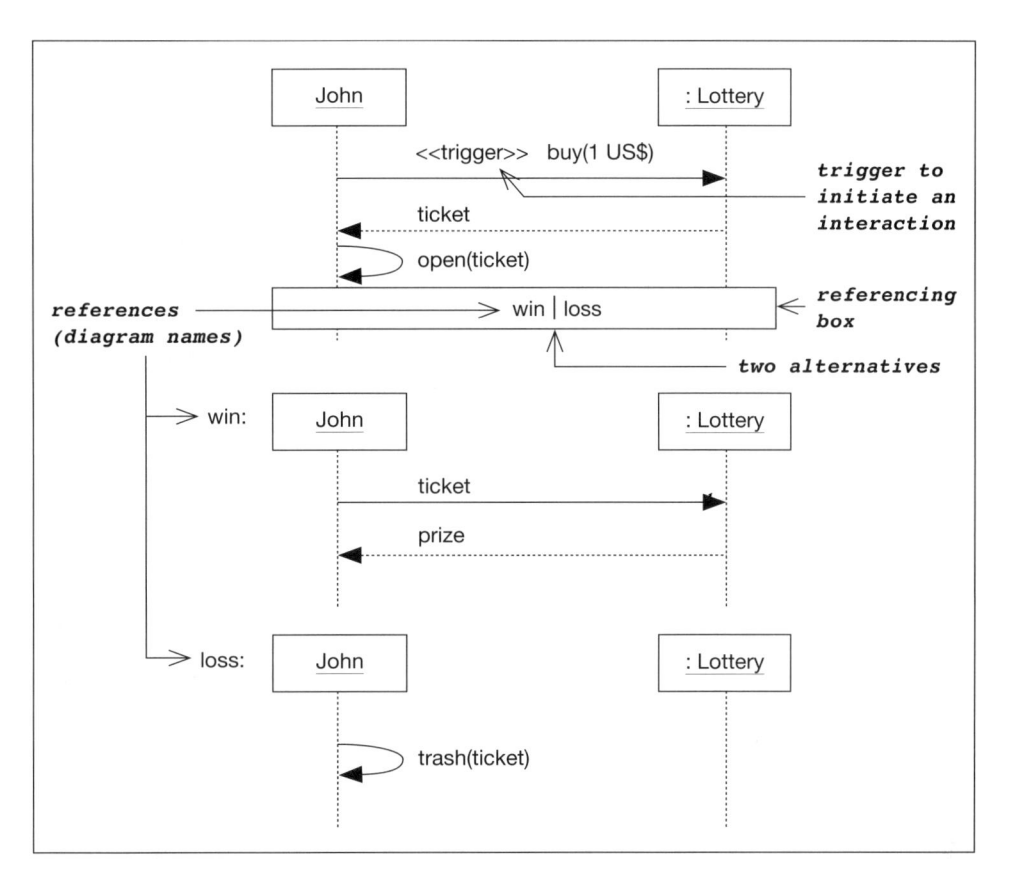

Figure 3.10 Alternatives and referencing in sequence diagrams in UML-F

number for an automated teller machine may be entered 1–3 times. A repetition factor of 0–1 is equal to being optional, '+', and the repetition factor 1 is redundant.

Because multiple messages are often sent to multiple objects, UML-F also allows the attaching of the repetition marker '*' to an object. In Figure 3.9 several :Account objects exist. Each of these objects is activated through one of the multiple method

---

[10] Both the optional '+' sign and he repetition sign '*' stem from regular expressions within the Backus–Naur notation. In sequence diagrams they are used for the very same purpose, namely extending the expressiveness of a sequence diagram from describing one exemplar interaction sequence to branching sets of possible sequences.

calls that are labeled balance(), and each reacts individually. If desired, a guard on the multiple method call may select a subset of objects that receive the message.

As stated above, a sequence diagram quickly tends to become overloaded with too many details. Thus, a technique for factoring common behavior into subsequence diagrams is useful. Other diagrams can reference these subsequence diagrams. This allows a structured view of interaction sequences and provides a way to reuse common interactions in different diagrams. To do this, it is necessary to identify sequence diagrams by name. Figure 3.10 exemplifies the referencing of two subsequence diagrams that describe alternative behaviors. Combinations of the operators described above are possible – for example, by attaching a repetition operator to a reference box the repetition of a whole sequence of messages can be described.

In practice, many sequence diagrams are used in a *trigger* mode. In a triggered sequence diagram, the first method invocation causes the rest of the interaction to happen. In the sequence diagrams above, the first message serves as a starting point for the interaction pattern to occur. We introduce the marker «trigger» to indicate that a message on the sequence diagram triggers the rest of the interaction.

To summarize the use of UML-F sequence diagram tags – sequence diagrams are the primary means of describing interactions between objects. A limited use of sequence diagrams can be found in Gamma et al. (1995) to illustrate interactions between the participating components of a pattern.

The form of sequence diagrams presented here affords improved expressiveness compared with sequence diagrams in standard UML. However, as sequence diagrams have to cope with two dimensions – structure and time – there are a number of interactions that still cannot be described: unordered messages, the explicit destroying of objects, and so on.[11] We have presented a subset of UML sequence diagrams augmented with techniques that prove particularly useful for describing interactions in frameworks. They include the use of boxes for referencing, '*' for repetition of objects and interactions, '+' for optional interactions, the «trigger» marker, and a new way of presenting alternatives. Table 3.7 summarizes these tags. The ideas for these extensions largely stem from approaches on augmentation of message sequence charts (MSC) and their

---

[11] There is a clear trade-off between the complexity of a notation and its ease of use. Unfortunately, there is no optimal solution and individuals have different preferences ranging from 'nice-to-have' to 'essential'. This conflict shows up in all UML notations but becomes more apparent in behavior notations, such as sequence diagrams.

unification with the UML, partly described in its standardization documents (ITU-TS, 1999) and Krüger (2000). They have not (yet) been integrated with the UML standard and are therefore regarded as UML-F specific extensions.

Tag	Applies to	Description
*	Message	The message can be repeated as often as desired. Zero occurrences are allowed.
*	Object	The object can exist multiple times (including zero). Typically, the denoted objects are the target of a repeated message arrow.
+	Message	The message is optional, occurring at most once.
(A–B)	Message	A more concise way to describe multiple occurrence of a message (here between A and B times).
«trigger»	Message	If the first message in a sequence diagram causes the subsequent interaction to occur, then it is called a trigger.

Table 3.7 UML-F tags for sequence diagrams

Of course, the use of '+' and (A–B) can be extended to objects as well. The use of references within sequence diagrams cannot be described as a standard UML tag extension. This, instead, is a so-called 'heavyweight' extension of UML since it directly affects the abstract syntax (the meta-model).

3.5 UML-F framework tags

The UML-F tags in the above sections are useful for any object-oriented model including frameworks. This section presents basic UML-F tags that are only useful in the context of frameworks. They are used by the framework developer to document the intended use of certain framework concepts for the application developer. These tags therefore give guidance to the application developer through the framework adaptation process. Furthermore, they give framework developers guidance for the enhancement of a framework, as they also allow one to document intentions to codevelopers. It is important to bear in mind the fact that framework developers are the masters of the framework and can therefore change the framework and its decorating tags, whereas application developers may not.

3.5.1 Framework and application classes

Many frameworks come together with prefabricated application classes that do not belong to the framework itself. These additional classes can be studied in order to understand the standard usage of a framework by examining and adapting their code, whereas the framework classes themselves are usually not subject to change.

The tag «application» marks application-specific classes. During the framework adaptation process, this tag can mark newly introduced classes as well. The «framework» tag marks classes and interfaces that are generally adapted through the definition of new subclasses and the implementation of interfaces. A third category of classes belongs to the utility level, as these classes are provided as basic classes by utility libraries or the runtime system. These may be tagged «utility». Figure 3.11 exemplifies their usage. If a package is marked with one of these tags, then all of its classes and interfaces are implicitly marked as such. Table 3.8 summarizes the meaning of these UML-F tags.

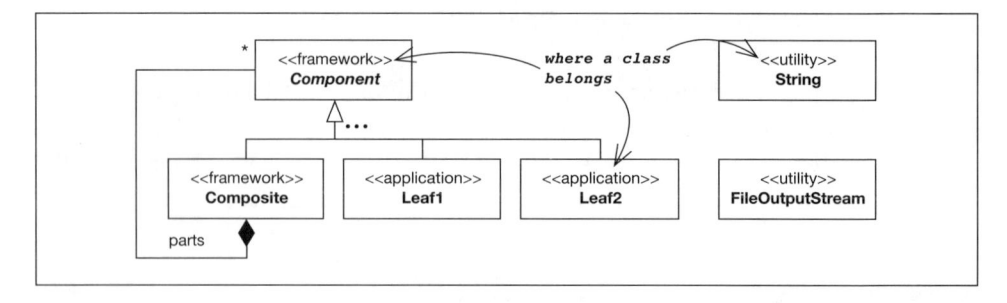

Figure 3.11 «framework», «application», and «utility» tags

Tag name	Applies to	Value type	Description
«application»	Class, package, interface	Boolean	The class/interface/package does not belong to a framework, but to an application.
«framework»	Class, package, interface	Boolean	The class/interface/package belongs to the framework.
«utility»	Class, package, interface	Boolean	The class/interface/package belongs to a utility library or the runtime system.

Table 3.8 UML-F class tags for discerning between framework and application components

3.5.2 Overview of adaptation tags

One important principle of framework design underlies the tags presented in this section: no framework element should be directly changed for an application by modifying its source code. This principle is necessary to enable reuse of the framework in different applications. However, this principle can only be applied if the framework is mature because the development of a framework usually goes hand-in-hand with the development of a number of applications.

In framework, classes, methods, and interfaces are adapted through the definition of new (sub)classes and the implementation of interfaces. The tags in Table 3.9 express whether an element is fixed (tag «fixed») or whether it can be adapted in subclasses. Two kinds of adaptations are distinguished: those made during runtime of a system (tag «adapt-dyn»); and those made during the design or evolution of a system (tag «adapt-static»). The following subsections discuss these tags in more detail.

Tag name	Applies to	Value type	Description
«fixed»	Class, method, generalization	Boolean	The element is fixed. Methods may not be changed in subclasses. In a generalization relation new subclasses may not be added.
«adapt-static»	Interface, class, method, generalization	Boolean	The element can be adapted during design time through subclassing or interface implementation. A method can be overridden in subclasses. New methods and attributes may be added to the subclass and existing methods may be overridden. During runtime the element is fixed.
«adapt-dyn»	Interface, class, method, generalization	Boolean	The interface, class, method can be changed at runtime, for example through dynamic loading of new subclasses. Additional subclasses typically override methods.

Table 3.9 UML-F tags for basic framework adaptations

Dynamic adaptations during runtime typically require extra effort and need special treatment. Not every implementation language and/or runtime system allows a dynamic adaptation. Java supports it through its meta-information system and the dynamic loading of classes.

3.5.3 Method adaptation tags

This section discusses the above tags in the context of methods. Methods can be «fixed», or can have the «adapt-static» or «adapt-dyn» tag attached to them.

The «fixed» tag

For many methods a framework already provides an implementation. To keep that implementation flexible, the method can be adapted through hook methods[12] that are called in the methods body. A method can be explicitly tagged as a «fixed» method if it should not be changed through adaptation or overriding, neither during runtime nor during design time.

If the framework itself provides more than one possible implementation of a «fixed» method in several subclasses, the application developer may choose (or the framework chooses) which implementation to use, but adding new implementations of that method are not allowed. Here, the «fixed» tag differs from the Java modifier final, which does not even allow framework subclasses to override a method. UML-F allows overriding of a «fixed» method within the framework, but the «fixed» tag also holds for the overridden subclass methods so that the application components cannot override it. Figures 3.12 and 3.13 illustrate the semantics of the UML-F tag «fixed».

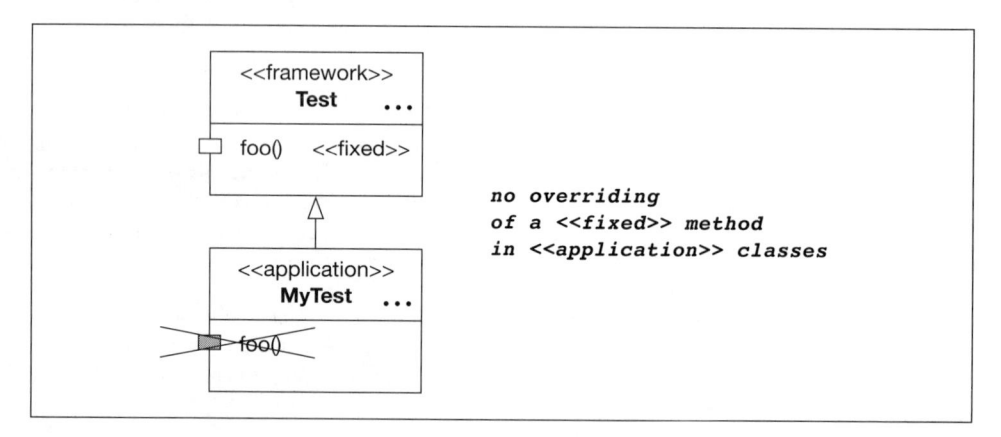

Figure 3.12 Constraint on overriding a «fixed» method

The «adapt-static» tag

The «adapt-static» tag allows the application developer to modify a method in a new subclass during design time (see Figure 3.14). This tag marks methods in

---

[12] Hook methods are described in detail in Chapter 4.

Chapter 3 Basic elements of the UML-F profile

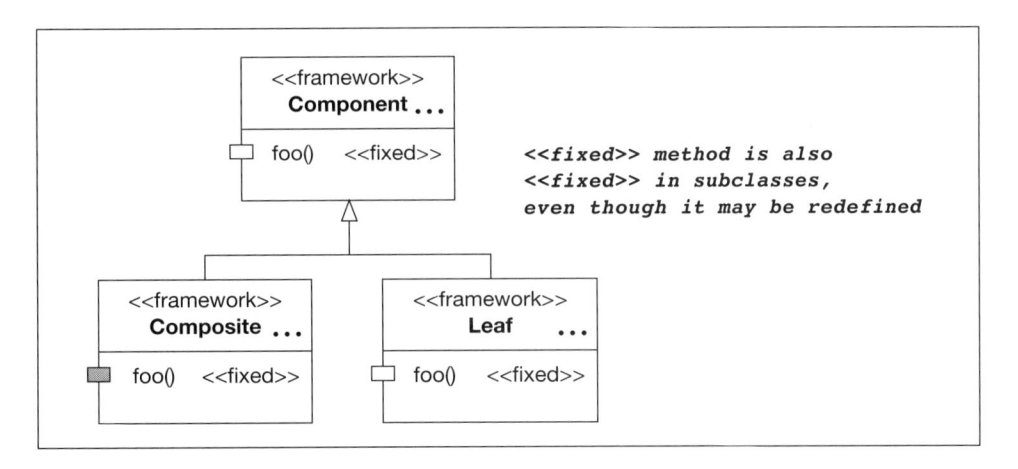

```
                    <<framework>>
                    Component ...

                    foo()   <<fixed>>        <<fixed>> method is also
                                             <<fixed>> in subclasses,
                                             even though it may be redefined


        <<framework>>           <<framework>>
        Composite ...           Leaf      ...

        foo()  <<fixed>>        foo()  <<fixed>>
```

Figure 3.13 Propagation of «fixed» tag to subclasses

framework classes that are intended to serve as a connection to the application. Such methods are often abstract, or provide only a dummy implementation. It is also possible that the default implementation of the method is rather elaborate and should be used through a super()-call if overridden.[13]

```
                              A           ...

                        foo() <<adapt-static>>    <<adapt-static>>
                                                  method can be
                                                  overridden in
                                                  subclasses


    A_sub1    ...        A_sub2    ...        A_sub3    ...

    foo() ✓              foo() ✓              foo() ✓
```

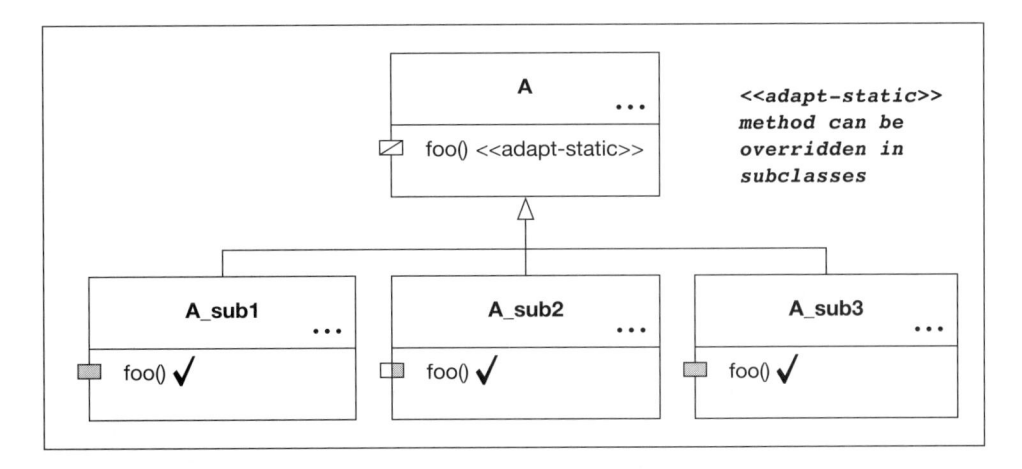

Figure 3.14 Overriding «adapt-static» methods

---

[13] As the «adapt-static» tag corresponds to overriding of methods in subclasses, we were tempted to introduce the tag «override» instead, but for the sake of uniformity we chose «adapt-static».

The «adapt-dyn» tag

On rare occasions implementations vary widely, even during system operation. Then it might not be possible to think of all cases up front. Instead, system designers offer a dynamic adaptation of the system. If the framework is designed in such a way that new implementations of a method can be added during runtime then that method can be marked as «adapt-dyn». Such a dynamic implementation occurs, for example, if the system should run without shutdowns.

Dealing with this form of adaptation is straightforward in languages such as Smalltalk and the Common Lisp Object System (CLOS). Java also provides the flexibility through its meta-information system and the dynamic loading of classes. A class that overrides an «adapt-dyn» method can be loaded while the system is running. A command interpreter is a workaround for dynamic adaptation in languages without an appropriate meta-information system (such as C++) and with runtime systems which lack dynamic loading capabilities. The dynamic adaptation is achieved by changing the command string.

Dynamic loading of methods introduces some overhead. So one should check carefully if the application of this technique is necessary. Furthermore, if the framework tags a method with «adapt-dyn», the framework itself should provide either a mechanism to load respective subclasses dynamically or an adaptable command interpreter as part of the framework.

Defaults

Methods in framework classes are marked as «fixed» by default – this adds a security level to framework use. If the framework developer wants to allow adaptation, this has to be enabled explicitly. Furthermore, in larger frameworks it appears that more than the half of the methods are meant to be «fixed». For methods, the «fixed» tag does carry over to subclasses, whereas the other two tags do not. Therefore an «adapt-dyn» method may be overridden by a «fixed» method in a subclass, but not vice versa.

A framework may have a large number of methods tagged as «adapt-static» or «adapt-dyn». It is not a requirement to actually adapt all these methods. Instead, the decisions as to which methods to adapt depend on the application being developed. The methodological guidelines that accompany a good framework – for example, in the form of a cookbook – should provide hints about adaptations for application-specific requirements.

3.5.4 Tags in the context of classes and interfaces

From a conceptual viewpoint, classes and interfaces share the characteristic that they define a type through their signature. During system modeling, classes and interfaces can be treated in a rather uniform way. Nevertheless, it makes no sense to apply the «fixed» tag to interfaces because an interface cannot provide a method implementation and any class implementing the interface therefore must be allowed to define its own method implementation.

The «fixed» tag

If none of the methods that a class provides are to be redefined in an application, then the class can be marked with the «fixed» tag (see Figure 3.15). The «fixed» tag for classes thus serves as a shortcut for attaching the tag to each of its methods. This allows the addition of new subclasses and the definition of new methods within these subclasses, but it does not allow the modification of any inherited methods. Although a class may be «fixed», the framework may provide a number of subclasses where methods are already overridden.

As a consequence of being a shortcut for attaching the tag to all methods, the «fixed» tag for classes does not carry over to its subclasses directly. Instead, it propagates only to all methods that are inherited (see Figure 3.16). The practical use of this tag is restricted to core classes in the inheritance hierarchy, whose methods are not intended for adaptations, and to highly specialized classes that have no subclasses at all (e.g. the String class in Java).

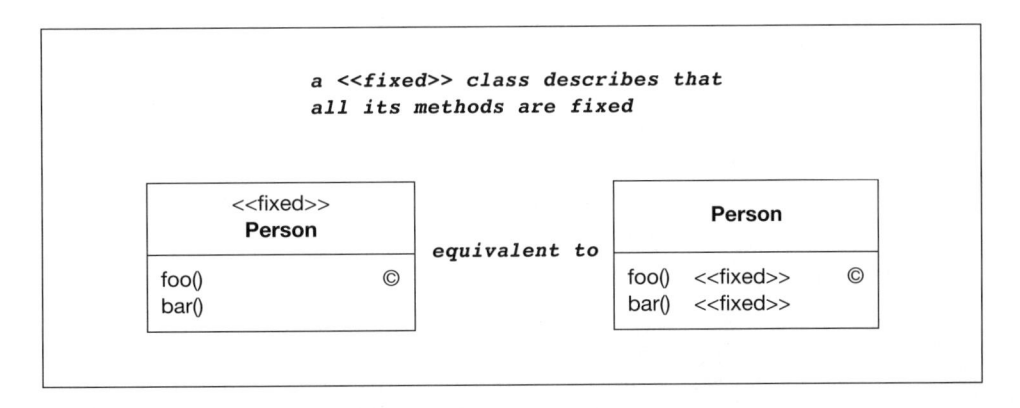

```
        a <<fixed>> class describes that
        all its methods are fixed

   ┌─────────────────┐                      ┌─────────────────────────┐
   │   <<fixed>>     │                      │        Person           │
   │    Person       │                      ├─────────────────────────┤
   ├─────────────────┤    equivalent to     │  foo()   <<fixed>>   ©  │
   │  foo()       ©  │                      │  bar()   <<fixed>>      │
   │  bar()          │                      └─────────────────────────┘
   └─────────────────┘
```

Figure 3.15 Marking a class as «fixed»

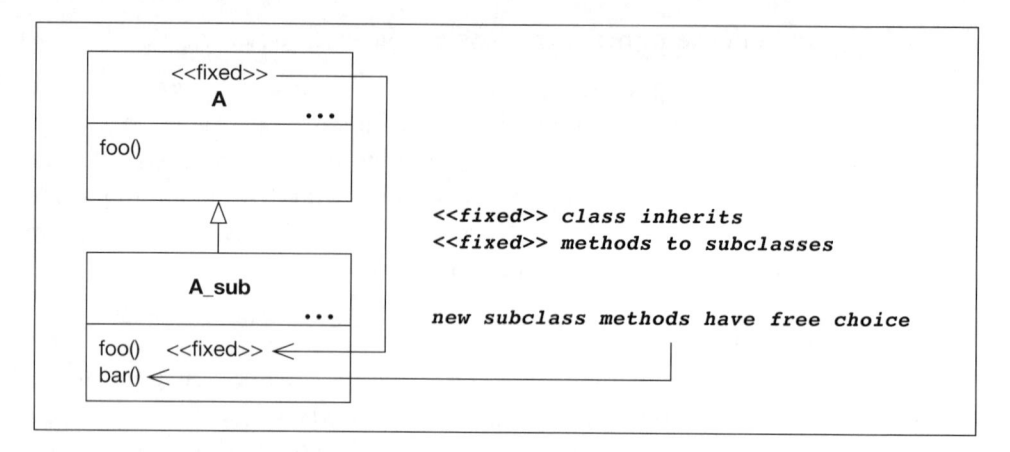

```
                ┌─────────────────────────────────────────┐
                │      <<fixed>>                          │
                │         A         ...                   │
                │   ┌──────────────┐                      │
                │   │ foo()        │                      │
                │   └──────────────┘      <<fixed>> class inherits
                │          △              <<fixed>> methods to subclasses
                │   ┌──────────────┐                      │
                │   │    A_sub     │      new subclass methods have free choice
                │   │        ...   │                      │
                │   │ foo()  <<fixed>>                    │
                │   │ bar()                               │
                │   └──────────────┘                      │
                └─────────────────────────────────────────┘
```

Figure 3.16 Tag «fixed» is not inherited directly between classes

The «adapt-static» tag

Marking a class or an interface with the «adapt-static» tag acts as a shortcut for marking all its methods as «adapt-static».[14] In this case, all its methods can be adapted by the application developer through adding (sub)classes. However, the «adapt-static» tag can be overruled for individual methods in the class. If a method is tagged as «fixed», then this method may not be adapted – explicit method tags overrule class tags when they are more restrictive than the class tag (see Figure 3.17). This means that if a class has the tag «adapt-static», then all its methods must be «adapt-static» or «fixed».

The «adapt-dyn» tag

Finally, the «adapt-dyn» tag can be attached to a class or an interface to express the possibility of dynamic adaptation during runtime. The use of «adapt-dyn» for a class/interface reveals the existence of at least one method with the same tag, thus encouraging dynamic loading of classes during runtime. The tag «adapt-dyn» applied to a class promotes to all its methods that are not marked differently. In practice, however, such classes often have only one or a few methods intended for dynamic adaptation.

---

[14] For the sake of readability, the following presentation mostly refers to 'classes' synonymously to 'interfaces', although a replacement of the terms 'class' by 'interface' would imply further changes of the description. For example, classes implement interface methods instead of overriding them.

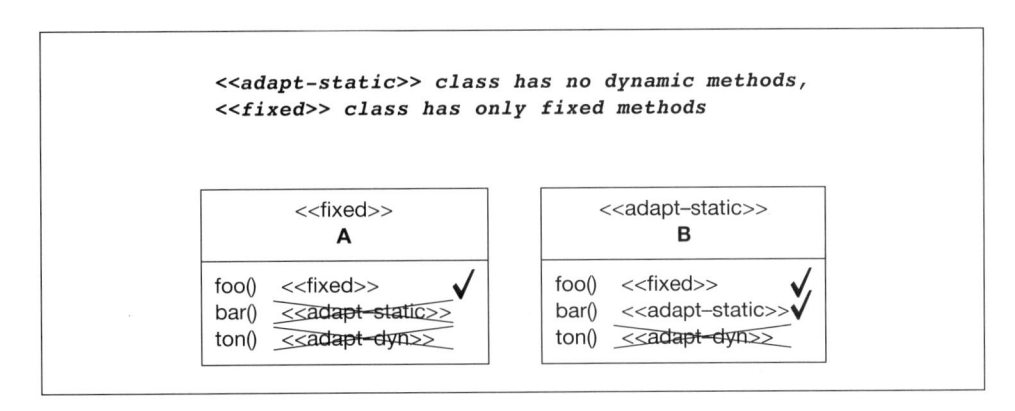

```
<<adapt-static>> class has no dynamic methods,
<<fixed>> class has only fixed methods
```

```
   <<fixed>>              <<adapt-static>>
       A                         B
 foo()  <<fixed>>      ✓    foo()  <<fixed>>       ✓
 bar()  <<adapt-static>>    bar()  <<adapt-static>> ✓
 ton()  <<adapt-dyn>>       ton()  <<adapt-dyn>>
```

Figure 3.17 Applying «fixed» and «adapt-static» tags to classes

3.5.5 Tags in the context of generalization

So far, the focus has been on tags for methods, classes and interfaces; and the tags for classes and interfaces as shortcuts for method tags. All these tags specify the degree of adaptability of particular methods in classes or interfaces. Thus, during a framework adaptation it is of interest to understand where classes should be added. For this purpose, UML-F provides the tags «fixed», «adapt–static», and «adapt–dyn» as attributes of generalization relationships.

The «adapt-static» tag

The «adapt-static» tag is applied to a generalization to express the idea that adding application-specific classes during design time is allowed. This tag allows the addition of new subclasses with application-specific features. In particular, a generalization relationship should be marked by «adapt-static» if the corresponding superclass should be adapted in subclasses. Figure 3.18 illustrates the use of this UML-F tag in the context of a generalization. As there is no detailed information about how and why to extend the generalization relationship, the information conveyed with the «adapt–static» tag is somewhat weak. Therefore, for example, the tags defined for the Composite pattern are based on the «adapt–static» tag, but include additional information on how to add classes to adapt the inheritance structure, as shown in Chapter 4.

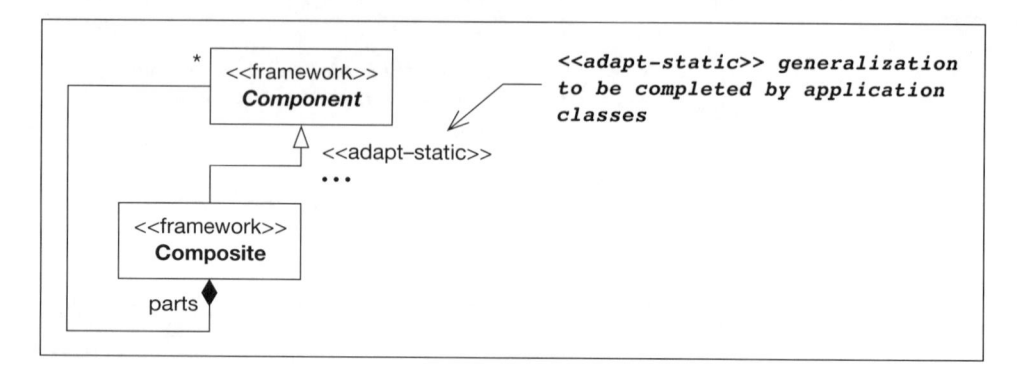

Figure 3.18 Explicit marking of a generalization

The «fixed» tag

Sometimes a framework is designed in such a way that no direct subclass is permitted to be added to a given class. Figure 3.19 illustrates the constraint imposed by the «fixed» tag.

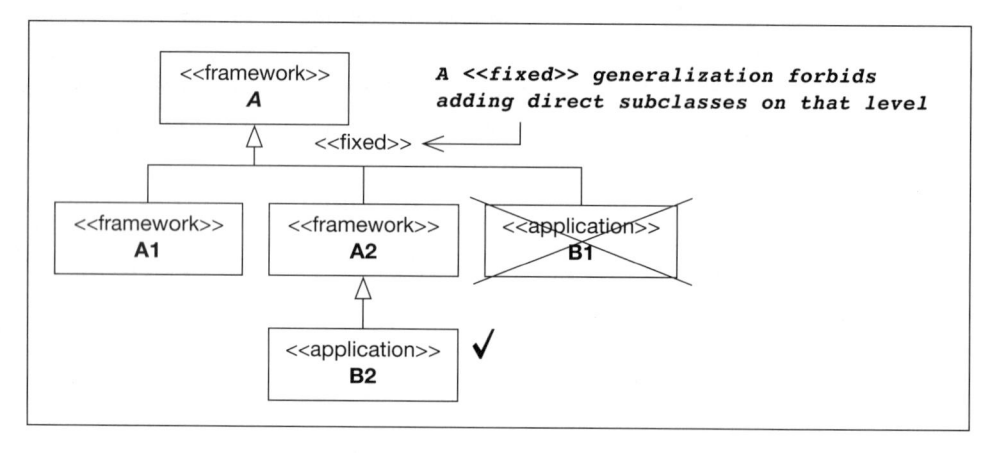

Figure 3.19 Semantics of a «fixed» generalization

As a second example, in the Visitor pattern (Figure 3.20, adapted from Gamma et al. 1995), an instance of class Visitor navigates through an object structure. The classes representing the objects that form the object structure should incorporate a fixed generalization if no additional subclasses of class Element are expected to be added. Another reason to prevent a generalization to be extended by the application developer is the existence of appropriate mechanisms to adapt its classes by composition or parameterization.

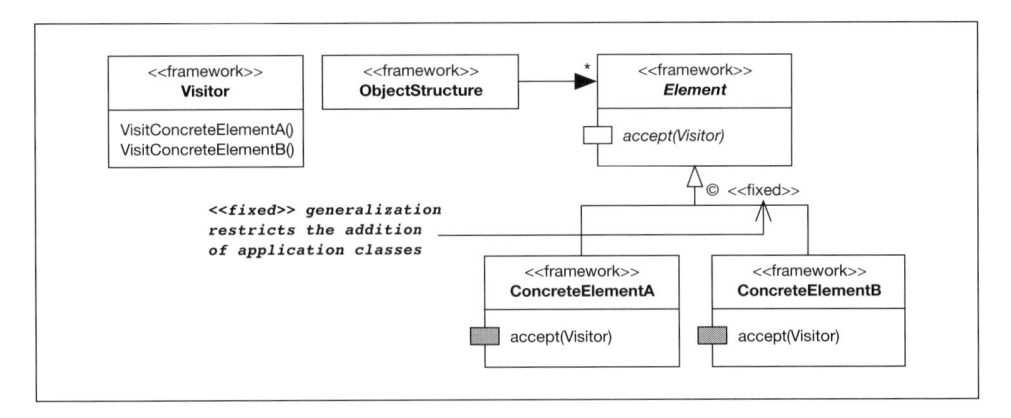

Figure 3.20 A sample «fixed» generalization in the Visitor pattern

As demonstrated above, the UML-F tag «fixed» expresses a restriction on the generalization relationship. The application developer cannot add direct subclasses, but can still add application-specific subclasses to already existing framework subclasses. The class diagram in Figure 3.21 exemplifies the abstract syntax of a programming language. Though the upper level generalization relationship is «fixed», the generalization relations between the subclasses of Nonterminal and their subclasses have the attribute «adapt–static», which allows language-specific extensions in the predefined Nonterminal categories Expression and Statement.

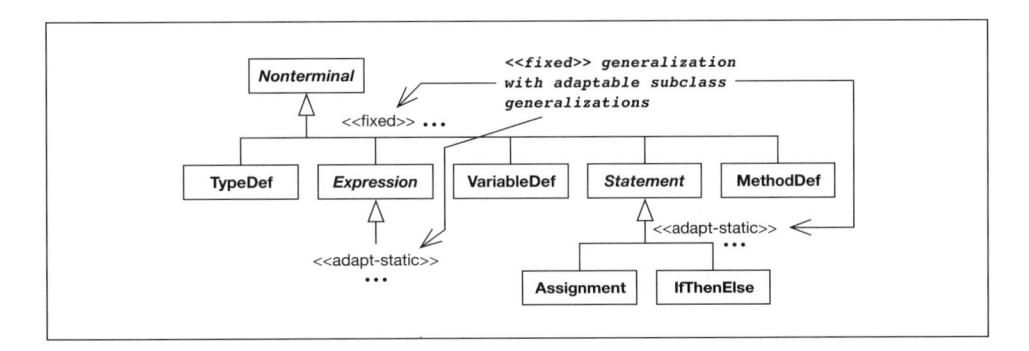

Figure 3.21 Combination of fixed and adaptable generalizations

The «adapt-dyn» tag

If the tag «adapt-dyn» is attached to a generalization, subclasses may be added during runtime. If a language and its runtime system support such extensions, an adaptation during runtime carries a risk of behavioral errors and exceptions that needs to be dealt with. Usually, the «adapt–dyn» tag is attached to a method, its defining class, and the generalization relationship altogether (see Figure 3.22). Omissions are possible because an attachment to the method is sufficient to convey the desired information.

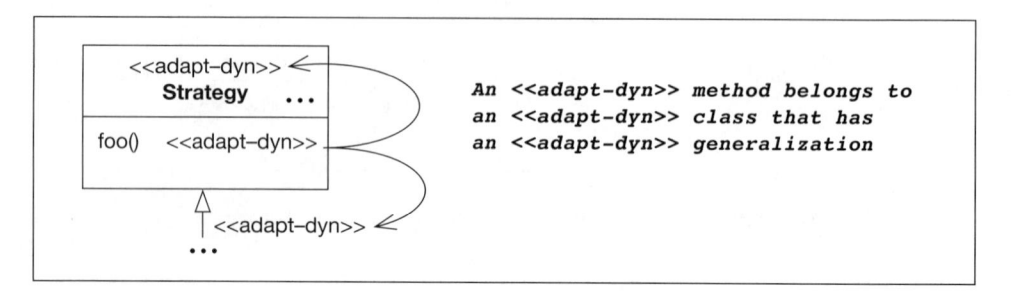

Figure 3.22 An «adapt–dyn» constellation

Promoting a tag from the superclass

If no tag is explicitly specified for a generalization, then the tag that implicitly applies depends on the tag of the superclass in that generalization. If the superclass is marked as «adapt–dyn» then the generalization is marked as «adapt–dyn». If the superclass is «fixed» or «adapt–static» then the generalization is «adapt–static». An explicit tag for the generalization, such as «adapt–static», always overrides the (invisible) promoted default.

As a convention, every class has a subclass tree and is therefore the root of a generalization relationship. If the subclass tree is empty, the generalization is empty too, but it still exists. Figure 3.23(a) shows how to mark a generalization relationship so that no subclasses can be defined. However, for this special case, UML-F provides a more intuitive notation, as shown in Figure 3.23(b). This is in accordance with the Java language which provides the modifier 'final' applicable to classes, indicating three constraints:

- the class is «fixed»
- the attached generalization relationship is «fixed»
- the generalization is empty – that is, no subclasses exist.

Standard UML already provides some constraints on generalizations.[15] The *complete* constraint roughly corresponds to UML-F's «fixed» tag, but with one important

Chapter 3 Basic elements of the UML-F profile

```
        <<framework>>           <<framework>>
        <<fixed>>               <<final>>
        Currency                Currency
            △
          © | <<fixed>>
           (a)                    (b)
```

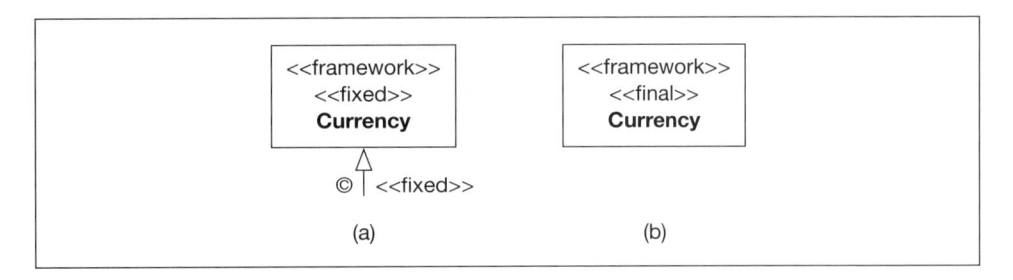

Figure 3.23 Equivalent representations ruling out the definition of subclasses

difference – the complete constraint applied to a class carries over to all subclasses and, therefore, does not allow the framework developer to decide which subclasses are adaptable. Thus, the inheritance structure of Figure 3.21 cannot be expressed within standard UML. The effect of the *complete* constraint, on the other hand, can be recreated by applying the «fixed» tag to all subclasses as well.

3.6 The UML-F mechanism for defining new tags

Though standard UML provides stereotypes, tagged values, and constraints as extension mechanisms, together with a set of predefined stereotypes and tagged values, it does not offer a suitable way of defining additional stereotypes or tagged values. This is comparable with a programming language that allows calling methods of predefined libraries but does not conveniently allow the definition of new ones. Any language – whether it is a natural language, a programming language, or a modeling language – needs to provide a mechanism for extending its vocabulary. In natural languages, new vocabulary can be expressed through already-known words. Programming languages provide definition mechanisms for classes, methods, etc. However, the UML 1.4 standard suggests the use of tables to introduce new stereotypes. UML-F clarifies and extends this technique by using a template that provides a simple but sound mechanism to introduce new tags. The presented mechanism combines a rigorous though informal description that defines the new tag in a sufficiently precise manner. Table 3.10 suggests a template for defining a new tag. In some ways this template structure resembles the description of a pattern.

---

[15] It was previously explained that the distinction between constraints, stereotypes, and tagged values is not sufficiently clear in the standard UML. UML-F therefore only uses tags – even for concepts similar to UML constraints.

There are two primary reasons for defining additional tags:

- The annotation of core construction principles and patterns in UML-F relies on tags. (The following chapters present these tags and their sample application.)
- Framework-specific tags can often be useful. Core abstractions in frameworks are good candidates for framework-specific tags. For example, all GUI frameworks contain an abstract class that represents visible objects such as sliders, buttons, and windows. The Java GUI frameworks Swing and AWT call that abstract class Component; ET++ provides the abstract class VObject. When dealing with such a framework, it can be useful to introduce shortcuts to mark a class that conforms to that abstraction by means of a tag, «Component» or «VObject». Another example where a framework-specific tag can be helpful is when framework-specific patterns are introduced. A corresponding tag marks the pattern instances in the framework.

Section name	Section purpose
Name	Defines the tag name, for example «VObject».
Applies to	Names the modeling element(s) that it may apply to. These are typically class, interface, method, attribute, and the like. If appropriate, a diagram shows the usage of the newly introduced tag.
Type	Explains which values the tag may assume. Tags are often of type Boolean. For example, «VObject» is equivalent to «VObject = true».
	Enumeration values can, for example, be denoted by #green, #red, #blue. Among others strings and integers are common tag types.
Motivation and purpose	What is the purpose of the tag? Where and how is it used?
Explanation of the effect	Informal, yet precise, explanations help the understanding of the meaning of a tag.
Expansion	Sometimes the tag serves as a shortcut. In this case, the effect of the tag can be described through an expanded diagram – for example, a «VObject» tag stands for a certain signature. If the tag stands for an interaction protocol, this could be described through sequence diagrams. Also (partial) method implementations can be shown here.
	If the tag can only be described partially through expansion, the expansion shall be shown and other semantic aspects should additionally be explained.
Discussion	A discussion of what the tag is good for, what the caveats are, and which related tags exist, is mandatory. It is of particular interest to describe how the new tag may interact with existing tags. It may be orthogonal, conflicting, or may imply another implicit tag on related modeling elements.

Table 3.10 Template for introducing a UML-F tag

The template in Table 3.10 is a modification of the template used by Gamma et al. (1995) to define a design pattern. We apply this template to introduce the subsequent layers of UML-F tags.

3.7 Summary

We have discussed the foundation of the UML-F profile, which comprises the concept of UML-F tags as a unified concept of standard UML tagged values and stereotypes. We have systematically introduced a number of UML-F tags that apply mainly to UML class diagram elements. Some of these tags, such as the incompleteness ('...') tag or the completeness ('©') tag, deal with the visual representation of a given model; others, such as «adapt-static» or «fixed», have implications for the model itself and the method of dealing with the tagged elements of the model.

For most of the tags that UML-F introduces, the standard stereotype form «tag-name» is used if the tag has implications for the model. An intuitive, iconic form (such as '...' or '©') is used if the tag has its implications for the visual representation.

The UML-F tags provided in this chapter are not fully independent of each other. Sometimes they imply, or even contradict, each other. In the following chapters, additional tags will be introduced as combinations of these basic tags to deal explicitly with framework core construction principles and with design patterns – both the patterns developed by the gang-of-four (GoF) authors (Gamma, Helm, Johnson and Vlissides), and any framework-specific ones.

Chapter 4

UML-F tags for framework construction principles and patterns

This chapter explores how to build and adapt object-oriented frameworks – that is, it presents the framework construction principles and patterns, and introduces the corresponding UML-F tags. What we call the construction principles of frameworks are independent of specific domains. Building frameworks by combining the basic object-oriented language constructs proves to be quite straightforward. However, this does not imply that frameworks are straightforward to develop. Instead, building such artefacts requires a thorough domain understanding. Good frameworks typically result from a tedious, iterative development process in which the interaction between software engineers and domain experts is a key element. (Chapter 7 provides hints and guidelines for the development and adaptation process in general.)

Many patterns written up in the pioneering pattern catalog (Gamma et al., 1995) by the GoF are frameworks that also rely on the few framework construction principles. This chapter discusses the relationship between the construction principles and the GoF catalog patterns and introduces the UML-F tags for annotating both the framework construction principles and the design patterns. Instead of listing the UML-F tags for each of the construction principles and patterns, we explain and exemplify how to derive the UML-F tags in a straightforward manner from their static structure.

Essential framework construction principles
Remember the definition of a framework as a piece of software that is extensible through the call-back style of programming. Object-oriented programming

languages support the call-back style of programming through inheritance or interfaces, combined with dynamic binding of methods. Adapting a framework thus means:

- modifying components according to specific needs by overriding methods of some framework classes in subclasses or by implementing interfaces; and/or
- assembling ready-made components.

The following sections discuss the two *construction principles* that assist these two styles of adaptation. The overriding of methods in white-box framework components corresponds to what we call the *Unification* construction principle. The assembly of ready-made components (black-box framework components) relies on what we call the *Separation* construction principle.

4.1 Unification principle – adaptation by inheritance

Hook methods can be viewed as placeholders that are invoked by more complex methods, usually called *template methods*[1] (Wirfs-Brock and Johnson, 1990; Gamma et al., 1995; Pree, 1995; Fayad et al., 1999a, b, c). The simple idea behind hook methods is that overriding hooks allows changes of the corresponding template method's behavior without having to alter the source code of the class to which the template method belongs.

The essential set of framework construction principles can be derived from considering all the possible combinations of template and hook methods within one class or in two classes. The reason why this becomes feasible is that the abstract concepts of templates and hooks fade out domain-specific semantics to show clearly the means of achieving extensibility in object-oriented technology. The rest of this chapter explores the flexibility afforded by the various template hook combinations and presents the corresponding UML-F tags. We use two case studies[2] to illustrate this construction principle.

Case study: Keeping the rounding of numbers flexible
Consider the convert() method in the Java class CurrencyConverter. It is a template method which invokes the hook method round() every time it has to round

---

[1] Template methods must not be confused with C++ template construct – this has a completely different meaning.

[2] The Java source code of most of the case studies in this book is available on the Web at *www.UML-F.net* – this, and the following chapters, assume a working knowledge of the Java programming language.

numbers (see Example 4.1). This hook method provides a four digit rounding after the comma as a default implementation. If the rounding policy of CurrencyConverter was to be changed without touching the existing source code, one would do so by defining a subclass that simply overrides the round() method. This elegantly changes the behavior of the convert() method without duplicating any source code. The convert() method actually calls back to the round() method. Overriding the round() method in a subclass redefines it, providing a different call-back routine to the convert() method. Note that we chose very simple rounding behavior to focus on the fundamentals of framework construction and adaptation.

```
public class CurrencyConverter {
    ...
    public void convert(...) {
        double result, value;
        ...
        switch (...) {
            case ... :
                ...
                result= round(value);
                break;
            case ... :
                ...
                result= round(value);
            ...
        }
        ...
    }
    public double round(double val) {
        ...
    }
    ...
}
```

Example 4.1 Currency conversion with rounding hook

Figure 4.1 shows a standard UML diagram that expresses the subclass relationship between CurrencyConverter and a sample subclass MyCurrConv. Class MyCurrConv overrides the hook method round().

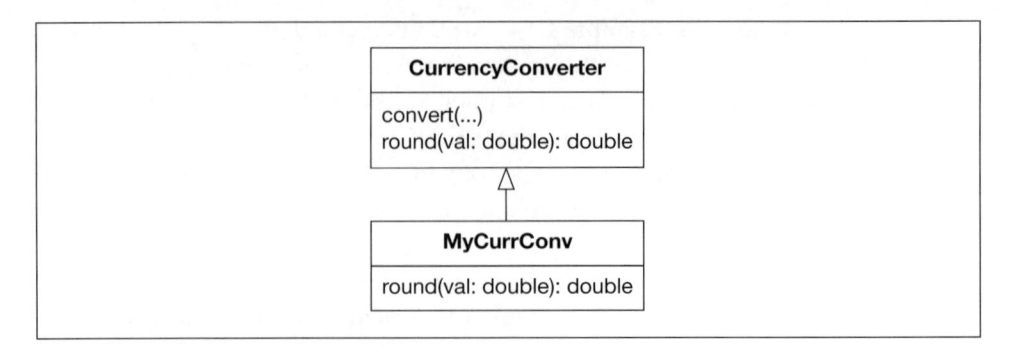

Figure 4.1 Adaptating CurrencyConverter by inheritance

Figure 4.2 illustrates schematically the basic object-oriented concept of overriding the hook method in MyCurrConv. This modification mechanism is supported directly by all object-oriented languages except C++.[3] Note that Figures 4.2 (a) and (b) are not UML diagrams.

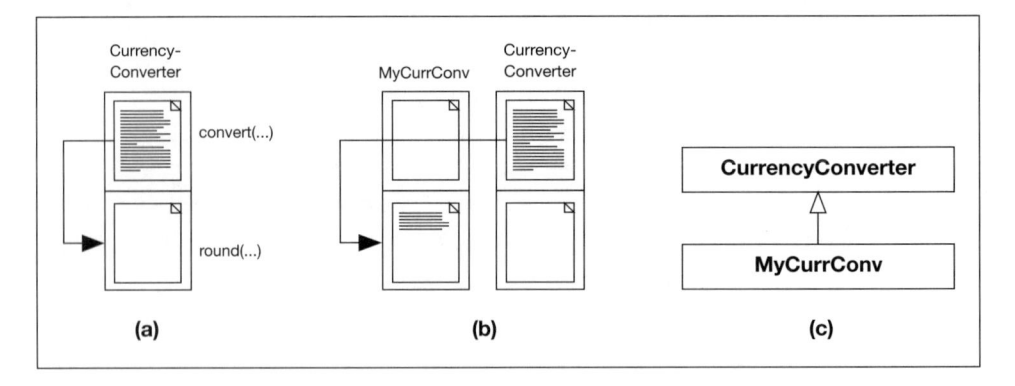

Figure 4.2 (a) Template method calling its hook method, (b) hook overriding, and (c) the corresponding UML class diagram

Case study: Keeping object creation flexible

Classes that rely on currency conversion have to create the appropriate instance, either of CurrencyConverter or one of its subclasses. Example 4.2 shows a class Account that creates a CurrencyConverter object in method sampleM().

---

[3] In C++, methods have to be explicitly marked as dynamically bound so that overridden hooks indeed modify their template method.

```
public class Account ... {
    ...
    public void sampleM(...) {
        ...
        CurrencyConverter currConv= new
            CurrencyConverter();
        ...
    }
    ...
}
```

Example 4.2 Fixed creation of a currency converter

If an Account object wanted to perform the currency conversion differently, (i.e. by means of another currency converter), the whole method sampleM() would have to be overridden or, even worse, the source code of sampleM() would be changed directly. To avoid this, Example 4.3 introduces the hook method createCurrConv(). The default implementation of createCurrConv() still creates an instance of CurrencyConverter. Nevertheless, the creation of a currency converter becomes flexible, as a subclass of Account just has to override the hook method to create a specific currency converter.

```
public class Account ... {
    ...
    public void sampleM(...) {
        ...
        CurrencyConverter currConv= createCurrConv();
        ...
    }
    public CurrencyConverter createCurrConv() {
        return new CurrencyConverter (...);
    }
    ...
}
```

Example 4.3 Currency conversion with rounding hook

Note that both case studies apply the same basic design principle, though the semantics of what is kept flexible differ. In case of the CurrencyConverter class, the hook method is round(). In case of Account, the hook method's name is createCurrConv(). In both cases, template and hook methods reside in one class. The fact that template and hook methods are in one class means that the behavior can only be modified by defining a subclass. So runtime adaptations are not feasible.

The Unification construction principle might be summarized as follows: generic behavior (that is, control flow that should be kept extensible) is packed into a hook method. The corresponding template and hook methods are in one class. The hook methods in the two examples above just differ in their names. Hook methods should be named according to the semantic aspects they keep flexible.

4.1.1 UML-F template and hook tags

The UML-F tags for marking template and hooks explicitly are «template» and «hook». In the currency converter example, method convert() in class CurrencyConverter is a template method invoking round() as its hook. Figure 4.3 shows the class CurrencyConverter with these UML-F tags annotating its methods convert() and round().

These UML-F tags can be used not only to mark methods but also to mark classes and interfaces. Attaching the «hook» tag to a class or interface means that it contains a hook method. The «template» tag has an analogous meaning, though it only makes sense to attach it to classes and not to interfaces as interfaces cannot provide implementations of methods. Figure 4.4 attaches both tags to class CurrencyConverter applying the UML-F tag rule that allows the listing of several tags within one set of enclosing guillemets.

CurrencyConverter	. . .
convert(...)	<<template>>
round(val: double): double	<<hook>>

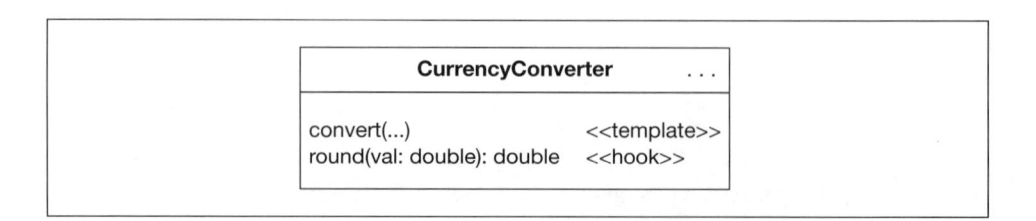

Figure 4.3 UML-F tags annotating template and hook methods

Chapter 4 UML-F tags for framework construction principles and patterns

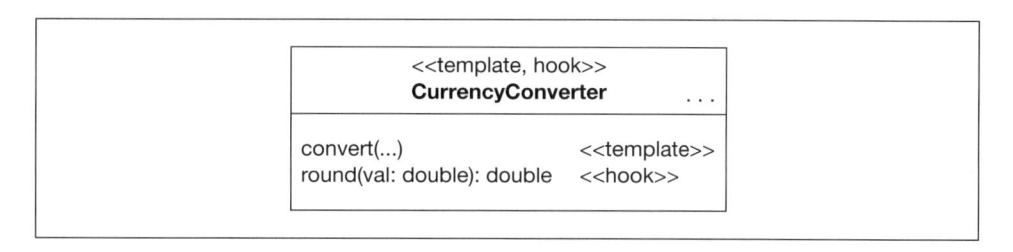

```
         <<template, hook>>
         CurrencyConverter              ...

  convert(...)                    <<template>>
  round(val: double): double      <<hook>>
```

Figure 4.4 UML-F tags attached to the class name and methods

Note that the context determines what is a template or what is a hook. Figure 4.5 shows class CurrencyConverter in the context of class Account. Here, method convert() is a hook method of the calcBalance() template method in class Account. Thus, method convert() is a template method in one context and a hook method in another context. Method calcBalance() can itself also become the hook method in the context of other classes.

Figure 4.6 attaches the name Rounding to the template and hook tags that form one logical group within one context. An explicit name for the tags provides the advantage of clear identification of related tags. Therefore the «hook» and «template» tags are of type String to allow the identification of the context they are used in.

```
     <<template>>                           <<hook>>
       Account          ...              CurrencyConverter    ...

  calcBalance(...)   <<template>>    convert(...)          <<hook>>
                                     round(val: double): double
```

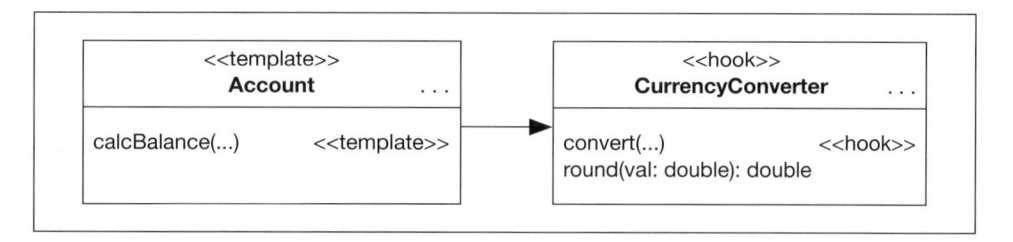

Figure 4.5 The context determines what is a template or hook method

```
         <<template, hook: Rounding>>
            CurrencyConverter              ...

  convert(...)                    <<template: Rounding>>
  round(val: double): double      <<hook: Rounding>>
```

Figure 4.6 Attaching a name to a group of related tags

Figure 4.7 shows the two tag groups Rounding and Conversion associated with the classes Account and CurrencyConverter, and some of their methods. The «template» tag serves as a hint for the application developer to leave the code untouched, whereas the «hook» tag serves as hint to adapt the code for application-specific needs. Chapter 5 describes how these UML-F annotations support framework adaptation. Tagging method convert() with both tags indicates that it depends on the context and the adaptation requirements whether it suffices to adapt only round() or the more complex convert() method instead.

The textual representation of several tag groups might get confusing quickly. To cope with numerous tag groups, a tool should allow the management of tag groups – for example, by offering a menu to select a group by name. Figure 4.8 shows how

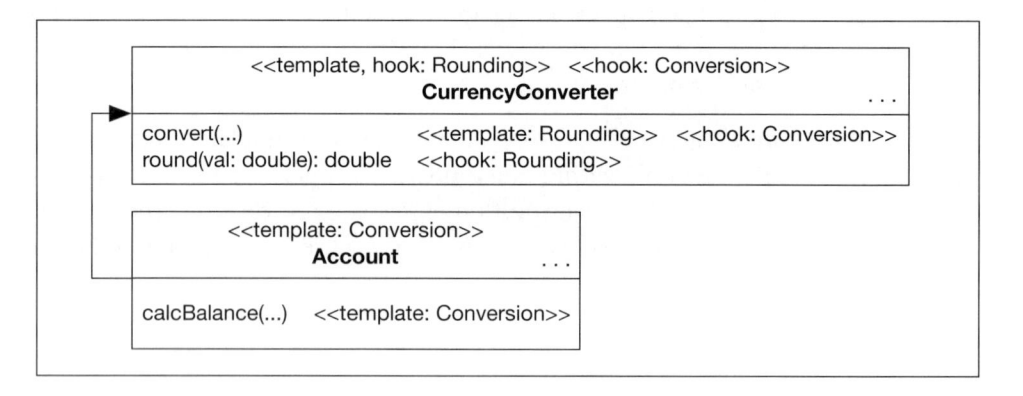

Figure 4.7   Textual marking of two tag groups

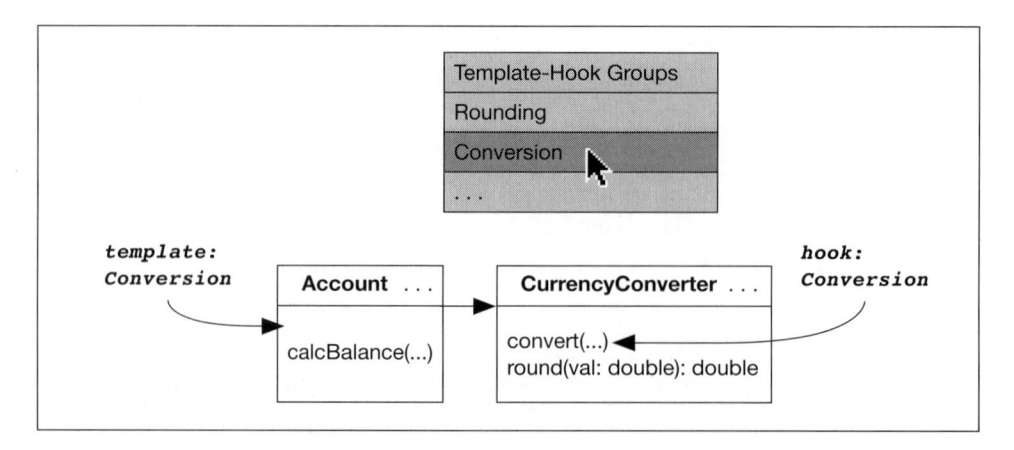

Figure 4.8   Selecting a tag group in a UML-F based tool

the user would interact with such a tool to highlight the group of tags labeled Conversion. The diagram proposes one possible visualization of the textual representation of the UML-F tags in the previous figures, relying on UML comments.

Definition of the UML-F template and hook tags

The Tables 4.1 and 4.2 summarize the UML-F template and hook tags according to the UML-F tag introduction mechanism (see Chapter 3). This completes the presentation of the template and hook tags above.

Tag	«hook».

Applies to	class, interface, method:
	
	`<<hook>>`
	ClassOrInterface
	`h()  <<hook>>`

Type	String.
Motivation and purpose	The tag makes it explicit that a method is a hook method, or that a class/interface contains a hook method. Framework adaptations often require the overriding of hook methods in subclasses. Thus the explicit marking helps to identify these framework variation points.
Informal explanation of effect	If the tag is attached to a class/interface it means that the class/interface contains at least one «hook» method. A string such as 'groupName' in «hook: groupName» is optional and can be used to mark templates and hooks that belong together. The string gives the template–hook group a name. If the tag is attached to a method it means that the method can be overridden in subclasses in order to add/modify application-specific code. If the hook method is part of an interface, a class that implements the interface provides the specific method implementation. A method with a hook tag can not only be called from the associated template method but from any method.

Expansion	The UML-F «hook» tag expands to the more basic UML-F tags «adapt–static» or «adapt–dynamic». These tags only indicate that an adaptation can take place. As a «hook» tag always comes with a corresponding «template» tag, the «hook» tag expresses more about a variation point than the basic tags.
	
	`<<adapt-static>>` `<<adapt-dynamic>>`
	H **H**
	`h() <<adapt-static>>` `h() <<adapt-dynamic>>`

Discussion	The «hook» tag is closely related to the «template» tag (see Table 4.2) and should never be used without a corresponding «template» tag. The explicit marking of framework classes/ interfaces/methods with the «hook» tag documents a framework's variation points.

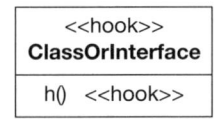

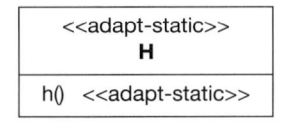

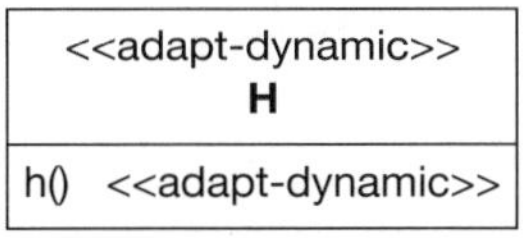

Table 4.1 Definition of the UML-F «hook» tag

Table 4.2 defines the «template» tag according to the UML-F tag introduction mechanism – note the symmetry between the two tags.

Tag	«template».
Applies to	class, method:
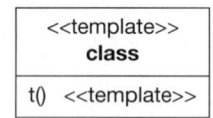	<<template>> **class** / t() <<template>>
Type	String.
Motivation and purpose	The tag makes it explicit that a method is a template method or that a class contains a template method. The overriding of hook methods adapts the corresponding template method. Such template and hook methods form a logical group. Thus the explicit marking helps to identify these framework variation points.
Informal explanation of effect	If the tag is attached to a class it means that the class contains at least one «template» method. A string such as 'groupName' in «template: groupName» is optional and can be used to mark template and hooks that belong together. The string gives the template–hook group a name. If the tag is attached to a method it means that the method is open for adaptations through the corresponding hook, but should not be overridden itself. If a method has both a template and a hook tag attached, then that method could possibly be overridden in the context in which it is a hook method.
Expansion	The UML-F template tag expands roughly to the more basic UML-F tag «fixed». The latter indicates that overriding the method is not an option. As a «template» tag always comes with a corresponding «hook» tag, the «template» tag expresses more about a variation point than the basic tag. <<fixed>> **T** / t() <<fixed>> ▲ <<fixed>> … A weaker form is relevant if class T also contains a hook method, because in this case only the template method is fixed, but subclasses are required to define hook methods: **TH** / t() <<fixed>>
Discussion	The «template» tag is closely related to the «hook» tag and should never be used without a corresponding «hook» tag. The explicit marking of framework classes/methods with the «template» tag documents a framework's variation points.

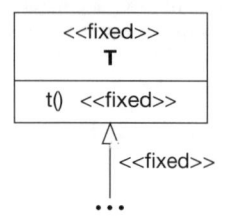

Table 4.2 Definition of the UML-F «template» tag

4.1.2 UML-F tags for the Unification construction principle

In the static structure of the Unification construction principle, the template method and its corresponding hook method reside in the same class that we call TH (see Figure 4.9). The procedure for deriving a tag name is to concatenate the construction principle name with each of the elements of the general structure of the construction principle. Thus, three UML-F tags annotate the Unification construction principle in a framework:

- «Unification–TH» marks the class
- «Unification–t» marks the template method
- «Unification–h» marks the hook method.

As a short cut we suggest using the tags «Unif–TH», «Unif–t», and «Unif–h». Compared to the bare-bone template and hook tags, stating explicitly that the Unification construction principle underlies a certain aspect of the framework provides more semantic information. In particular, a person who is familiar with the Unification construction principle might, for example, infer the degree of flexibility associated with that construction principle – adaptations have to be accomplished in subclasses and thus require an application restart. This semantic aspect cannot be formally defined within UML-F.

Figure 4.10 applies the Unification tags to annotate class CurrencyConverter. As with the template and hook tags, any name can be defined for a group of tags. We chose the name Rounding for the Unification construction principle in this case.

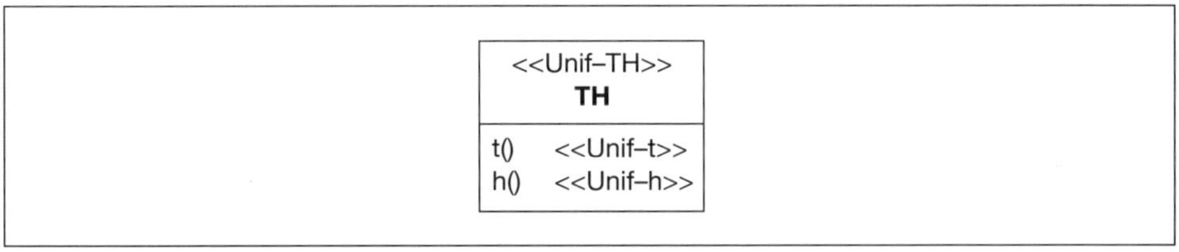

```
           <<Unif–TH>>
              TH
        ─────────────────
        t()    <<Unif–t>>
        h()    <<Unif–h>>
```

Figure 4.9   Static structure of the Unification construction principle

```
        <<Unif–TH: Rounding>>
           CurrencyConverter
─────────────────────────────────────────
 convert(...)
 round(val: double): double   <<Unif–t: Rounding>>
                              <<Unif–h: Rounding>>
```

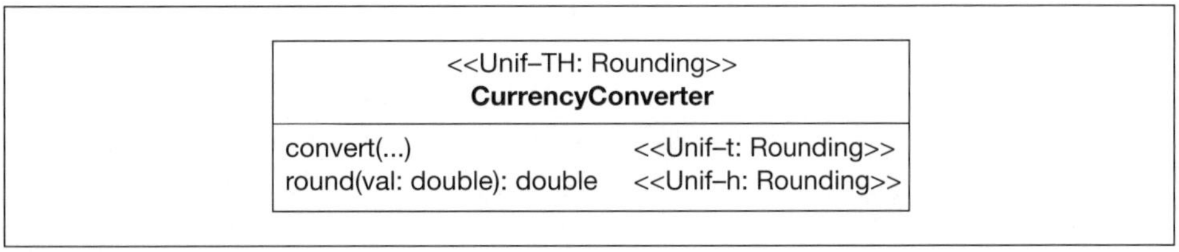

Figure 4.10   UML-F annotation of a sample application of the Unification construction principle

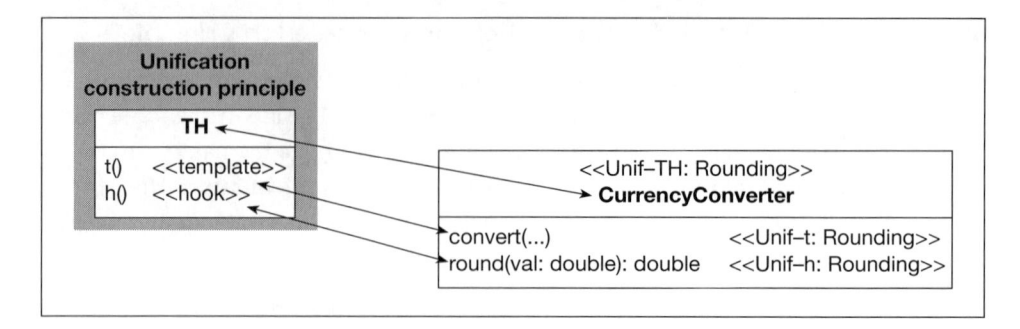

```
                  Unification
             construction principle
             ┌─────────────────────┐
             │        TH ◄─────────┼──────┐
             ├─────────────────────┤      │                    <<Unif–TH: Rounding>>
             │  t()   <<template>> │◄─────┼────────────────►   CurrencyConverter
             │  h()   <<hook>>     │◄──┐  │
             └─────────────────────┘   │  │   convert(...)               <<Unif–t: Rounding>>
                                       └──┼── round(val: double): double <<Unif–h: Rounding>>
```

Figure 4.11   Rationale behind the Unification UML-F tags

Conceptually, UML-F tags that correspond to the static structure of a framework construction principle provide a means of pinpointing the methods and classes in a framework that apply a particular design. Figure 4.11 illustrates this aspect. The arrows express the mapping of the structural components of the Unification construction principle to their manifestation in a certain part of a framework.

Definition of the UML-F Unification tags

Table 4.3 summarizes the UML-F Unification tags. The table documents all three tags that form a logical unit.

Tags	«Unification–TH», «Unification–t», «Unification–h»; or their abbreviations «Unif–TH», «Unif–t», «Unif–h».
Apply to	class («Unification–TH»), method («Unification–t», «Unification–h»); see Figure 4.9.
Type	String.
Motivation and purpose	The tags highlight the application of the Unification construction principle in a framework by marking the corresponding template and hook methods as well as the class to which these methods belong.
Informal explanation of effect	The Unification construction principle implies that the adaptation of the framework variation point requires the overriding of the hook method.
Expansion	The Unification tags «Unification–t» and «Unification–h» expand to the UML-F «template» and «hook» tags (see Figure 4.11).
Discussion	The three UML-F Unification tags must always be used together. Several instances of the «Unification–h» tags are possible if the «Unification–t» method calls them all.

Table 4.3   Definition of the UML-F Unification tags

4.2 Separation principle – adaptation through composition

The Separation construction principle places the template and hook methods in separate classes. Let's rework the CurrencyConverter example. The hook method round() becomes part of another class RoundingPolicy. The class with the hook method is, in most cases, an abstract class or a Java interface (see below). An instance of CurrencyConverter refers to an object of static type RoundingPolicy through an instance variable rPol. Further, CurrencyConverter typically offers a method that allows a change of the rounding policy. This is method defineRoundingPolicy() in Example 4.4. In other words, the behavior of the template method convert() in CurrencyConverter can be changed by plugging in any specific RoundingPolicy object through the method defineRoundingPolicy().

```
public class CurrencyConverter {
    RoundingPolicy rPol= new DefaultRPol();
    ...
    public void convert(...) {
        double result, value;
        ...
        switch (...) {
            case ... :
                ...
                result= rPol.round(value);
                break;
            case ... :
                ...
                result= rPol.round(value);
                ... break;
        }
        ...
    }
    public void defineRoundingPolicy(RoundingPolicy
        rp) {
        rPol= rp;
    }
    ...
}
public abstract class RoundingPolicy {
    public abstract double round(double val);
```

```
}
public class DefaultRPol extends RoundingPolicy {
    public double round(double val) {
        ... // do a four digit after comma rounding of
        //      'val'
    }
}
```

Example 4.4 Separation of template and hooks

The main difference between the Unification and Separation construction principles is the ease of extension. The Unification principle requires overriding of the hook method in a subclass in order to change the behavior of the template method. Common object-oriented languages and their runtime systems do not allow such modifications at runtime. The Separation principle on the other hand only requires an object instantiation and a redefinition of a reference that can be done at runtime. Any of the subclasses of RoundingPolicy might be instantiated and plugged into the CurrencyConverter object. Runtime adaptations of the template method behavior are easier with the Separation principle.

4.2.1 Compositional adaptation with predefined black-box components

Figure 4.12 shows three subclasses of RoundingPolicy. The connecting line between classes CurrencyConverter and RoundingPolicy expresses an association that corresponds to the instance variable rPol in class CurrencyConverter. The italic style of the class name RoundingPolicy and method round() marks the class and its

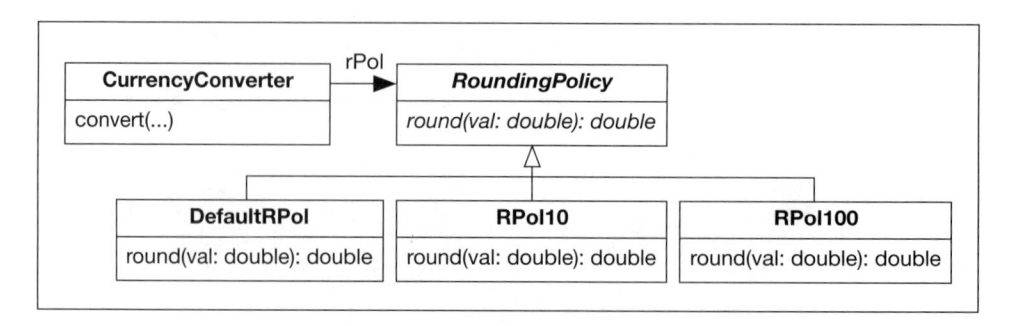

Figure 4.12 UML diagram showing sample rounding policies

method as abstract – this is standard UML. The rounding behavior of the three subclasses DefaultRPol, RPol10, and RPol100 is as follows: DefaultRPol rounds a number to four digits after the comma; RPol10 rounds the decimal place; RPol100 rounds by the hundreds. Plugging in one of these rounding policies in a currency converter object adapts the rounding behavior of the template method convert() accordingly. Example 4.5 presents a source code fragment that accomplishes these adaptations, assuming that the end-user chooses a rounding policy via a menu.

```
...                     // the local variable 'currConv' refers
                        // to an instance
                        // of class CurrencyConverter
switch (...) {          // menu selection
        case ... :
                currConv.defineRoundingPolicy(new
                    DefaultRPol());
                break;
        case ... :
                currConv.defineRoundingPolicy(new
                    RPol10());
                break;
        case ... :
                currConv.defineRoundingPolicy(new
                    RPol100());
                break;
}
```

Example 4.5 Plugging in different rounding components

4.2.2 Extending a set of black-box components at runtime

Figure 4.13 shows the UML diagram of three subclasses of RoundingPolicy and an additional subclass SpecialRPol. SpecialRPol rounds the decimal place for numbers up to 50,000 and rounds by the hundreds for larger numbers. SpecialRPol should be defined, implemented and plugged into a CurrencyConverter instance while the application that uses currency conversion is running. In other words, the class SpecialRPol was not available when that application was started. While the

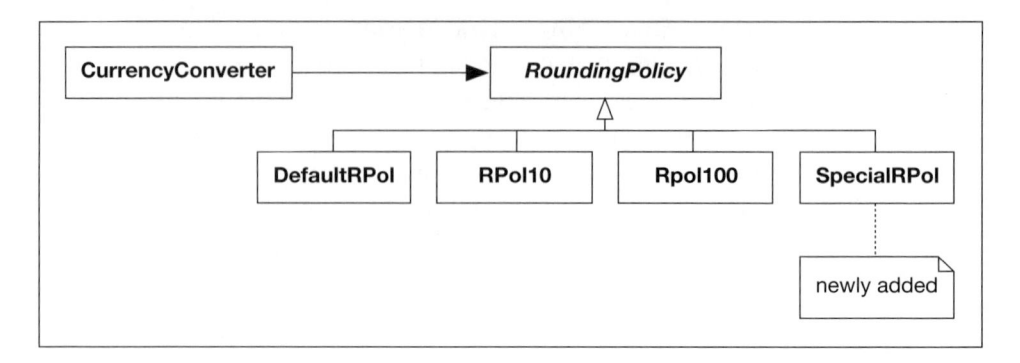

Figure 4.13 Sample rounding policies

application is running, the additional class SpecialRPol is implemented and an instance of it should be used to adapt a CurrencyConverter object.

This requires the dynamic loading and linking of a class to a running application, and the instantiation of a class whose name is not known in advance. A simple user interface for plugging in additional rounding policies could be a dialog box that allows entering the class name as string (see Figure 4.14).

Java offers the dynamic loading and linking of classes and its meta-information system suffices for instantiating classes whose names are specified as strings. Example 4.6 shows the source code fragment that instantiates a rounding policy based on the class name that is provided as string. The static forName() method of class Class searches for the Java byte code in certain directories, if the class is not yet linked to the running application. Method forName() then generates an instance of class Class whose method newInstance() creates an instance of the class that was specified as string.

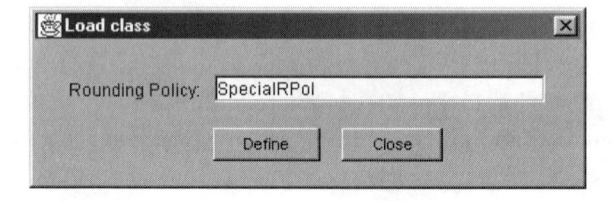

Figure 4.14 Dialog box for plugging in a rounding component that is not known a priori

```
public RoundingPolicy createRoundingPolicy(String
                                           className) {
    Object aRPol;
    try {
        Class aClass= Class.forName(className);
        aRPol= aClass.newInstance();
    } catch (Exception e) { return null; }
    if (aRPol instanceof RoundingPolicy)
        return (RoundingPolicy)aRPol;
    else
        return null;
}
//
...
String clName= read the text entered in the dialog
               entry field (see Fig. 4.14)
RoundingPolicy rPol= createRoundingPolicy(clName);
if (rPol != null)
        currConv.defineRoundingPolicy(rPol);
...
```

Example 4.6 Instantiating and plugging in rounding components

4.2.3 UML-F tags for the Separation construction principle

In the Separation construction principle, the template and the hook methods are defined in separate classes coupled via an association. The class containing h() could also be a Java interface. Figure 4.15 illustrates this combination of template and hooks. As a consequence, UML-F provides a means of marking these items (T, H, t(), and h()), and in particular whether class H is supposed to be extended in the framework adaptation process.

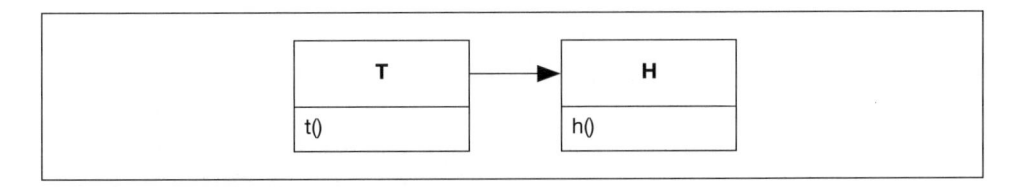

Figure 4.15 Separation of template and hook methods

Analogous with the Unification construction principle, the static structure of the Separation construction principle determines the corresponding UML-F tags. Figure 4.16 shows the static structure of the Separation construction pattern annotated with the UML-F tags for that construction pattern. As can be seen, there are four concepts that need to be documented using UML-F tags.

- «Separation–T» marks the class that contains the template method
- «Separation–H» marks the class that contains the hook method
- «Separation–t» marks the template method
- «Separation–h» marks the hook method.

As a short cut we suggest using the tags «Sep–T», «Sep–H», «Sep–t», and «Sep–h».

Figure 4.17 applies the Separation tags to annotate the conversion design aspect of classes Account and CurrencyConverter. Though again not mandatory, we chose the name Conversion for that application of the Separation construction principle and explicitly group the tags.

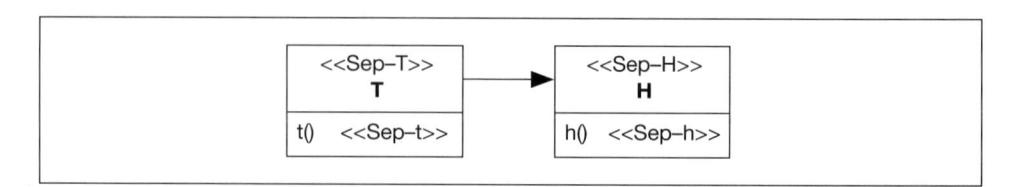

Figure 4.16 Static structure of the Separation construction principle

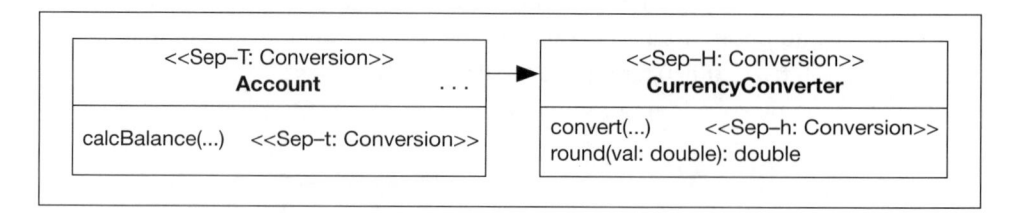

Figure 4.17 Sample UML-F annotation of a Separation construction principle

The mapping between a construction principle and classes or methods of a framework allows adequate documentation, and as a consequence, better understanding of a framework. Figure 4.18 shows this mapping schematically. The use of tags makes for a more compact textual mapping which is equally informative. Beyond a simple marking of the templates and hooks, the Separation and Unification UML-F tags express semantic information which is inherent in these construction principles.

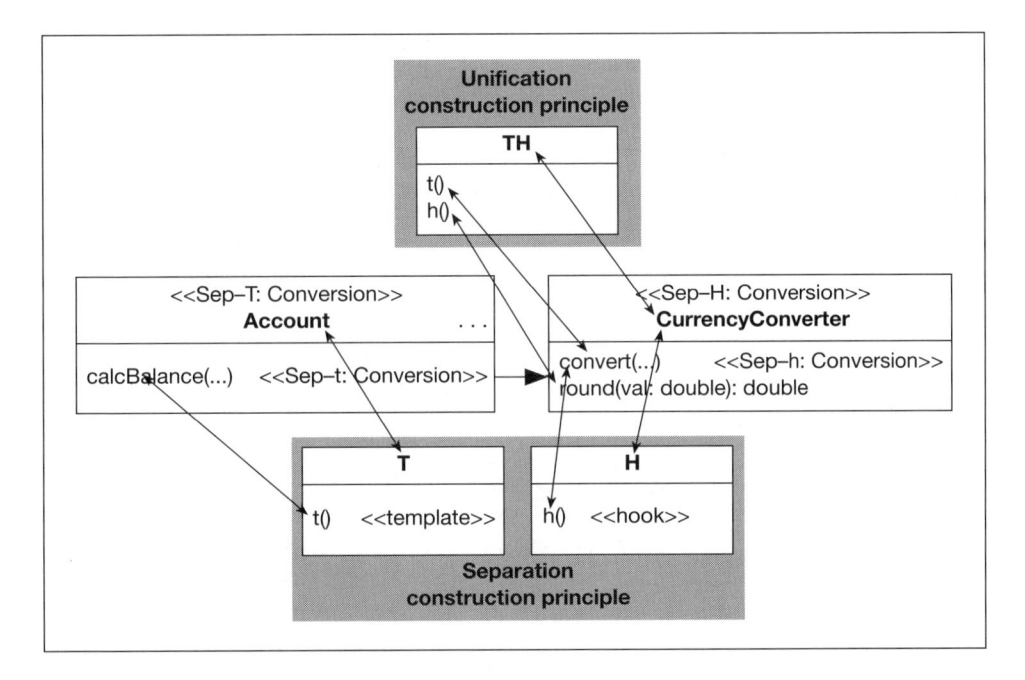

Figure 4.18 Mapping construction principles onto a sample framework

Analogous with the proposed tool support for template and hook tags, Figure 4.19 exemplifies how a tool could exploit UML-F tags for framework construction principles. If a user would like to view instances where the Separation construction principle was applied, they select one incarnation from a pop-up menu by name. Based on the selection, the tool might establish hyperlinks that link the corresponding classes/interfaces and methods. Figure 4.19 illustrates this linkage. As an alternative view, the structural components of the construction principle might be highlighted, for example by labels and lines with arrow heads as in Figure 4.18.

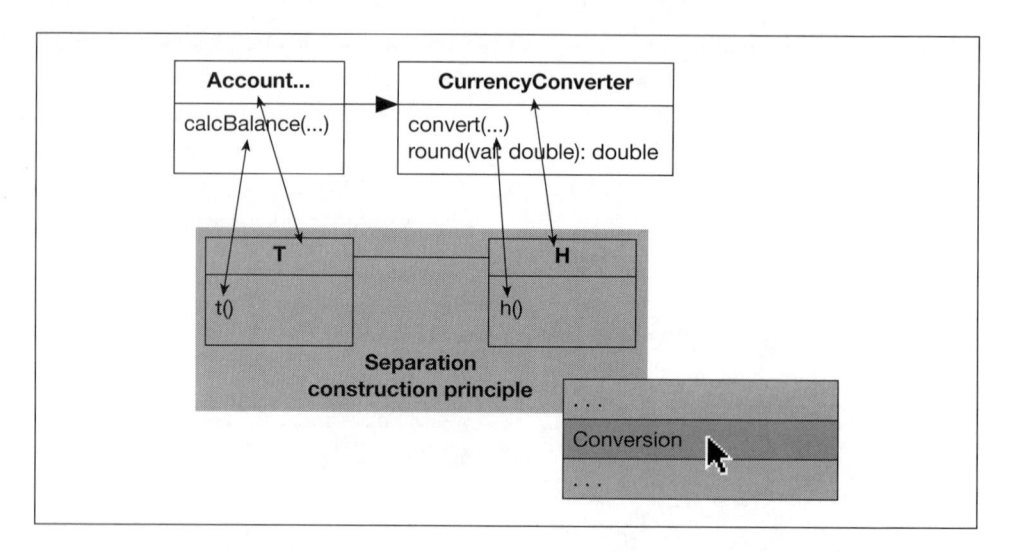

Figure 4.19 Tool-assisted mapping of the structure of a pattern to framework spots

Definition of the UML-F Separation tags

Table 4.4 summarizes the UML-F Separation tags. The table documents all four tags that form a logical unit.

Tags	«Separation–T», «Separation–H», «Separation–t», «Separation–h»; or their abbreviations «Sep–T», «Sep–H», «Sep–t», «Sep–h».
Apply to	class («Separation–T», «Separation–H»), method («Separation–t», «Separation–h»), interface («Separation–H»); see Figure 4.16.
Type	String.
Motivation and purpose	The tags highlight the application of the Separation construction principle in a framework by marking the corresponding template and hook methods as well as the classes/interfaces to which the particular methods belong to.
Informal explanation of effect	The Separation construction principle implies that the adaptation of the framework variation point can be accomplished by plugging in specific instances of classes of static type «Separation-H». If the framework does not provide appropriate classes of static type «Separation-H», additional ones have to be defined by overriding of the hook method(s).
Expansion	The Separation tags «Separation–t» and «Separation–h» expand to the more basic UML-F template and hook tags (see Figure 4.18).
Discussion	The four UML-F Separation tags must always be used together. Several instances of the «Separation–h» tags are possible, if the «Separation–t» method calls them.

Table 4.4 Definition of the UML-F Separation tags

4.3 Terminology and concept excursion: abstract classes, abstract coupling, Java interfaces

Classes that define common behavior for a set of subclasses usually do not represent instantiable classes but abstractions thereof – they are called *abstract classes*. It does not make sense to generate instances of abstract classes since some methods are abstract and have empty or no implementations. The general idea behind abstract classes is clear and straightforward.

- Properties (that is, attributes and methods) of similar classes are defined in a common superclass.

- Some methods of the resulting abstract class can be implemented, while only empty or no implementations can be provided for others, which are termed *abstract methods*. The RoundingPolicy class is so simple that it only contains one abstract method, round(). Though abstract methods cannot be implemented, their names and parameters create a *standard class signature* for all descendants, since descendants cannot change the method interface. Instances of all descendants of an abstract class understand at least all messages that are defined in the abstract class. (A descendant class inherits from another class, but not necessarily as a direct subclass.)

Sometimes the term *protocol* is used for this standardized signature – instances of descendants of a class A support the same signature as supported by instances of A. Conceptually, a signature and a Java interface are the same. The differences between an abstract class and a Java interface are explained below.

4.3.1 Abstract classes and abstract coupling

The purpose of an abstract class A is to provide a signature[4] so that other pieces of software, such as a component B, can be implemented based on the signature of A. B relies on the signature supported by the abstract class – that is, B is *abstractly coupled* with the abstract class A. In an adapted framework an implementation for the signature of the abstract class A is provided through a concrete subclass A1, which the component B does not know of. Most importantly, these components interact properly, that is without change and recompilation, with instances of all future extensions of the abstract classes.

In general, the key is to find useful abstractions so that software components can be implemented without knowing the specific details of the concrete objects they

---

[4] In addition to that, abstract classes can also implement methods and define instance variables. Java interfaces can only provide a signature.

rely on. Framework development projects corroborate that difficulty, as it sometimes takes years to refine abstractions.

Usually an instance variable maintains a coupling relation between two classes. Other possibilities are global variables or temporary relations by passing object references via method parameters. As the actual coupling between abstractly coupled classes is a rather irrelevant implementation detail, this issue is not discussed in further detail. The same is true for the implementation of a UML association between two classes.

Note that the Separation principle is closely related to abstract coupling. Both terms can be used interchangeably in most contexts. A small difference is that the Separation principle does not require the class with the hook to be an abstract one. For example, the rounding policy case study could abandon the abstract class RoundingPolicy. Instead, the CurrencyConverter could be coupled with the concrete class DefaultRPol. RPol10, RPol100, and SpecialRPol would then be subclasses of DefaultRPol.

4.3.2 Java interfaces

Java supports a separation of interface and class definitions. In other typed object-oriented languages, such as C++, the type hierarchy is only defined by (and is identical to) the class hierarchy – only descendants of a class A are type compatible to A. Java breaks this up by offering the interface language construct. C# also provides the interface construct. Thus the following discussion applies to C# as well.

Interface and class definitions both represent type definitions. Therefore the class hierarchy in Java acts as type hierarchy. But classes can additionally implement one or more interfaces. So additional types can be defined independently of the class hierarchy.

In Java, interfaces are defined similarly to classes with the keyword interface instead of class. Analogous with abstract methods, only the signature of a method is defined, not its implementation. So neither method implementations nor any state variables (instance variables or attributes in UML terminology) are present in an interface. Example 4.7 shows the definition of an interface and a class that implements this interface. If a class definition says it implements an interface, it has to implement all methods specified in the particular interface. Classes can implement several interfaces by separating the list of interfaces with commas.

```
public interface SampleInterface {
    public void method1();
    public void method2() ;
}
public class A extends AnotherClass implements
    SampleInterface {
    public void method1() { // implementation of
                            // method1
    }
    public void method2() { // implementation of
                            // method2
    }
    ...
}
```

Example 4.7 Sample interface definition and implementation

Variables of static type[5] SampleInterface can refer to instances of classes that implement the interface (see Example 4.8). There is another difference between class and interface hierarchies. In Java, a class can only inherit from one other class (single inheritance), while an interface can inherit from any number of interfaces (multiple inheritance). As interfaces only define method signatures, multiple inheritance of interfaces causes no problems as no method implementations are inherited.

```
...
SampleInterface si;
si= new A();
...
```

Example 4.8 Type compatibility

---

[5] In statically typed languages, such as Java, C#, and C++, a variable has exactly one static type as specified in the variable declaration in the (static) program text. On the other hand, a variable can have any number of dynamic types. The dynamic type of a variable is the type of the object the variable refers to. In the context of interfaces, a variable wih the static type of an interface can refer to any object that is an instance of a class that implements that interface.

From the perspective of construction principles, Java interfaces are equivalent to abstract classes. Thus, it does not matter whether a class is coupled with an abstract class or an interface. In case of an abstract class, subclasses define the specific behavior in the overridden methods. In case of an interface, any class in the class hierarchy can implement the interface, no matter whose subclass it is. The implementation of interface methods corresponds to the overriding of abstract methods in abstract classes.

The abstract class RoundingPolicy in the earlier case study could, and probably should, become an interface. A rule of thumb is to prefer interfaces, if the resulting entity does not have a minimum number of method implementations that justifies an abstract class definition. The consequence of defining RoundingPolicy as an interface would simply be that the classes DefaultRPol, RPol10, RPol100, and SpecialRPol would not be subclasses of RoundingPolicy, but would implement its round() method. Figure 4.20 shows the corresponding UML diagram. Any class that offers an appropriate round() method could implement the RoundingPolicy interface.

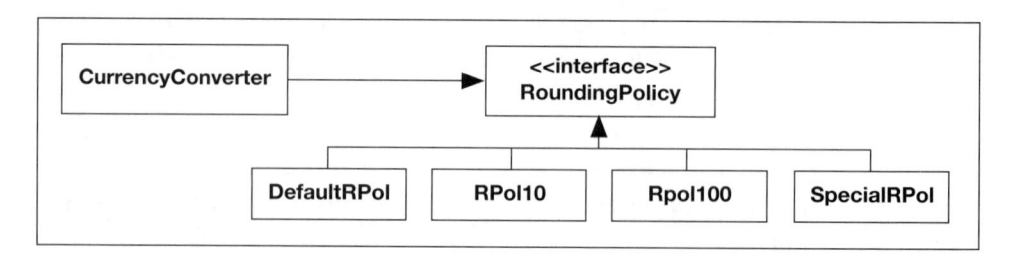

Figure 4.20   RoundingPolicy as an interface

Example 4.9 summarizes the modifications in the source code. There are no changes necessary in class CurrencyConverter.

```
public class CurrencyConverter {
    RoundingPolicy rPol= new DefaultRPol();
    ...
    public void convert(...) {
        double result, value;
        ...
```

```
            switch (...) {
                case ... :
                    ...
                    result= rPol.round(value);
                    break;
                case ... :
                    ...
                    result= rPol.round(value);
                ...
            }
            ...
        }
        public void defineRoundingPolicy (RoundingPolicy rp) {
            rPol= rp;
        }
        ...
    }
    public interface RoundingPolicy {
        public double round(double val);
    }
    public class DefaultRPol implements RoundingPolicy {
        public double round(double val) {
            ... // do a four digit after comma rounding
                // of 'val'
        }
    }
```

Example 4.9 Hook as Java interface

4.4 Hooks as name designators of pattern catalog entries

Hook methods form the points of predefined refinement that we call variation points or hot spots (Pree, 1995). Framework adaptation takes place at these variation points. Depending on hook placement and template–hook method combination more or less flexibility can be achieved.

Every framework incorporates the two essential construction principles, Unification and Separation, no matter how simple or how complex the particular template and hook methods are. Fine-grained classes apply the same construction principles as complex classes in order to introduce flexibility. They differ only in the granularity, the semantics of the hooks (often expressed in a hook's name), the number of provided defaults for a hook, and the number of template–hook pairs. Thus we can take a fresh look at widely known pattern catalogs. As the focus of the following considerations lies on the pioneering pattern catalog by Gamma et al. (1995), the reader should be familiar with these patterns. In the following, when we refer to the pattern catalog or the GoF patterns we mean the 23 patterns published in the book by Gamma et al. (1995).

Many entries in the pattern catalog can be regarded as small frameworks,[6] consisting of a few classes, that apply the essential construction principles in various more or less domain-independent situations. These catalog entries are helpful when designing frameworks and they illustrate typical hook semantics. In general, the names of the catalog entries are closely related to the semantic aspects that are kept flexible by provided hooks.

4.4.1 GoF patterns with a template–hook unification

The catalog pattern Template Method discusses the basic concept of template and hook methods in a quite generic way analogous with the Unification construction principle. The Factory Method pattern keeps the creation of objects flexible and relies on a unification of template and hook methods in one class. The template and hook methods are in class Creator, the hook method has the name factoryMethod(). The hook semantics determine the pattern name. Figure 4.21 annotates the structure of the Factory Method pattern (see Gamma et al., 1995) and points out which of the methods in class Creator is the template and which one is the hook method.

The Abstract Factory pattern results from the Factory Method pattern by separating template and hook methods in two classes. This is analogous with keeping the hook method round() in the same class as the template method versus separating the two methods.

---

[6] These are Template Method, Factory Method; Bridge, Abstract Factory, Builder, Command, Interpreter, Observer, Prototype, State, Strategy; Composite, Decorator, Chain of Responsibility

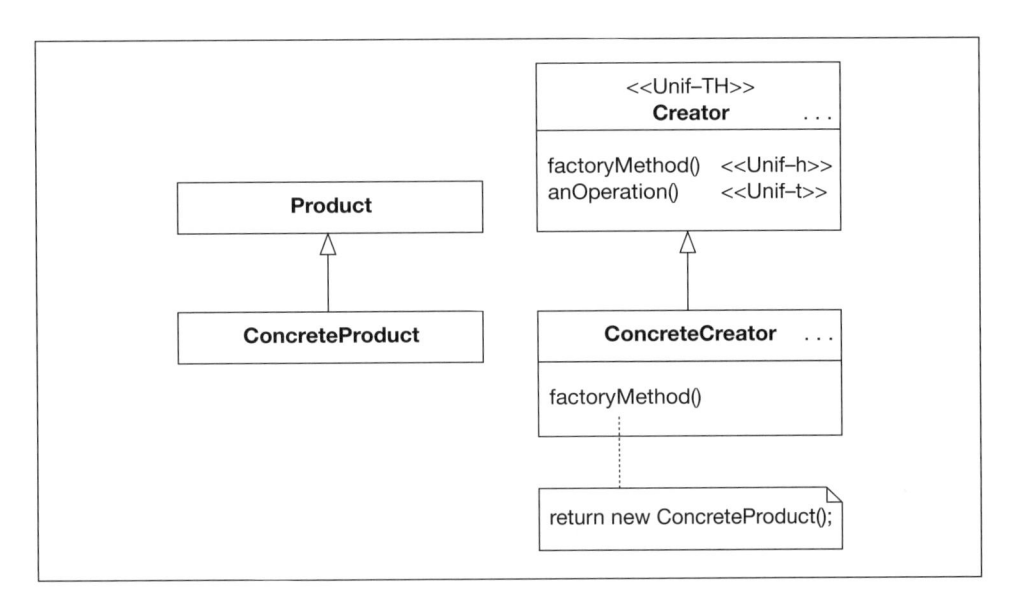

Figure 4.21 Unification-based Factory Method pattern

4.4.2 GoF patterns with a template–hook separation

A significant portion of the framework-centered pattern catalog entries relies on a separation of template and hooks, that is on the basic Separation principle. The catalog pattern Bridge discusses the abstract coupling mechanism generically. Other catalog entries that use template–hook separation introduce more specific semantics for their hooks: Abstract Factory, Builder, Command, Interpreter, Observer, Prototype, State, and Strategy. The names of these catalog patterns correspond to the semantics of a particular hook method or the corresponding class. Table 4.5 relates these GoF pattern names to the name of the class containing the hook, the hook method name, and the name of the class containing the template as used in the pattern description in the catalog. The hook semantics are summarized from a table in Gamma et al. (1995). The method names start with a capital letter as in the GoF pattern catalog.

Catalog entry	Class with hook	Hook method	Class with template	Hook semantics
Abstract Factory	AbstractFactory	CreateProduct()	Client	Families of product objects.
Builder	Builder	BuildPart()	Director	How a complex object is created.
Command	Command	Execute()	Invoker	When and how a request is fulfilled.
Interpreter	AbstractExpression	Interpret(...)	Client	Interpretation of a language.
Observer	Observer	Update()	Subject	How the dependent objects stay up to date.
Prototype	Prototype	Clone()	Client	Class of object that is instantiated.
State	State	Handle()	Context	States of an object.
Strategy	Strategy	AlgorithmInterface()	Context	An algorithm.

Table 4.5 Naming issues of catalog entries

Of these Separation-based patterns, the Abstract Factory, Builder, Observer, State, and Strategy patterns represent rather generic examples of hook semantics. In particular, the necessity to keep object creation flexible – as in the two patterns Abstract Factory and Builder – is likely to occur in many frameworks.

4.4.3 GoF patterns with recursive template–hook combinations

Besides the unification and separation of template and hooks, three principles result from template–hook combinations that allow recursive graph compositions of objects – for example, in trees and lists. For the sake of completeness, we include the derivation of these principles as a result of considering the possible template–hook combinations. The pattern catalog discusses the details of how and when to apply these construction principles.

In the pattern catalog entry Composite, the class with the template method (T) inherits from the class with the hook method (H). The association between the two classes is a zero to N relationship – that is, a T object can refer to any number of H objects (see Figure 4.22(a)). The name Composite expresses the core characteristic

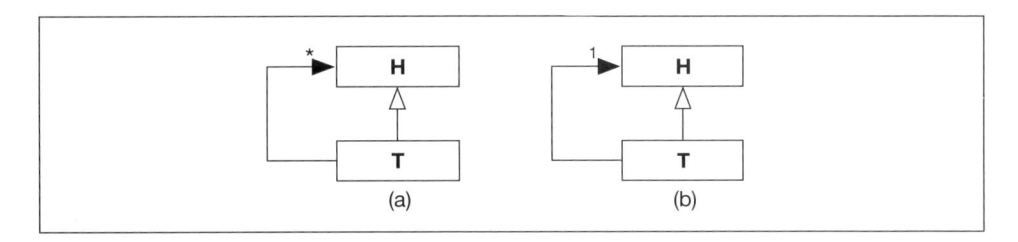

Figure 4.22 Core class structure of (a) Composite and (b) Decorator patterns

of this construction principle, namely that a tree hierarchy of objects can be built and treated in the same way as a single object.

The recursive composition where template and hooks are separated and where a T object can refer to zero or one H object (see Figure 4.22(b)) represents the Decorator pattern. The name expresses that objects can be dynamically adorned with additional behavior. Note that T need not be a direct subclass of H – that is, several other classes might be in between T and H. This is valid for both class diagrams (a) and (b) in Figure 4.22.

Finally, a kind of degenerated recursive composition where template and hooks melt in one class TH, and where a TH object can refer to zero or one other TH object (see Figure 4.23) is the Chain of Responsibility pattern in the catalog.

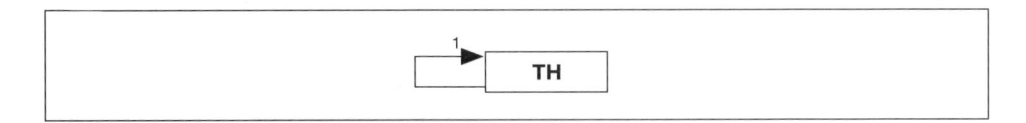

Figure 4.23 Class structure of the Chain of Responsibility pattern

4.5 UML-F tags for framework patterns

Analogous with the Unification and Separation construction principles, the structure of a GoF pattern determines the particular set of UML-F tags. In the case of the GoF framework patterns, each pattern description has a section labeled Structure which shows a class diagram. The class and method names in such a diagram, together with the pattern name, form the set of UML-F tags: «PatternName–methodName», «PatternName–ClassName»; and for potential future Java- or C#-based versions of the GoF catalog or other pattern catalogs,

«PatternName–InterfaceName». In situations where associations and attributes play a role, tags of the form «PatternName-associationLabel» and «PatternName-attributeName» are present as well.

This section illustrates the straightforward mechanism for the GoF patterns Factory Method, Composite, and Strategy as well as for a domain-specific pattern called Calculation.

Consider the layered relationship between the UML-F tag sets[7] for the design patterns, construction principles, and the template and hook tags (see Figure 4.24). The figure does not show the lower level UML-F tags «fixed», «adapt–static», and «adapt–dynamic» on which the template and hook tags are loosely based. In addition to presenting the sample UML-F tag sets for Factory Method, Composite, Strategy, and Calculation, this section discusses the layered relationships in further detail.

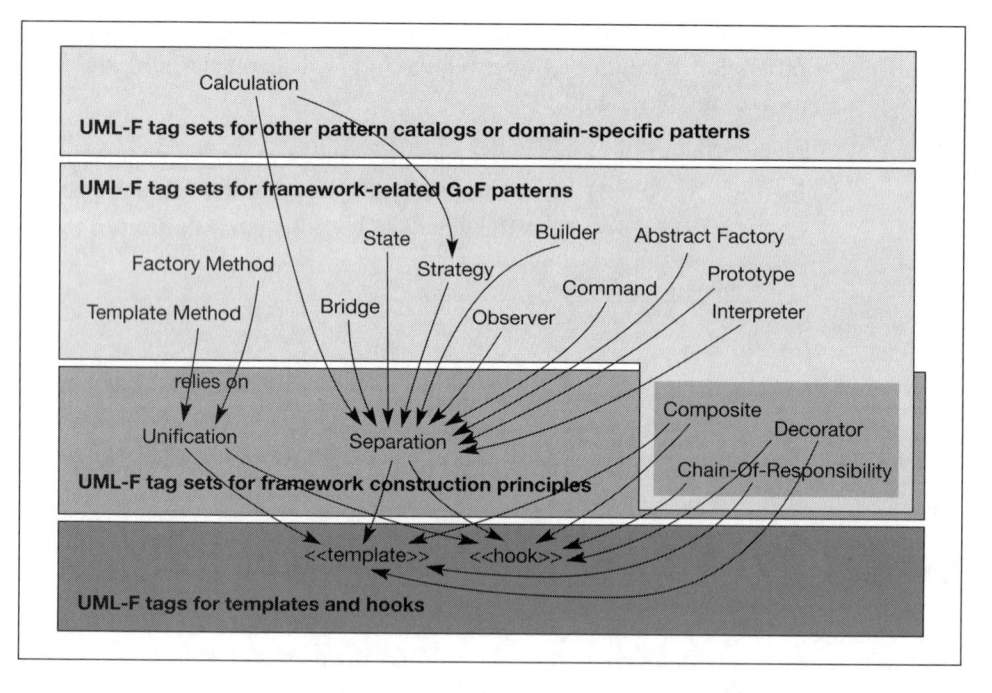

Figure 4.24 Layers of UML-F tag sets

---

[7] The tags of a construction principle or pattern form one tag set. For example, the three tags of the Unification principle form the Unification tag set.

The essential framework construction principles Unification, Separation, Composite, Decorator, and Chain of Responsibility represent the possible combinations of templates and hooks in one or two classes/interfaces. Since the GoF patterns Composite, Decorator, and Chain of Responsibility are identical with those core framework construction principles which result from combinations of templates and hooks via inheritance, we suggest the GoF names and structure of these three patterns as the basis from which to derive the UML-F tag sets. This section illustrates that derivation for the Composite pattern. Appendix B presents the tag sets for the Decorator and Chain of Responsibility patterns.

Though the other GoF framework patterns and domain-specific patterns rely on either Unification or Separation of templates and hooks, framework developers needing to express the richer semantic information inherent in these patterns, do so by annotating a framework by means of the corresponding UML-F tag sets. The application of one of these patterns expresses the intended use and adaptation possibilities beyond the static structure to which a pattern is often reduced. The semantics of a pattern tag are defined through its structural and behavioral constraints, as well as its intended use.

4.5.1 UML-F tags for the Factory Method pattern

Figure 4.25 shows the static structure of the Factory Method pattern according to the GoF catalog. Note that the diagrams in the catalog adhere to the Object Modeling Technique (Rumbaugh et al., 1994) notation which significantly influenced UML but which is no longer used in its original form. All the diagrams in this book adhere to the UML notation.

According to the static structure of the Factory Method pattern,[8] the UML-F tag set consists of these tags:[9]

- «FacM–*Creator*»
- «FacM–*facM*»
- «FacM–anOp»
- «FacM–Product»
- «FacM–ConcreteProduct»

---

[8] The tags adopt the Java convention of using uppercase first letters in class/interface names and lowercase first letters in method names. The use of the italics style indicates an abstract class, an interface, or an abstract method.

[9] We use the abbreviations FacM for Factory Method, and anOp for anOperation.

- «FacM– ConcreteCreator»
- «FacM–facM».

One could argue that the subclasses of Creator and Product are, in some cases, not appropriate for documenting that pattern. So an alternative, shorter list of UML-F tags would be: «FacM–*Creator*», «FacM–*facM*», «FacM–anOp», «FacM–Product».

Figure 4.26 attaches the UML-F Unification tags to the methods of class Creator. This illustrates in detail the relationship between the tag sets of the Factory Method pattern and the Unification construction principle. It also demonstrates the additional semantic information provided by the Factory Method pattern. For example, the Unification pattern does not deal with a Product class.

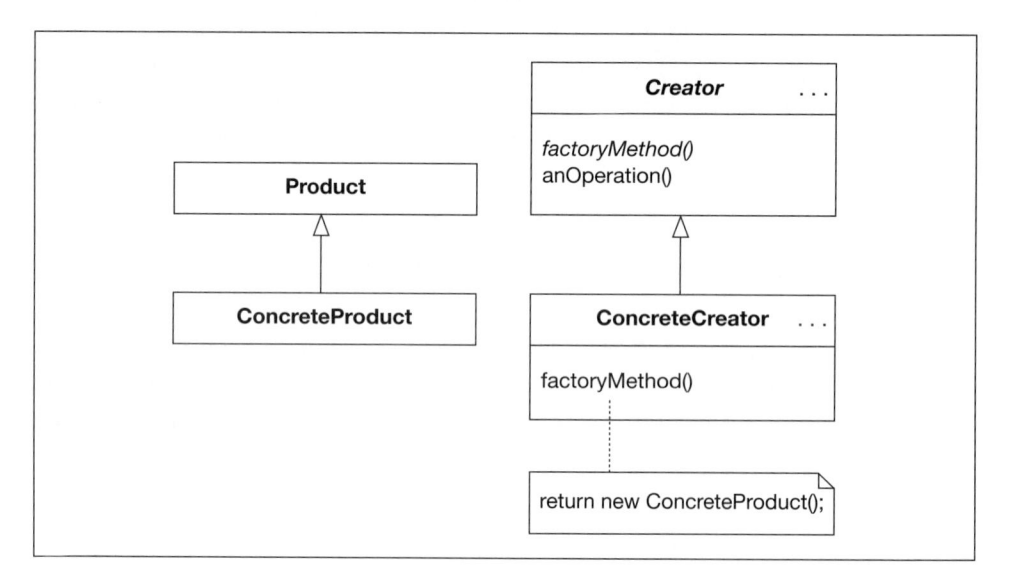

Figure 4.25 Structure of the Factory Method pattern (adapted from Gamma et al., 1995)

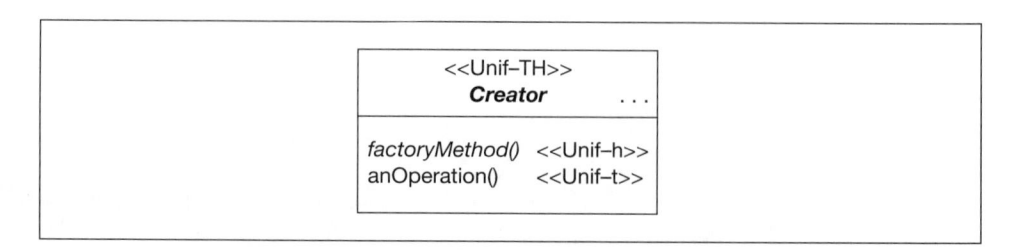

Figure 4.26 Application of the Unification construction principle in the Factory Method pattern

Definition of the UML-F Factory Method pattern tags

Table 4.6 summarizes the UML-F tags of the GoF Factory Method pattern.

Tags	«FacM–*Creator*», «FacM–*facM*», «FacM–anOp», «FacM–Product», «FacM–ConcreteProduct», «FacM–ConcreteCreator», «FacM–facM».
Apply to	class («FacM–Creator», «FacM–Product», «FacM–ConcreteProduct», «FacM–Concrete-Creator»), method («FacM–*facM*», «FacM–anOp», «FacM–facM»), interface («FacM–Product»).
Type	String.
Motivation and purpose	The tags highlight the application of the Factory Method pattern in a framework by marking the corresponding methods as well as the classes/interfaces belonging to that pattern.
Informal explanation of effect	The Factory Method pattern implies that the creation of an instance of static type Product is deferred to a subclass of Creator. The subclass has to override the method marked by the tag «FacM–*facM*».
Expansion	The Factory Method pattern tags «FacM–*Creator*», «FacM–*facM*», and «FacM–anOp» expand to the more basic UML-F Unification tags «Unif–TH», «Unif–t» and «Unif–h» (see Figure 4.26).
Discussion	The UML-F Factory Method pattern tags «FacM–*Creator*», «FacM–*facM*», «FacM–anOp», and «FacM–Product» must always be used together. The tags «FacM–ConcreteProduct», «FacM–ConcreteCreator», and «FacM–facM» are optional and can only be used in conjunction with the former list of tags.

Table 4.6 Definition of the UML-F Factory Method pattern tags

4.5.2 UML-F tags for the Strategy pattern

Figure 4.27 shows the static structure of the Strategy pattern according to the GoF catalog (Gamma et al., 1995). The original structure diagram shows three subclasses of the abstract class Strategy: ConcreteStrategyA, ConcreteStrategyB, and ConcreteStrategyC. In most situations where UML-F tags are attached to framework spots, these exemplar subclasses are not relevant. Thus, we reduce the structure of the pattern to the one shown in the class diagram in Figure 4.27. This demonstrates that class diagrams in the structure section of the GoF catalog don't have to be transformed 1:1 into UML-F tag sets. Using the basic tag «adapt-static» to mark the generalization relation explicitly as extensible demonstrates the intention of this pattern in a more general form than only through exemplar class diagrams. The appropriate use of UML-F tags provides additional descriptive power.

Another aspect of the structure of the Strategy pattern is the fact that the association between the Context and the Strategy classes has the label 'strategy'.

This can also be included in the UML-F tag set. So the UML-F tag set for the Strategy pattern is:[10]

- «Strategy–Context»
- «Strategy–anOp»
- «Strategy–strategy»
- «Strategy–*Strategy*»
- «Strategy–*algInt*»
- «Strategy–ConcreteStrategy»
- «Strategy–algInt».

or in a more abbreviated version: «Strat–Ctxt», «Strat–anOp», «Strat–strat», «Strat–*Strat*», «Strat–*algInt*», «Strat–ConcreteStrat», «Strat–algInt». An alternative shorter tag set would drop the tags of the concrete subclass(es) of Strategy.

The Strategy pattern relies on the Separation construction principle. Figure 4.28 attaches the UML-F Separation tags to the methods of the classes Context and Strategy.

Figure 4.29 shows the UML-F diagram of the case study where the rounding of class Converter is kept flexible by means of the Strategy pattern. The annotation applies

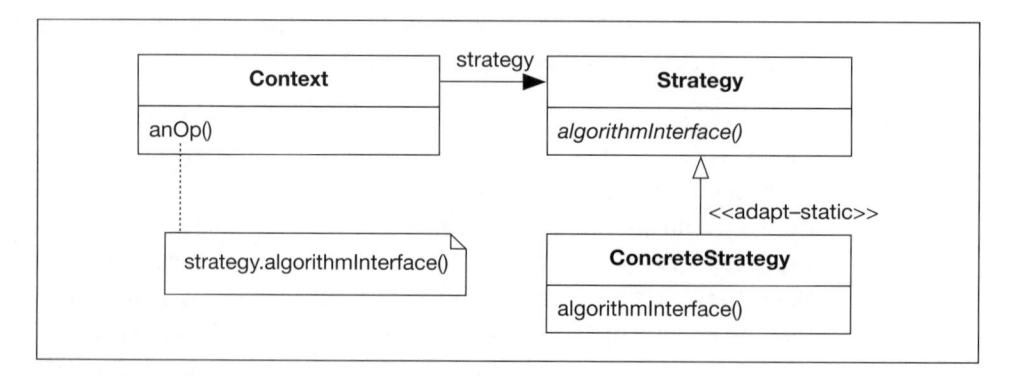

Figure 4.27 Structure of the Strategy pattern (adapted from Gamma et al., 1995)

---

[10] We use the abbreviations Int for Interface, and alg for algorithm. Further abbreviations could be Ctxt for Context, and Strat for Strategy.

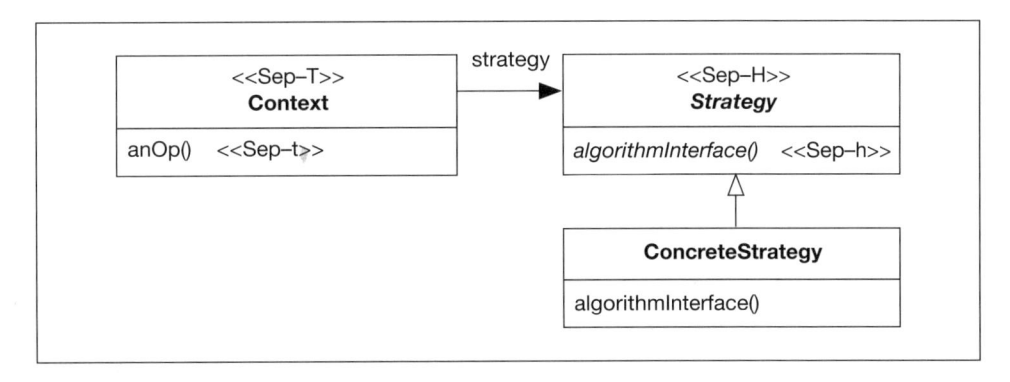

Chapter 4 UML-F tags for framework construction principles and patterns 101

Figure 4.28 The Strategy pattern is based on the Separation construction principle

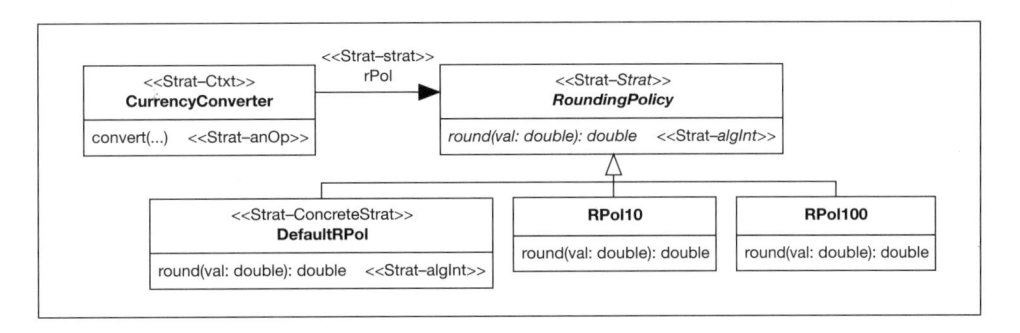

Figure 4.29 UML-F diagram with Strategy pattern tags

the UML-F tags «Strat–ConcreteStrat» and «Strat–algInt» for a specific subclass of Strategy only to class DefaultRPol.

Again, a tool could be based on the UML-F pattern tags as was illustrated in the cases of the template and hook tags, and the Unification and Separation tags. Figure 4.30 illustrates this for the Strategy pattern. Let us assume that the group of UML-F tags has the name Rounding (not shown in Figure 4.29). A user would select a particular incarnation of the Strategy pattern by name. The tool would, for example, define the hyperlinks that link the methods and classes comprising the pattern structure to the corresponding framework spots and vice versa. As a consequence, tools that support UML-F would typically offer a view of various pattern structures, such as the one in the gray box for the Strategy pattern.

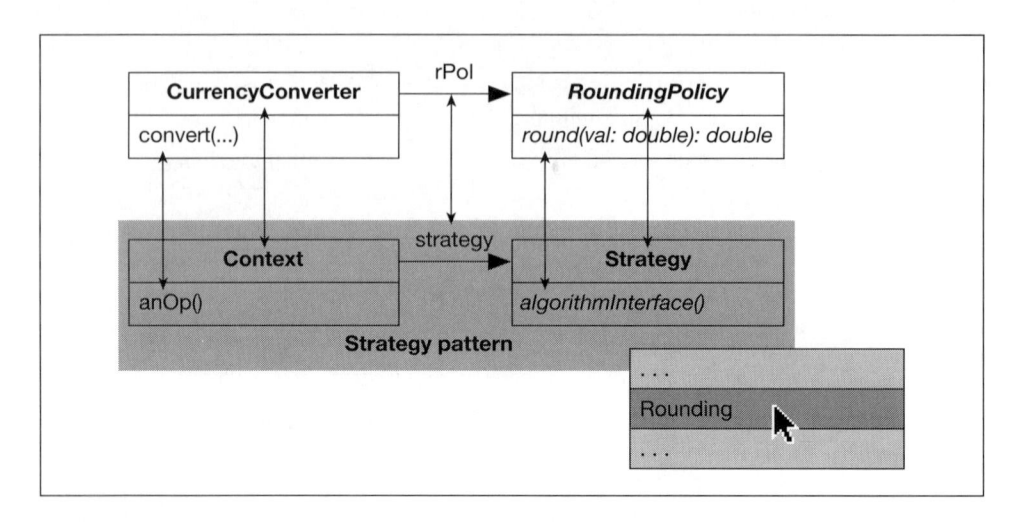

Figure 4.30 Tool-assisted mapping of the structure of a pattern to framework spots

Definition of the UML-F Strategy pattern tags

Table 4.7 summarizes the UML-F tags of the GoF Strategy pattern.

Tags	«Strategy–Context», «Strategy–anOp», «Strategy–strategy», «Strategy–*Strategy*», «Strategy–*algInt*», «Strategy–ConcreteStrategy», «Strategy–algInt»; or their abbreviations «Strat–Ctxt», «Strat–anOp», «Strat–strat», «Strat–*Strat*», «Strat–*algInt*», «Strat–ConcreteStrat», «Strat–algInt».
Apply to	class («Strategy–Context», «Strategy–*Strategy*», «Strategy–ConcreteStrategy»); method («Strategy–anOp», «Strategy–*algInt*», «Strategy–algInt»); interface («Strategy–Context», «Strategy–*Strategy*»); association («Strategy–strategy»).
Type	String.

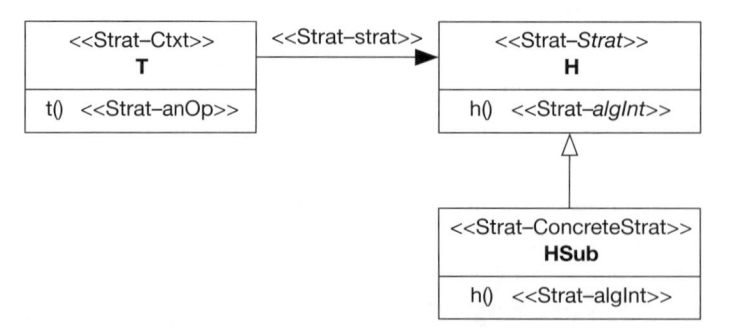

Motivation and purpose	The tags highlight the application of the Strategy pattern in a framework by marking the corresponding methods as well as the classes/interfaces belonging to that pattern.
Informal explanation of effect	The Strategy pattern implies that the handling of a request in a Context object is deferred to a subclass of Strategy, or a class that implements the interface Strategy. Specific Strategy classes override/implement the abstract method marked by the «Strategy–algInt» tag.
Expansion	The Strategy pattern tags «Strategy–Context», «Strategy–anOp», «Strategy–*Strategy*», and «Strategy–*algInt*» expand to the more basic UML-F Separation tags «Sep–T», «Sep–t», «Sep–H», and «Sep–h». The figure above illustrates this, though the templates and hooks are not explicitly marked by the Separation tags.
Discussion	The UML-F Strategy pattern tags «Strategy–Context», «Strategy–anOp», «Strategy–*Strategy*», and «Strategy–*algInt*» must always be used together. The tags «Strategy–strategy», «Strategy–ConcreteStrategy», and «Strategy–algInt» are optional and can only be used in conjunction with the former list of tags.

Table 4.7 Definition of the UML-F Strategy pattern tags

4.5.3 UML-F tags for the Composite pattern

Figure 4.31 shows the static structure of the Composite pattern according to the GoF catalog (Gamma et al., 1995). The getChild(int) method in the classes Component and Composite has been dropped as this represents a quite specific way of accessing the objects in the Composite object tree. The resulting UML-F tags are[11]:

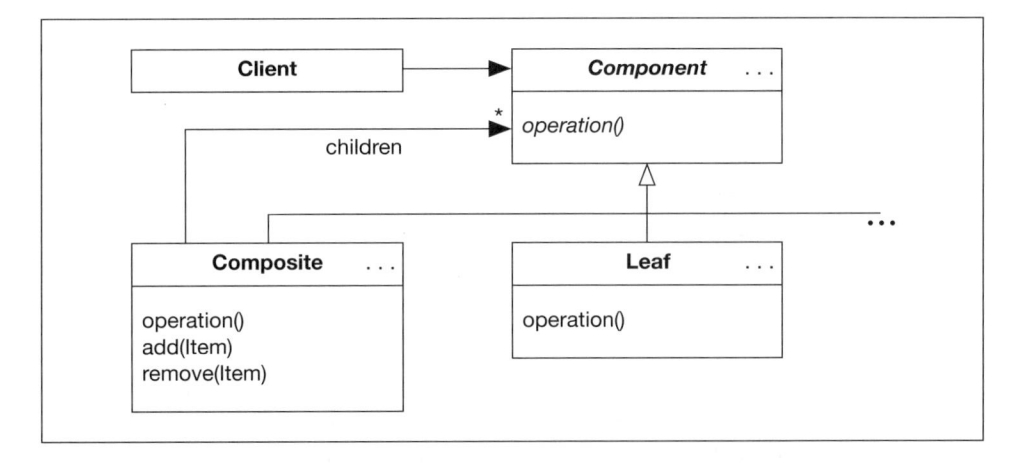

Figure 4.31 Structure of the Composite pattern (adapted from Gamma et al., 1995)

---

[11] We use the abbreviations op() for operation(), add() for add(Item), and remove() for remove(Item).

- «Composite–Client»
- «Composite–*Component*»
- «Composite–*op*»
- «Composite–Composite»
- «Composite–children»
- «Composite–op»
- «Composite–add»
- «Composite–remove»
- «Composite–Leaf».

The Client and Leaf tags could be omitted in a shorter tag set.

Consider as an example the classes Item and Folder in Figure 4.32. Folder manages any number of objects of static type Item (such as TextDoc and DrawDoc instances) because the association between Folder and Item has the cardinality *. Folder also manages any future specializations of Item, such as VoiceDoc. As Folder is a subclass of Item, Folder instances can also manage any number of other folders. Thus, Folder allows the definition of a tree hierarchy of objects – this is a core characteristic of the Composite pattern.

The schematic annotations point out that class Item corresponds to H and class Folder to T at the abstraction level of templates and hooks. The names of the template and hook methods are the same in the Composite pattern. The template method typically iterates over the collection of managed objects. In the case of the getSizeInBytes() method, the hook method is an abstract method that defines that the size of an item should be calculated. The corresponding template method in class Folder iterates over the collection of items and adds the results to calculate the overall size of a folder. Though the method has a recursive flavor by passing the method call getSizeInBytes() on to all objects in the object tree, it is not a recursive method in the classic sense. Due to the structure of a template method in the Composite pattern, the composed tree can be treated as one object – the methods forward the corresponding messages along the tree.

The methods addItem(...) and removeItem(...) provide basic support for managing the contained items. More elaborate solutions would, for example, provide methods for iterating over the contained items.

Figure 4.33 shows a sample object tree. The root Folder object manages another Folder instance and a TextDoc instance. The other Folder instance contains a DrawDoc instance and a TextDoc instance. Due to the forwarding mechanism

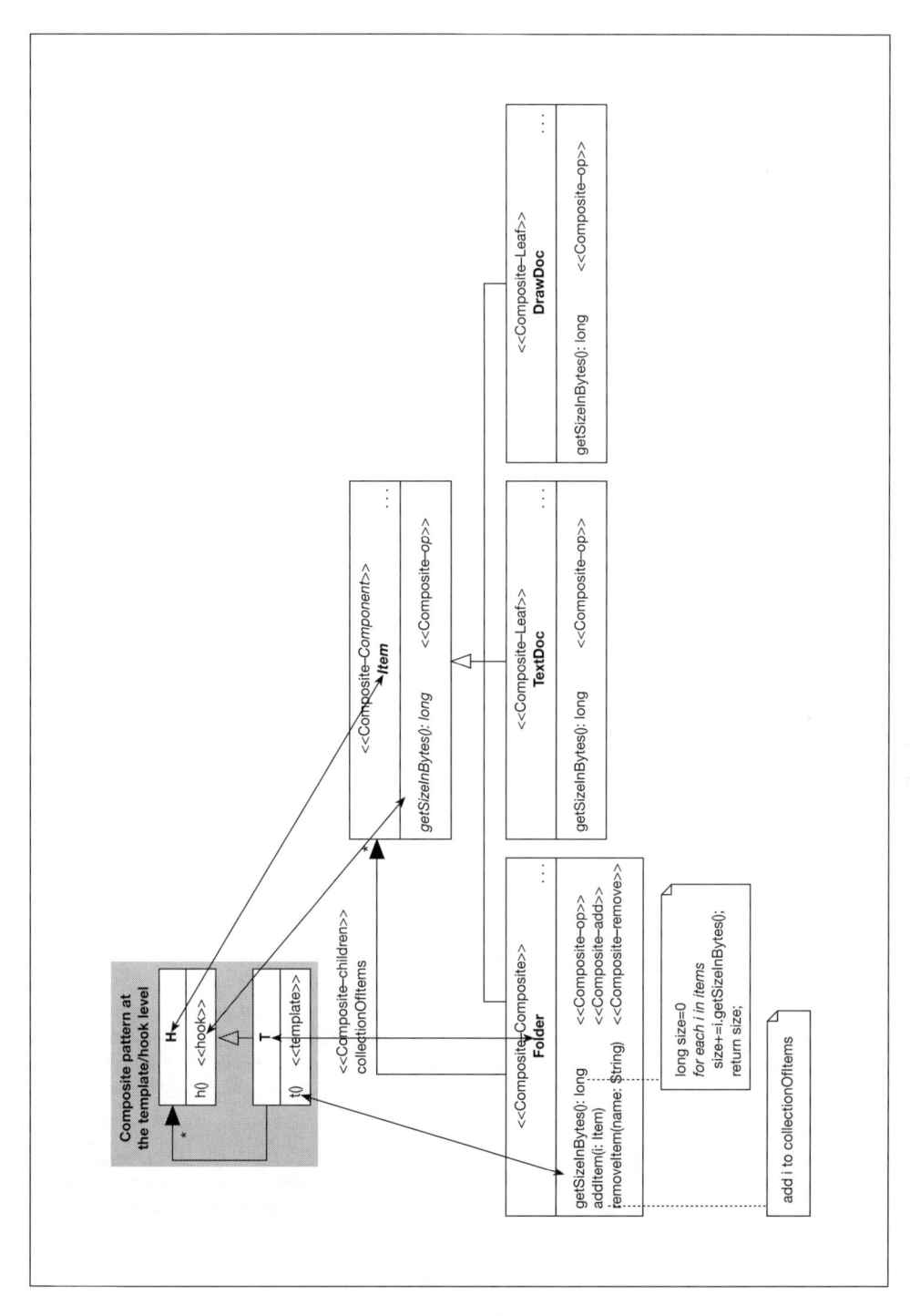

Chapter 4 UML-F tags for framework construction principles and patterns

Figure 4.32 Sample application of the Composite pattern

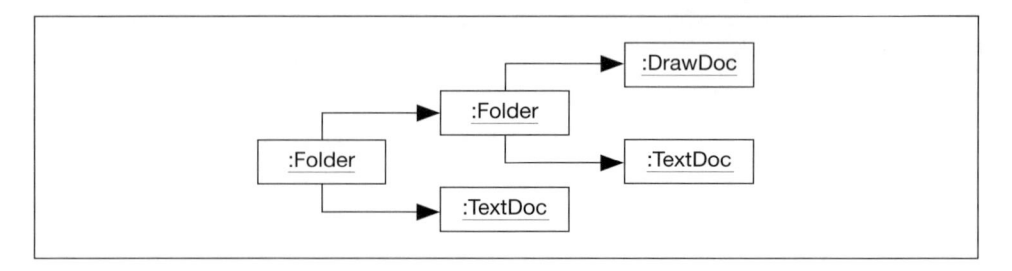

Figure 4.33 Sample object tree

inherent in each template method, messages flow through the object tree from the root down to the leaves. So a Folder object can be treated in the same way as a single object of static type Item.

Definition of the UML-F Composite pattern tags
Table 4.8 summarizes the UML-F tags of the GoF Composite pattern.

Tags	«Composite–Client», «Composite–*Component*», «Composite–*op*», «Composite–Composite», «Composite–children», «Composite–op», «Composite–add», «Composite–remove», «Composite–Leaf».
Apply to	class («Composite–Client», «Composite–*Component*», «Composite–Composite», «Composite–Leaf»); method («Composite–*op*», «Composite–op», «Composite–add», «Composite–remove»); interface («Composite–Client», «Composite-*Component*») ; association («Composite–children»); see Figure 4.32.
Type	String.
Motivation and purpose	The tags highlight the application of the Composite pattern by marking the corresponding methods as well as the classes/interfaces and associations belonging to that pattern.
Informal explanation of effect	The Composite pattern implies that a tree of Component objects form a Composite object. The Composite object can be treated as a single object. The Leaf classes override/implement the methods of class/interface Component. If Leaf classes are added, the methods marked as «Composite–*op*» have to be overridden/implemented and can be annotated by the tag «Composite–op». The Composite class implements the methods for managing a tree of Component objects. These methods are marked by the tags «Composite–add» and «Composite–remove».
Expansion	The Composite pattern tags «Composite–*Component*» and «Composite–*op*» correspond to the hook class[12] and the hook method, «Composite–Composite», and «Composite–op» to the template class and template method. Figure 4.32 illustrates this expansion.

---

[12] That is, the class containing a hook method.

Discussion	The UML-F Composite pattern tags «Composite–*Component*», «Composite–*op*», «Composite–Composite», «Composite–children», «Composite–add», and «Composite–remove» must always be used together. «Composite–Client», «Composite–op», and «Composite–Leaf» are optional and can only be used in conjunction with the former list of tags.

Table 4.8 Definition of the UML-F Composite pattern tags

4.5.4 UML-F tags for a domain-specific pattern

Frameworks contain numerous patterns that are not published in pattern catalogs, but which rely on one of the framework patterns, and thus on the essential framework construction principles. In many situations it might be useful to introduce UML-F tag sets that refer explicitly to these domain-specific patterns. The definition of these domain-specific UML-F tag sets works in the same way as for the pattern tags. The structure of a domain-specific pattern defines the tags. The structure of a domain-specific pattern should also be annotated by GoF pattern tags or the tags of the core construction principles. This ensures an explanation of the domain-specific pattern in terms of already understood designs.

The following example illustrates the introduction of a domain-specific pattern. Chapter 7 provides another example where the introduction of a domain-specific pattern is appropriate. The case study below assumes that a framework needs to keep various calculation algorithms flexible, with rounding as one specific calculation algorithm. Figure 4.34 shows the structure of the Calculation pattern. The UML-F tags for the Calculation pattern are:

- «Calculation–Calculator»

- «Calculation–calcOp»

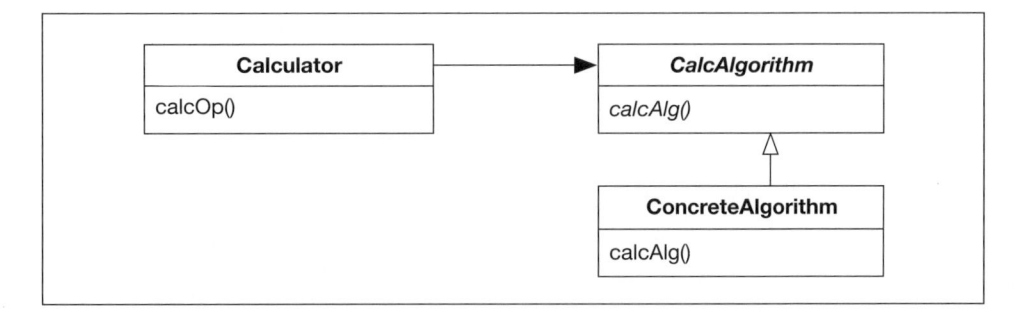

Figure 4.34 Structure of the Calculation pattern

- «Calculation–*CalcAlgorithm*»
- «Calculation–*calcAlg*»
- «Calculation–ConcreteAlgorithm»
- «Calculation–calcAlg».

Figure 4.35 annotates the Calculation pattern by means of the UML-F tags for the Strategy pattern. This points out that the Calculation pattern is a refinement of that GoF pattern. An alternative annotation of the Calculation pattern with the UML-F tags for the Separation construction principle would have served the same purpose.

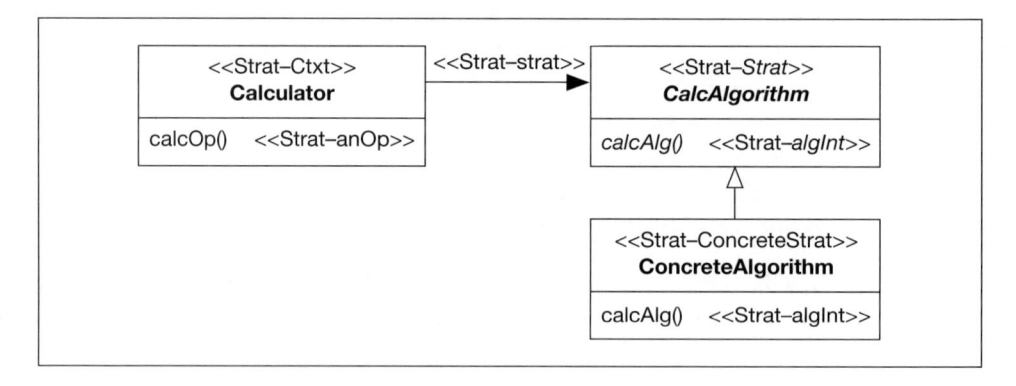

```
   <<Strat–Ctxt>>           <<Strat-strat>>        <<Strat–Strat>>
     Calculator         ─────────────────▶         CalcAlgorithm
   ─────────────────                              ─────────────────
   calcOp()  <<Strat–anOp>>                       calcAlg()  <<Strat–algInt>>
                                                         △
                                                         │
                                              <<Strat–ConcreteStrat>>
                                                ConcreteAlgorithm
                                              ─────────────────
                                              calcAlg()  <<Strat–algInt>>
```

Figure 4.35   Calculation pattern annotated with the Strategy pattern tags

Figure 4.36 applies the UML-F Calculation pattern tags to the currency converter example. The Calculation pattern tags could annotate any framework spot that keeps a calculation flexible.

```
   <<Calculation–Calculator>>              <<Calculation–CalcAlgorithm>>
      CurrencyConverter        ─────▶            RoundingPolicy
   ─────────────────────                    ──────────────────────────
   convert(...)  <<Calculation–calcOp>>    round(val: double): double  <<Calculation–calcAlg>>
```

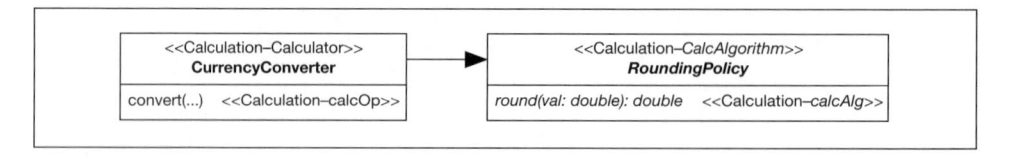

Figure 4.36   UML-F annotation of the currency converter design

Definition of the UML-F Calculation pattern tags

Table 4.9 summarizes the UML-F tags of the Calculation pattern.

Tags	«Calculation–Calculator», «Calculation–calcOp», «Calculation–*CalcAlgorithm*», «Calculation–*calcAlg*», «Calculation–ConcreteAlgorithm», «Calculation–calcAlg».
Apply to	class («Calculation–Calculator», «Calculation–*CalcAlgorithm*», «Calculation–ConcreteAlgorithm»); method («Calculation–calcOp», «Calculation–*calcAlg*», «Calculation–calcAlg»); interface («Calculation–*CalcAlgorithm*»):
	<<Calculation–Calculator>> **T** — t() <<Calculation–calcOp>> ⟶ <<Calculation–*CalcAlgorithm*>> **H** — h() <<Calculation–*calcAlg*>> △ <<Calculation–ConcreteAlgorithm>> **HSub** — h() <<Calculation–calcAlg>>
Type	String.
Motivation and purpose	The tags highlight the application of the Calculation pattern in a framework by marking the corresponding methods as well as the classes/interfaces belonging to that pattern.
Informal explanation of effect	The Calculation pattern keeps the calculation algorithm flexible. Specific algorithms are implemented in subclasses of the CalcAlgorithm class or in classes that implement the CalcAlgorithm interface. They override/implement the method «Calculation–*calcAlg*».
Expansion	The Calculation pattern tags «Calculation–Calculator», «Calculation–calcOp», «Calculation–*CalcAlgorithm*», «Calculation–*calcAlg*», «Calculation–ConcreteAlgorithm», and «Calculation–calcAlg» expand to the Strategy pattern tags «Strategy–Context», «Strategy–anOp», «Strategy–*Strategy*», «Strategy–*algInt*», «Strategy–ConcreteStrategy», and «Strategy–algInt» (see Figure 4.35).
Discussion	The UML-F Calculation pattern tags «Calculation–Calculator», «Calculation–calcOp», «Calculation–*CalcAlgorithm*», and «Calculation–*calcAlg*» must always be used together. The tags «Calculation–ConcreteAlgorithm» and «Calculation–calcAlg» are optional and can only be used in conjunction with the former list of tags.

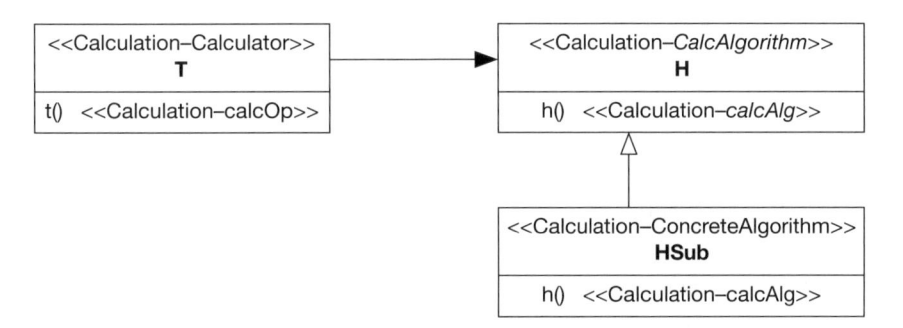

Table 4.9 Definition of the UML-F Calculation pattern tags

4.5.5 UML-F tags for non-framework GoF patterns?

This book focuses on how to support framework development and adaptation with the UML-F profile. The mechanism for defining UML-F tags for framework-related patterns in the catalog might be extended to the other patterns in the catalog as well – one could simply take their structure and define the UML-F tag set. In principle, there is no objection to supporting the annotation of these GoF patterns in UML-F. On the other hand, that might become tricky in some cases. For example, the GoF Façade pattern actually deals with the problem of defining an interface for a subsystem. The structure of that pattern only shows the name Façade in a box that encloses a subsystem of unnamed classes. Thus, the resulting UML-F tag «Façade–Façade» would not really help. On the other hand, the Proxy pattern is an example where the tag definition would make sense. One could argue that the Proxy pattern should be regarded as framework pattern which relies on the Separation construction principle. To conclude, it is up to the developer to choose further GoF patterns, or patterns from other catalogs, and to define the corresponding UML-F tags according to their structure. In this sense UML-F provides the mechanism for defining pattern tags without prescribing certain tag sets or restricting them. Applying the standardized template table for the definition of tags allows a systematic and easily conveyable definition of new tag sets.

4.6 How essential framework construction principles scale

The framework construction principles are independent of the complexity of template and hook methods. In other words, the construction principles can be applied recursively to compose larger units that can be extended depending on the applied construction principle. Why is that the case? What constitutes a template method and a hook method is a matter of viewpoint. By definition, a hook method is elementary compared to the template method in which the particular hook method is used. In another context, the template method can become a hook of another template method. For example, convert() in class CurrencyConverter is a template method invoking round() as its hook (see Figure 4.37).

In the context of class Account, another method, for example calcBalance(), is the template method that calls convert() of a CurrencyConverter object as its hook (see Figure 4.38). Method convert() which is a template method in one context becomes a hook in another context. Method calcBalance() can again become the hook method in the context of another class. In other words, hooks are not necessarily tiny methods, but scale up to more complex behavior.

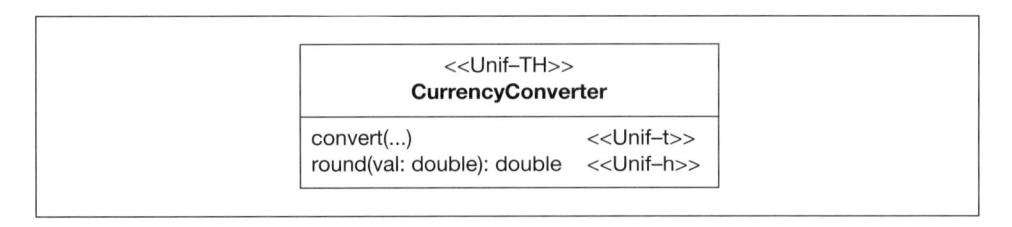

```
┌─────────────────────────────────────────────────┐
│              <<Unif–TH>>                        │
│            CurrencyConverter                    │
│─────────────────────────────────────────────────│
│   convert(...)                   <<Unif–t>>     │
│   round(val: double): double     <<Unif–h>>     │
└─────────────────────────────────────────────────┘
```

Figure 4.37 Template and hooks in class CurrencyConverter

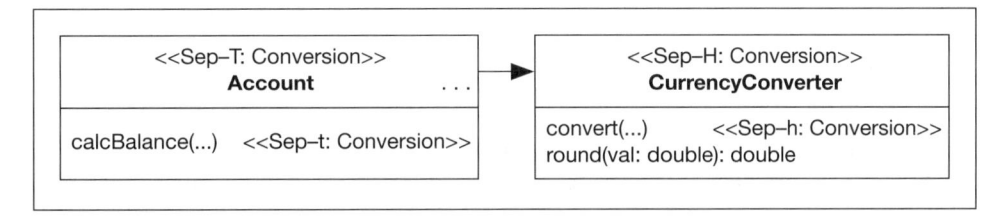

```
┌──────────────────────────────┐     ┌──────────────────────────────────┐
│   <<Sep–T: Conversion>>      │     │    <<Sep–H: Conversion>>         │
│        Account               │ ──▶ │       CurrencyConverter          │
│──────────────────────────────│     │──────────────────────────────────│
│ calcBalance(...)  <<Sep–t:   │     │ convert(...)   <<Sep–h: Conversion>> │
│            Conversion>>      │     │ round(val: double): double       │
└──────────────────────────────┘     └──────────────────────────────────┘
```

Figure 4.38 Template and hooks in classes Account and CurrencyConverter

4.6.1 Finding a balance between template and hook methods

Ideally, programmers only have to override the most elementary hook method to adjust the behavior of the outermost template method. In the example above, overriding CurrencyConverter's method round() should suffice to adjust calcBalance(), at least the rounding aspect of this method. Various authors (e.g. Weinand et al., 1989) refer to this framework design principle as the narrow inheritance interface principle.

Unfortunately, designing classes with narrow inheritance interfaces involves conflicting goals – good design of class interfaces in the realm of frameworks should find the optimal balance between flexibility and the effort required to adapt classes. If a template offers too many hooks it might get too complex to adapt. A class that provides powerful template methods which are only based on a few hooks implies minimal effort for adaptation. Behavior is adapted by overriding some or all of these hooks in subclasses. However, powerful template methods could sacrifice the flexibility of a class. If their hook methods are not sufficient to modify the template method's behavior, a class becomes inflexible, implying that the whole template method has to be overridden. In the example above, method calcBalance() has to be overridden as a whole if it does not offer the appropriate hooks.

Thus, template methods have the potential to reduce adaptation effort without sacrificing flexibility, but add the danger of making classes too rigid, which then increases the adaptation effort.

The design of framework classes/interfaces typically requires many iterations, caused by the use of a framework in specific situations. During such iterations, some template methods might appear to be too rigid, so that more hook methods have to be integrated. It is also possible that the actual use of the defined classes provides insight into how to come up with additional template methods. If programmers have to implement similar control flow repeatedly in the course of adapting a framework, additional template methods should be defined in framework classes.

It is impossible to lay down general guidelines for getting template methods right from the start. Above all, it is important to grasp the conflicting goals of combining template and hook methods according to the narrow inheritance principle. The optimum balance depends on domain-specific adaptations of frameworks.

4.7 Summary

This chapter completes the introduction of UML-F tags. It has introduced the five framework construction principles: Unification, Separation and those with a recursive flavor that have the same name as in the GoF catalog: Composite, Decorator, and Chain of Responsibility. We have presented the UML-F tags for the Unification, Separation and Composite construction principles. In addition, we chose the Factory Method and Strategy patterns from the GoF catalog and a domain-specific pattern called Calculation to illustrate the UML-F tag introduction mechanism. Instead of listing the UML-F tags for each of the construction principles and patterns, the chapter explains and exemplifies how to derive the UML-F tags in a straightforward manner from their static structure. Thus, understanding the tag definition mechanism is a key goal of this chapter. Appendix B complements it and introduces the UML-F tags for the other GoF framework patterns.

Chapter 5

Framework adaptations of UML-F pattern annotations

An efficient adaptation of a framework requires an explicit representation of its key structures and intentions. A framework user has to understand at least portions of the framework architecture, be aware of the variation points, and adapt them to meet the requirements of the application being developed. (By the term 'framework user' we mean the developer who uses a framework to produce a specific application.) Thus, frameworks should provide appropriate documentation of their structure and collaborations, and should provide a means of guiding application developers through the adaptation process.

So-called 'cookbooks' (Goldberg, 1984; Krasner and Pope, 1988; Johnson, 1992) consist of a number of 'recipes' that guide the framework adaptation process. The recipes describe, in an informal way, the use of a framework to accomplish specific tasks. The adaptation of variation points that rely on the framework construction principles follows generic recipes. This chapter presents the cookbook recipes that correspond to the Unification, Separation, and Composite construction principles. In other words, the recipes describe how to adapt the variation points that are annotated by the UML-F tags for these framework construction principles. They are also valid for the UML-F pattern tags that rely on the framework construction principles.

5.1 Cookbooks for framework adaptation

Framework-centered development is an incremental, iterative process. Starting from a given framework, classes are added and changed until the desired application emerges. Applications may be seen as living and growing organisms that constantly gain functionality during the development process. Framework documentation in the form of cookbook recipes don't need to cover all aspects in detail. An appropriate cookbook should, on one hand, cover the overall picture – the structure, the important collaborations, the intention, and overall functionality of its parts – and on the other hand include a solid discussion of tricky and complex mechanisms of the framework.

UML-F class and object diagrams represent an appropriate mechanism to describe the static structure of a framework. UML-F sequence diagrams describe interaction patterns. Many of the UML-F tags make variation points explicit and simultaneously give hints about how to adapt those variation points. Experience has proven that marking parts of the framework with UML-F tags provides useful assistance to the application developer for locating, understanding, and adapting variation points. However, diagrams are not enough. Informal text should be used to explain the rationale behind the architecture, as well as domain-specific constraints such as which variation points are optional and which must be adapted. Thus, cookbook recipes usually intertwine diagrams with informal textual descriptions.

In order to provide adequate assistance in adapting a framework, a cookbook should provide the following (see Figure 5.1).

- *A guided tour through the architecture*: the guided tour is particularly useful for an understanding of the framework. It allows the application developer to gain efficient access to the key elements of the framework. The guided tour offers a path through the framework that incrementally allows a developer to understand the framework and its internal architecture.

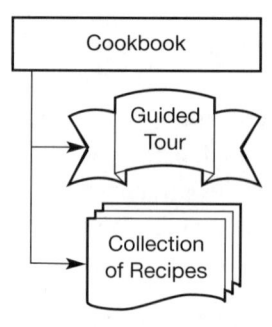

Figure 5.1 Cookbook aspects

- *A collection of recipes*: the recipes describe particular adaptations of the framework. Variation points are described in one or more recipes. A recipe may provide pointers to related recipes, guiding the order in which the adaptations should be performed.
- *Domain-specific UML-F tags*: the cookbook might introduce domain-specific UML-F tags that allow a concise description of certain aspects of the framework. These tags are used by the recipes (and therefore are not shown on Figures 5.1).

Recipes can be classified into three categories. (The case study in Chapter 6 illustrates these recipe types.)

- *Basic recipes*: these focus on a particular variation point, explaining how to adapt it.
- *Recipes for choosing among alternatives*: these discuss issues that help to choose between alternative adaptations. Such recipes often refer to basic recipes for the actual adaptation.
- *Composite recipes*: these provide guidance though complex tasks, partitioning them into subtasks. Composite recipes refer to a number of other recipes and suggest a particular order. Such recipes are comparable with process patterns as proposed by Ambler (1998) which form a vital part of *Catalysis* (D'Souza and Wills, 1998).

Cookbook recipes, with their inherent references to other recipes, lend themselves to presentation as hypertext. Recipes do not usually explain the internal design and implementation details of a framework, only the necessary information to guide the adaptation.

Table 5.1 proposes a *recipe template*. However, to match specific needs, additional sections may be provided in the recipe, or given ones may be omitted. 'Sample adaptations' and 'source code samples' might be such additional sections, beefed up by UML-F diagrams.

Recipe 'Name: Short explanation of the recipe', typically beginning with "How to …"	
Intent	The motivation and the intent of the recipe
Classes	■ Which framework classes are involved and need to be understood? ■ Which framework classes should be adapted? ■ UML-F diagrams are useful here.
Related recipes	■ Which related recipes are involved, either as subrecipes or as alternatives?
Steps to apply	The sequence of steps that must be applied, e.g. 1. Create a new subclass of A. 2. Override method foo() in the newly created subclass, but call super() at the end. 3. …
Discussion	Discussion of alternatives including caveats, possible problems, and alternative recipes.

Table 5.1 Recipe template

5.2 A sample cookbook recipe

Reconsider the RoundingPolicy variation point realized through the Separation construction principle (Figure 5.2). It provides an abstract class *RoundingPolicy* together with three specific implementations of the hook method round() in subclasses. Let us assume this example is part of a framework and let us define a recipe for its adaptation. What is required for adapting the rounding variation point?

If the framework provides all the required implementations of RoundingPolicy, an adaptation by composition is feasible. In this case, the application developer plugs an appropriate instance of a RoundingPolicy subclass into a CurrencyConvertor object. If the UML-F «fixed» tag is attached to the generalization, additional rounding policies cannot be defined.

If, instead, the framework does not provide a complete set of subclasses of the RoundingPolicy class, the generalization should be marked as «adapt-static» or «adapt-dyn». The application developer can then use one of the predefined classes, but can also add specific ones. The cookbook recipe in Table 5.2 describes this straightforward adaptation.

Figure 5.2

```
┌─────────────────────────────────────────────────────────────────┐
│   <<Sep–T>>                    <<Sep–H>>                        │
│  CurrencyConverter     ───►   RoundingPolicy                    │
│  +convert()  <<Sep–t>>        +round()    <<Sep–h>>             │
│                                    △                            │
│                    ┌───────────────┼───────────────┐            │
│   DefaultRPol              RPol10              RPol100          │
│   +round()                 +round()            +round()         │
└─────────────────────────────────────────────────────────────────┘
```

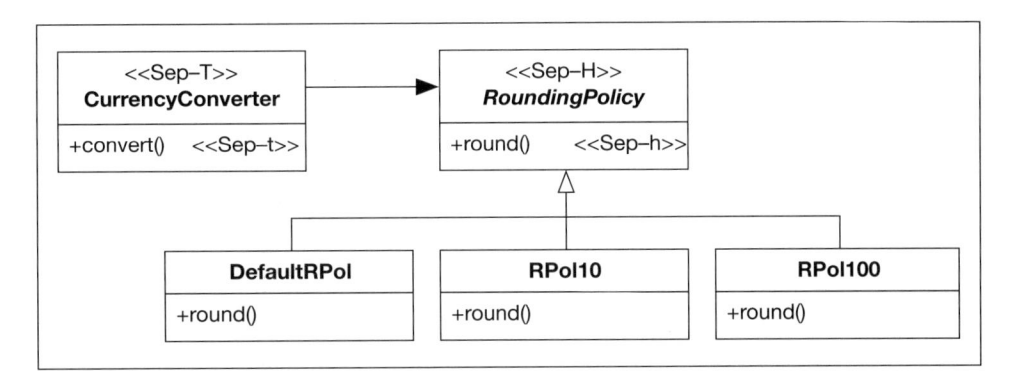

Figure 5.2 Keeping the rounding policy flexible by means of the Separation construction principle

---

Recipe 'CurrencyConverter: How to adapt the rounding behavior'

Intent	To adapt the rounding behavior of a currency converter.
Classes	■ CurrencyConverter provides the common conversion behavior in the convert() template method. ■ RoundingPolicy represents the variation point that can be redefined. ■ See Figure 5.2 for a UML-F class diagram.
Steps to Apply	1. Things to know about the CurrencyConverter functionality: 　■ The convert() method is used to convert between currencies. It may be invoked by various clients of the framework. 　■ The convert() method's responsibility is to perform the conversion and to round the result. 　■ Method round() is used only in the context of convert(). 2. Determine whether there is already a subclass of RoundingPolicy that provides the desired rounding algorithm. The framework provides DefaultRPol, Rpol10, and RPol100. 3. If these three are not appropriate rounding policies, define a new subclass of RoundingPolicy. 　■ Implement the round() method accordingly. 　■ You cannot invoke super() within your implementation of the round() method, since the base class only provides an abstract method. 4. Ensure that your new class is being used: the rounding class is selected by passing it as parameter to the constructor of the CurrencyConverter class.
Discussion	See discussion above.

Table 5.2 Cookbook recipe for adapting the rounding policy of a CurrencyConverter instance

Figure 5.3 presents a sample adaptation. The tag «adapt-static» explicitly indicates that the application developer may add new classes. Furthermore, some existing classes (such as RPol10) have been omitted in the diagram – instead, an «application» class RPolByBase has been added. The presentation tag © is attached to that class to indicate that all methods and instance variables provided by it are shown. Class RPolByBase allows the definition of the rounding base dynamically, thus providing additional flexibility.

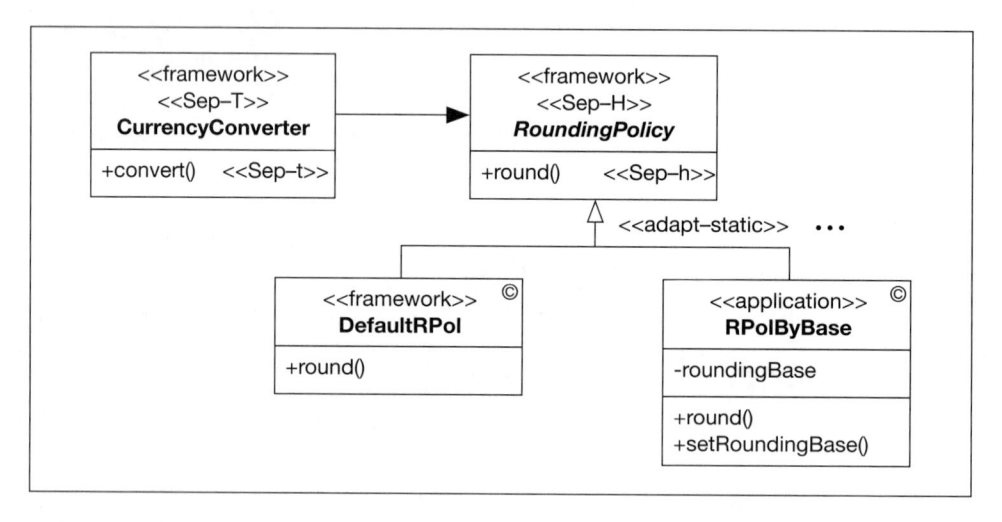

Figure 5.3 A sample adaptation following the cookbook recipe

The UML-F tags indicate that the rounding policy variation point is based on the Separation pattern. Thus, a generic recipe for the Separation pattern would usually suffice for adapting variation points that rely on that construction principle. If more specific recipes are required, they could build on generic recipes. Sections 5.3–5.5 introduce the generic recipes for the Unification and Separation construction principles and for the Composite pattern.[1] For understanding and adapting the Decorator and Chain of Responsibility patterns, we refer to the GoF pattern catalog (Gamma et al., 1995).

Generic recipes for the adaptation of UML-F annotated variation points allow an efficient definition of more elaborate recipes for patterns and framework variation

---

[1] As the Composite, Decorator, and Chain of Responsibility construction principles overlap with the GoF patterns, we use the term 'pattern' for them – for example, Composite pattern instead of Composite construction principle.

points. More specific recipes, which rely on and build on the generic recipes, typically add domain or framework-dependent information such as default implementations for the variation points, possible side effects, relevant constraints, and related variation points.

5.3 Recipe for adapting the Unification construction principle

The Unification construction principle consists of one class marked as «Unif-TH». It contains both the template method, marked as «Unif-t», and the hook method, marked as «Unif-h». Figure 5.4 shows the structure of this pattern and Table 5.3 describes the corresponding generic recipe. Though variation points based on the Unification construction principle are straightforward to adapt, the generic recipe serves as a checklist.

Recipe 'Generic adaptation for the Unification construction principle'	
Intent	The recipe describes how to adapt a variation point that is designed according to the Unification construction principle. Framework-specific considerations are not provided here.
Classes	■ «Unif-TH» indicates the class that needs to be refined. No other framework classes are involved directly. ■ See Figure 5.4 for the UML-F class diagram.

Steps to Apply	1. Understand the template/hook relationship («Unif–t», «Unif–h»).
	   ■ Determine when and where in the template method the hook is invoked. Is the hook called more than once?
	   ■ What is the hook method's responsibility, and how do changes affect the template?
	   ■ Is the hook method used by another method in the «Unif-TH» class, or from outside?
	2. Determine whether there is already a subclass that provides the desired or a similar functionality. Could that be refined?
	3. If not, build a new subclass of the class marked by the UML-F tag «Unif–TH».
	   ■ Implement the hook method in the newly defined subclass, indicated by the «Unif-h» tag by providing the desired functionality.
	   ■ Determine whether you can reuse the provided default implementation through calling the inherited method. This is only possible if the inherited method is not abstract.

Discussion	The Unification construction principle doesn't allow the hook implementation to change during runtime. The «Unif–TH» base class may provide a default implementation for the «Unif–h()» method.

Table 5.3   Adaptation of a variation point based on the Unification construction principle

Part I The UML-F profile

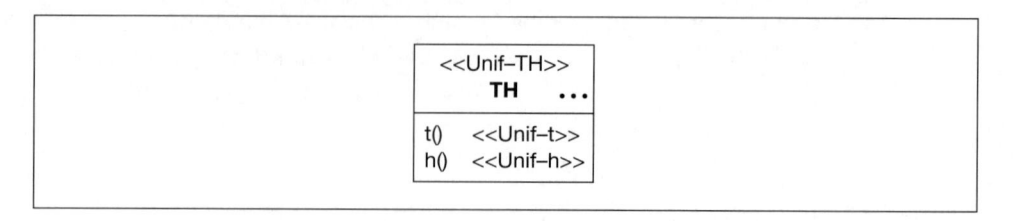

```
        <<Unif–TH>>
            TH     ...
    t()    <<Unif–t>>
    h()    <<Unif–h>>
```

Figure 5.4   The structure of the Unification construction principle

5.4 Recipe for adapting the Separation construction principle

Figure 5.5 shows the structure of the Separation construction principle and Table 5.4 describes the corresponding generic recipe.

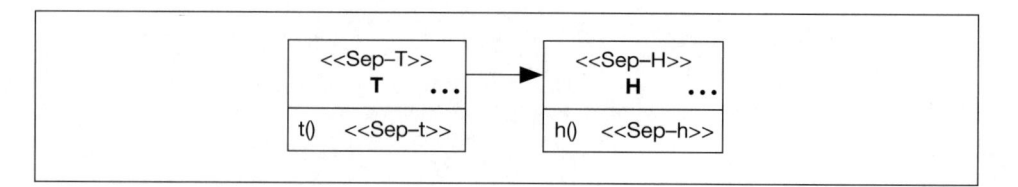

```
    <<Sep–T>>              <<Sep–H>>
        T       ...    ──▶     H       ...
    t()  <<Sep–t>>         h()  <<Sep–h>>
```

Figure 5.5   The structure of the Separation construction principle

Recipe 'Generic adaptation for the Separation construction principle'	
Intent	The recipe describes how to adapt a variation point that is designed according to the Separation construction principle. Framework-specific considerations are not provided here.
Classes	■ «Sep–T» marks the class with the template method, which is indirectly modified. ■ «Sep–H» indicates the corresponding hook class/interface that has to be overridden/implemented. ■ See Figure 5.5 for the UML-F class diagram.
Steps to Apply	1. Understand the template–hook relationship and the consequence of separating these methods. ■ Determine when and where in the template method «Sep–t» the hook «Sep–h» is used. Is the hook used more than once? ■ What is the hook method's responsibility, and how do changes affect the template? ■ Is the hook method used by another method in «Sep–T», in «Sep–H», or outside?

2. How is the association between template and hook(s) established? Determine whether there is already a (sub)class of «Sep–H» that provides the desired or a similar functionality. Could that be refined?
3. If not, define a new (sub)class that inherits from «Sep–H», or that implements it in the case where it is an interface.
   - Implement the hook method in the newly defined subclass, indicated by the «Sep–h» tag providing the desired functionality.
   - Determine whether you can reuse the provided default implementation through calling the inherited method. This is only possible if the inherited method is not abstract.
4. Instantiate (i.e. create an instance of) the appropriate «Sep–H» class and plug it into the «Sep–T» instance – for example, by invoking a defineH() method of a T object.

Discussion The «Sep-H» class may provide a default implementation for the hook method «Sep-h» that could be reused through super() calls.
Comparing the «Separation» with the «Unification» construction principles, it is apparent that the Separation's ability to dynamically replace hook objects increases flexibility but also introduces some overhead (see Chapter 4).

Table 5.4 Adaptation of a variation point based on the Separation construction principle

5.5 Recipe for adapting the Composite pattern

Chapter 4 introduced the tags of the Composite pattern. We use the prefix 'C' as a shortcut for Composite in the UML-F tags. Figure 5.6 shows the structure of the pattern and Table 5.5 presents the generic cookbook recipe.

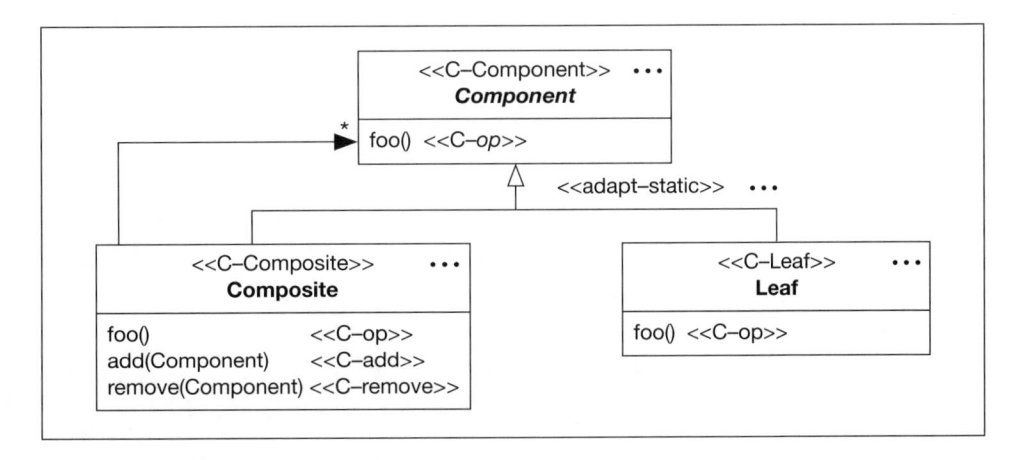

Figure 5.6 The structure of the Composite pattern

Recipe 'Generic adaptation for the Composite pattern'	
Intent	The recipe describes how to adapt a variation point that is designed according to the Composite pattern. Framework-specific considerations are not provided here.
Classes	- «C–Component» is the top-level class in the hierarchy, representing a single object or a tree of objects. - «C–Composite» provides the management of «C–Component» objects. - Usually some specific «C–Component» classes already exist. They are tagged as «C–Leaf». This recipe describes how to add more of them. - See Figure 5.6 for the UML-F class diagram.
Steps to Apply	1. For each method «C–op» understand its responsibilities. - Determine when and where the operation «C–op» is used. Is it used by more than one client method? 2. Determine whether there is already a (sub)class of «C–Leaf» that provides the desired or a similar functionality. Could that be refined? 3. If not, define a new subclass of «C–Component». Provide implementations of the methods marked with «C–op» if necessary. Determine whether you can reuse the provided default implementation through calling the inherited method. This is only possible if the inherited method is not abstract.
Discussion	See the discussion of the Composite pattern in Gamma et al. (1995). Particularly relevant are the following aspects: "Clients can treat composite structures and individual objects uniformly." They do not have to know whether they are dealing with a leaf or a composite component.

Table 5.5   Adaptation of a variation point based on the Composite pattern

5.6 Automating the adaptation of UML-F pattern annotations

So-called 'wizards' (Microsoft, 2001) and active cookbooks (Pree, 1995) support framework adaptations by means of tools that are tailored to a specific framework. As the cookbook recipes for the essential construction principles are generic, generic tool support can be provided for the particular adaptation task. A Unification wizard, for example, would basically ask the framework user to provide the subclass name and would then generate a skeleton of a class that overrides the hook method – it might also check whether the hook method is called from other methods within the class or from outside. The wizards for the other essential construction principles would follow the steps listed in the generic cookbook recipes in an analogous way.

Such UML-F-based adaptation tools could also offer the possibility of specifying adaptation steps or constraints specific to a particular variation point. An appropriate tool would guide a framework user through the adaptation of each UML-F annotated variation point that the user desires to adapt. A prototype of such a tool is described in (Fontoura, 1999).

5.7 Summary

The well-known concept of framework cookbooks can be combined with UML-F annotations of construction principles and patterns. Generic recipes for the Unification and Separation construction principles and the Composite pattern have been presented to illustrate the application of the framework cookbook concept. The generic recipes indicate that a tool could be provided to help automate the adaptation of frameworks that are annotated by UML-F tags.

The definition of a 'guided tour' through an entire framework is highly framework-dependent. It provides an overview and then gradually digs deeper into the framework details. Alongside a guided tour, UML-F diagrams help to pinpoint the variation points. Chapter 6 exemplifies the application of UML-F in the context of a cookbook. It introduces the JUnit testing framework and illustrates the JUnit adaptation process.

PART II

UML-F @ work

Though the use of UML-F tags has already been exemplified as they were introduced, this second part illustrates the benefits of UML-F in the context of larger frameworks. Chapter 6 annotates the JUnit framework, which was designed and developed by Kent Beck and Erich Gamma (Beck and Gamma, 1998b). The purpose of JUnit is to automate the testing of Java components. The case study shows how UML-F enhances framework description and supports framework adaptation.

Chapter 7 completes the book by considering the framework development and adaptation process as a whole. It presents a selection of practical hints and guidelines that are intended to assist in the design, development, and adaptation of frameworks. Similar to the relationship between UML and the Unified Process, (Jacobson et. al., 1998) UML-F forms the notational basis of a framework development process. Chapter 7 provides that perspective in the context of a framework that was designed and implemented for the European Space Agency to model spacecraft control systems.

Chapter 6

UML-F based documentation and adaptation of the JUnit testing framework

JUnit (Beck and Gamma, 1998a; Fowler, 2000) is a Java framework that assists in the definition of automated tests. Testing is an important and obligatory part of the eXtreme Programming approach for software development (Beck, 1999; Beck and Fowler, 2000). This chapter provides a brief UML-F based documentation of JUnit and a set of JUnit adaptation cookbook recipes. It shows how they can be used to guide its adaptation process. Thus, it illustrates how UML-F annotations and cookbook recipes assist in framework adaptation, demonstrating an effective way to support the required adaptation steps.

In this chapter we use a simplified version of JUnit. The source code for this version and for the sample adaptations described in this chapter is available at http://www.UML-F.net. Since the chapter focuses on a sample use of UML-F, it deliberately omits some details of the JUnit framework and its design. The Java source code of the complete version of the JUnit framework, and additional documents, are available at the JUnit's web site http://www.junit.org

6.1 An overview of JUnit

JUnit allows programmers to define tests in a compact way, to reuse code in related test cases, to compose test cases into test suites, and to manipulate and visualize test results. The goal of JUnit is to reduce the amount of code that has to be written by a developer who wants to test Java applications. The following are the main parts of the framework.

- *Test cases*: each test case describes one particular test. Adding new test cases is the most frequent JUnit adaptation. JUnit provides the TestCase class, which defines a standard interface for test cases. TestCase is the most important abstraction in JUnit.

- *Test suites*: the number of test cases can grow quickly, thus JUnit allows test cases to be composed into test suites in order to organize a larger number of test cases. TestSuite objects are composed of test cases and other test suites, thus allowing for hierarchical and efficient test management.
- *Test results*: JUnit keeps track of the results of executed test cases. Since there are different kinds of reporting mechanisms, it keeps the way that the test results are reported flexible. Overriding the TestResult class allows the desired manipulation of test results (for example, storing the results of the tests in a database for project control purposes, or creating HTML files that report the test activities). The default behavior provided by JUnit is to count the number of executed tests.

Figure 6.1 provides an overview of the framework. The following subsections describe each entity in more detail, highlighting the JUnit variation points and providing recipes for their adaptation. For an appropriate marking of JUnit classes, we introduce the «JUnit» tag in Table 6.1. It can be regarded as shorthand for «framework=JUnit», denoting that the class it is attached to belongs to the framework JUnit.

Tag	«JUnit».
Applies to	Classes, interfaces, packages, methods, and attributes.
	<<JUnit>> **Test** <<application>> **NewClass** / attribute <<JUnit>> / foo() <<JUnit>>
Type	Boolean.
Motivation and purpose	The tag denotes that the origin of the tagged element is the JUnit framework.
Explanation of effect	The tag is used to make it explicit that a class/interface belongs to the JUnit framework. Methods and attributes that are originally defined in the JUnit framework, but represented in application classes, may also be annotated with that tag – though the tag holds only for methods whose implementation is not overridden in application subclasses.
Expansion	The tag can be seen as a short cut for «framework=JUnit» or «package=JUnit».
Discussion	The «JUnit» tag does not apply to methods whose signature is inherited from JUnit and whose method body is overridden.

Table 6.1 Introducing the «JUnit» tag

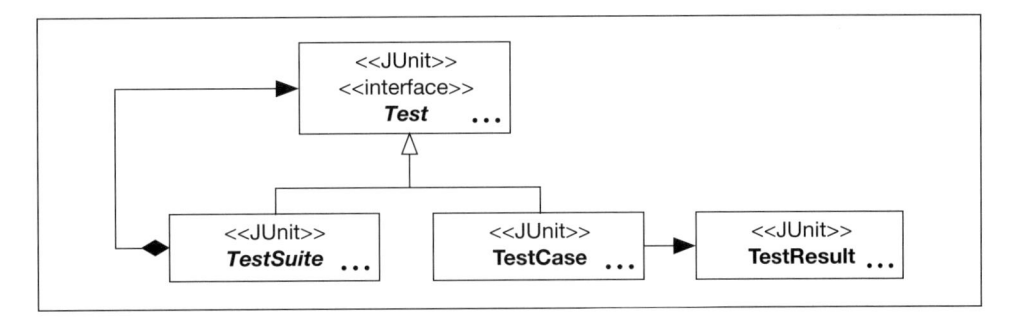

Chapter 6 UML-F based documentation and adaptation of the JUnit testing framework

```
        <<JUnit>>
      <<interface>>
         Test      ...

  <<JUnit>>        <<JUnit>>        <<JUnit>>
  TestSuite ...    TestCase ...     TestResult ...
```

Figure 6.1 Overview of the core JUnit classes

The following subsections discuss the concepts underlying the mentioned classes. Section 6.2 presents adaptation recipes for each of JUnit's variation points.

6.1.1 Test cases

JUnit builds on the observation that any test case consists of potentially three parts: the *initialization*, the *test check*, and a *clean up*. The initialization part defines a so-called test fixture. A test fixture is an object structure that is used as a starting point for testing. Fixtures that may be used by several test cases should be created in the initialization part for reuse purposes.

The test check applies one or several method calls on the fixture created in the initialization part. Afterwards it verifies whether certain constraints are met. Have certain changes of the object structure and values been conducted? Do invariants still hold? These checks primarily rely on the assert() method provided by JUnit. The assert() method succeeds if the evaluation of the parameter yields the boolean value True.

Finally, the third part cleans up a test. It is used mainly to close files and database connections and to make unused objects available for garbage collection.

Figure 6.2 annotates the TestCase class with the Unification tags. Method run() has a standard implementation, calling the other three methods in the order setUp(), runTest(), and tearDown() (see Example 6.1). The three «Unif-h» methods could be abstract because their intention is to be overridden in subclasses to define actual tests. However, all three provide an empty default implementation allowing a subclass not to have to define these methods if they aren't necessary. For example, when no clean up code is required tearDown() doesn't need to be overriden.

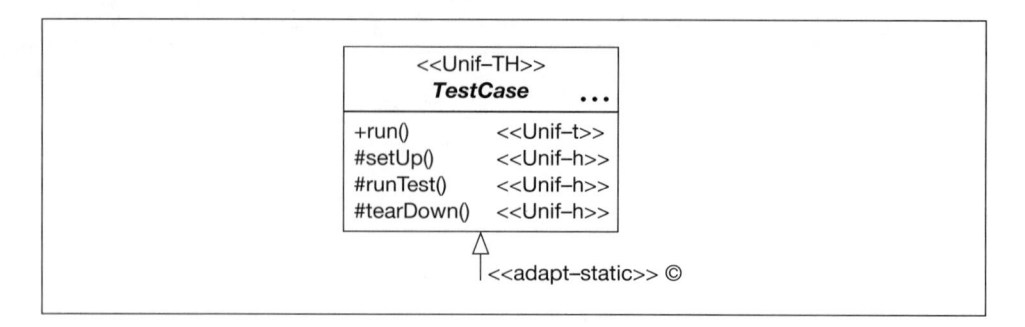

```
                    <<Unif–TH>>
                     TestCase        ...
                 +run()        <<Unif–t>>
                 #setUp()      <<Unif–h>>
                 #runTest()    <<Unif–h>>
                 #tearDown()   <<Unif–h>>
                         △
                         |<<adapt–static>> ©
```

Figure 6.2   JUnit's TestCase class

Test cases should override the hook methods. Code reuse among tests can be achieved by building subclasses and reusing a subset of these methods. For example, reuse of the initialization and clean up methods allows different tests to operate on the same data. Reuse of runTest() allows a test to operate on different data.

```
public void run() {
    setUp();
    runTest();
    tearDown();
}
```

Example 6.1   Simplified run() method of JUnit's class TestCase (from Beck and Gamma, 1998a)

6.1.2 Test suites

Defining and running only a single test would be insufficient for checking a software system. Therefore, a larger number of tests needs to be defined and managed. The Composite pattern allows the definition of test suites as composite tests that can be treated as individual tests. Thus, test suites may contain test cases and test suites. Additional subclasses of Test are not allowed. The tag «fixed» attached to the generalization hierarchy expresses this restriction (see Figure 6.3).

The implementation of the run() method in class TestSuite invokes the run() method for each contained Test (see Example 6.2). The UML-F sequence diagram in Figure 6.4 describes this behavior, using '*' to indicate that several Test objects are in a test suite and to make the repeated invocation of the run() method explicit.

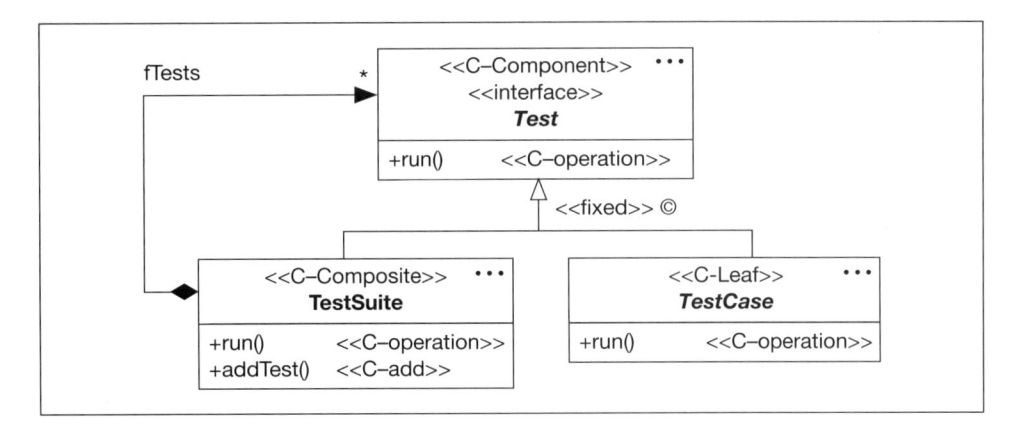

Chapter 6 UML-F based documentation and adaptation of the JUnit testing framework

Figure 6.3 TestSuite design structure

```
public void run() {
      for (Enumeration e = fTests.elements();
                            e.hasMoreElements();) {
          Test test = (Test) e.nextElement();
          test.run();
      }
}
```

Example 6.2 The code of the run() method in class TestSuite (from Beck and Gamma, 1998a)

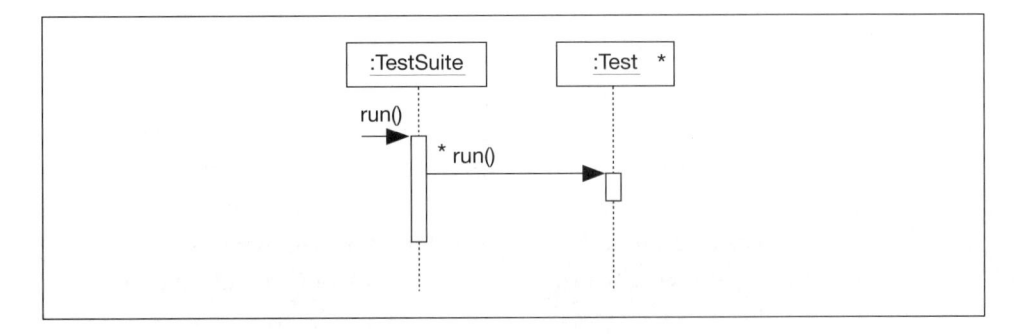

Figure 6.4 Interaction between a TestSuite object and its contained Test objects

6.1.3 Reporting the test results

JUnit distinguishes between failures and errors. Failures are situations where a test does not yield the expected result. Usually, a failure is detected by applying the assert() method to check whether a constraint holds. Errors, instead, are unanticipated bugs in the code being tested, or in the test cases themselves. The TestResult class is responsible for reporting failures and errors in different ways.

Analogous with a test case, a test result object is able to execute an initialization code before it starts keeping track of each test case, and to execute a wrap up code at the end of each test case. TestResult offers four methods: startTest() containing the initialization code; addFailure() which is invoked every time a failure occurs; addError() which is invoked every time an error happens; and endTest() which does the wrap up. Example 6.3 shows the implementation of the run(TestResult) method in class TestCase in more detail. The test result object is handed through the test objects as a parameter of the run(TestResult) method.

```
public void run(TestResult result) {
    result.startTest(this);
    setUp();
    try { runTest(); }
    catch (AssertionFailedError e) {
        result.addFailure(this, e); }
    catch (Throwable e) {
        result.addError(this, e); }
    finally { tearDown();
        result.endTest(this); }
}
```

Example 6.3 The run method of class TestCase (from Beck and Gamma 1998a)

The earlier Examples 6.1 and 6.2 show simplified versions of the parameter-less run() method. In the actual implementation, both methods call the run(TestResult) method after they have created a TestResult object on their own. The UML-F sequence diagram in Figure 6.5 describes the behavior of the run(TestResult) method, showing the three alternative outcomes of an invoked test.

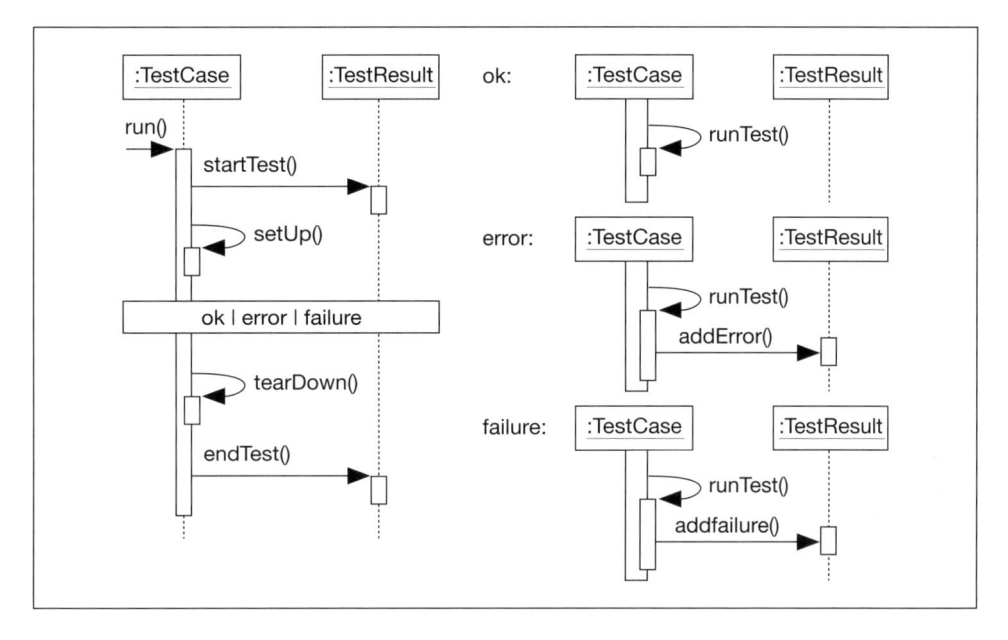

Chapter 6 UML-F based documentation and adaptation of the JUnit testing framework 133

Figure 6.5 Sequence diagram for the run(TestResult) method in class TestCase

In order to define a test-reporting mechanism that is different from the default implementation, the developer is allowed to override the appropriate methods of class TestResult. The JUnit designers have applied the Separation construction principle to achieve the required flexibility for each aspect of a test result – that is, initializing the component, adding failures or errors, and finalizing the reporting. The UML-F diagram in Figure 6.6 illustrates that aspect of JUnit.

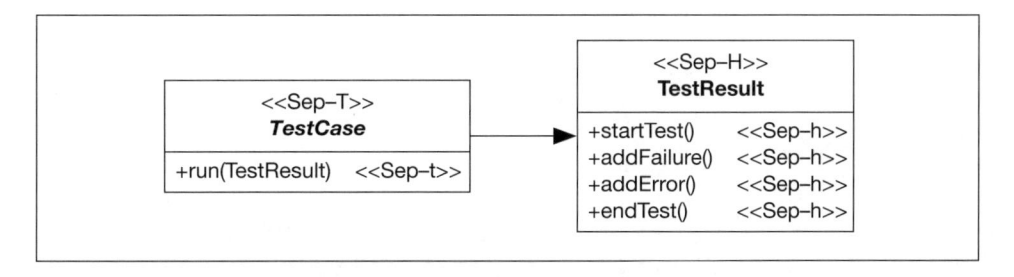

Figure 6.6 TestResult design based on the Separation construction principle

6.2 Recipes for defining new tests

The following recipes describe how to adapt the JUnit framework. This section presents the cookbook recipes for adapting the three main components of JUnit:

- the definition of test cases
- their combination into test suites
- the adaptation of test reporting mechanisms.

Additionally, sample adaptations of JUnit demonstrate how to apply the cookbook recipes. The adaptations rely on test cases for a simple complex number class introduced in Example 6.4 and the UML-F diagram in Figure 6.7. It offers methods for accessing its attributes (the real and imaginary part of a complex number), as well as for adding and multiplying complex numbers.

```
class ComplexNumber {
    private double fReal;
    private double fImaginary;
    public ComplexNumber(double re, double im) {
        fReal = re;
        fImaginary = im;
    }
    public double getReal() {
        return fReal;
    }
    public double getImaginary() {
        return fImaginary;
    }

    ...

    public ComplexNumber add(ComplexNumber c) {
        return new ComplexNumber (
            getReal() + c.getReal(),
            getImaginary() + c.getImaginary());
    }
    public ComplexNumber multiply(ComplexNumber c) {
        double re = getReal()*c.getReal() -
                getImaginary()*c.getImaginary();
        double im = getImaginary()*c.getReal() +
                getReal()*c.getImaginary();
```

```
            return new ComplexNumber(re, im);
    }

    public boolean equals(Object anObject) {
        if (anObject instanceof ComplexNumber) {
            ComplexNumber c = (ComplexNumber)
                                       anObject;
            return ((c.getReal() == getReal()) &&
                (c.getImaginary() == getImaginary()));
        } else
            return false;
    }
}
```

Example 6.4 Java source code of class ComplexNumber

```
        <<application>>
        ComplexNumber       ...
    ─────────────────────────────
    –double fReal
    –double fImaginary
    ─────────────────────────────
    +getReal()
    +getImaginary()
    +add(ComplexNumber)
    +multiply(ComplexNumber)
    +equals(Object)
```

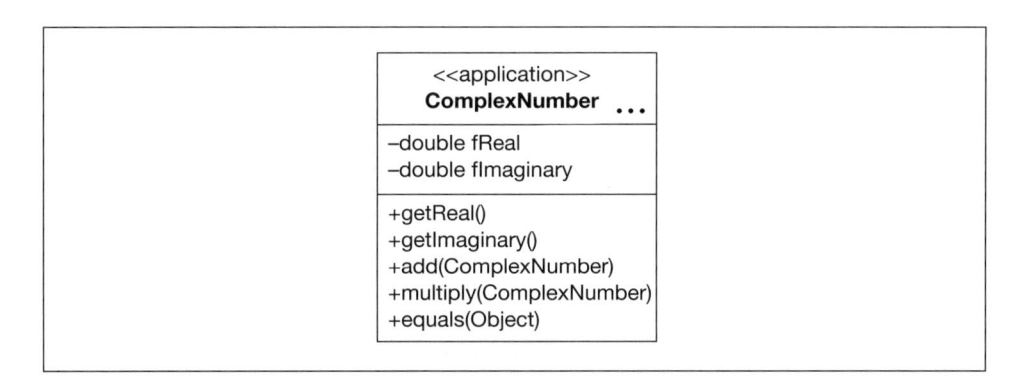

Figure 6.7 The UML-F diagram of class ComplexNumber

6.2.1 Recipe for creating automated tests in JUnit

The main purpose of JUnit is to facilitate the creation of automated tests for Java programs. This adaptation is therefore the most common one. The adaptation is straightforward, and we structure its description into four recipes: one composite recipe that provides an overview; and three basic recipes that refine the first one by explaining how to define test cases and how to group test cases into test suites. Table 6.2 shows the cookbook recipe 'How to create automated tests in JUnit'.

Recipe 'JUnit 1: How to create automated tests in JUnit'	
Intent	To define test cases for Java applications.
Classes	TestCase and TestSuite.
Related recipes	■ 'JUnit 1.1: How to define a test case', or ■ 'JUnit 1.1A: How to define test cases as inner classes' together with ■ 'JUnit 1.2: How to compose a test suite'.
Steps to Apply	1. Understand the functionality to be tested and plan the tests that are needed. 2. Apply the recipe 'JUnit 1.1: How to define a test case' to create the appropriate test cases. Repeat this step, as often as necessary, but you may also adapt previously defined tests to reuse parts for new tests. 3. Alternatively to step 2, apply the more sophisticated recipe 'JUnit 1.1A: How to define test cases as inner classes' allowing the definition of several test cases in a single class file. 4. Add the test cases to a given test suite or group them into a new test suite by applying the recipe 'JUnit 1.2: How to compose a test suite'.
Discussion	For discussion of the details refer to the subrecipes. Usually step 2 (creating a test) is applied repeatedly to gain a suite of tests. Typically, new tests are defined on the basis of older ones. In particular, setUp() and tearDown() methods are candidates for reuse. The alternative step 3 is more compact if a number of related tests has to be defined.

Table 6.2 Recipe providing an overview for adapting JUnit

JUnit provides standard ways for reporting test results. Moreover, adaptation of the result reporting is done only once per project. Therefore, the adaptation of the test result reporting mechanism is addressed independently later in this chapter.

According to step 1 of the recipe, we have to figure out what has to be tested. We suggest at least one test for each calculation method. This might be useful, for example, if the underlying data structure changes in the future. Furthermore, the equals() method deserves several tests. Thus, the following may be an appropriate test plan:

- One test for add, with arbitrary, non-zero data.
- One test for multiply, with arbitrary, non-zero data.
- Four tests for the equals method:

    1. Two equal numbers, represented by distinct objects;

    2. Two different numbers with a non-zero real part only;

    3. Two different numbers with a non-zero imaginary part only;

    4. The object passed as parameter for comparison is not a ComplexNumber.

The next section presents the recipes for test cases and test suites, so that we can adapt JUnit for the tests sketched above.

6.2.2 Cookbook recipe for the definition of a test case

Since the design of the TestCase variation point is based on the Unification construction principle (see Figure 6.2), its adaptation requires the creation of a subclass and the overriding of its hook methods («Unif–h»). As the run() method is the template method (UML–F tag «Unif–t») it should not be overridden. Table 6.3 describes the cookbook recipe for adapting the JUnit class TestCase. It augments the generic recipe for the Unification construction principle presented in Chapter 5 with JUnit-specific constraints.

Recipe 'JUnit 1.1: How to define a test case'	
Intent	To create a test case.
Classes	TestCase.
Steps to Apply	1. Decide what is to be tested, and choose an appropriate test setting. The following questions may help. ■ Which functionality is to be tested? A method call or an interaction between several related components? ■ What is the test data (fixture) to operate on? ■ What is the expected outcome? 2. Is there similar code in test cases that can be reused? In particular, take a look at the setUp(), runTest(), and tearDown() methods. 3. Define a new subclass, either as a direct subclass of TestCase or a subclass of some other appropriate subclass of TestCase. 4. Define the attributes needed to hold the object structures (fixtures) needed for the test. 5. Optional: override setUp(). The default implementation in TestCase is empty. If subclassing another test, setUp() may adapt the result of a super.setUp() call or reuse the inherited method. 6. Override runTest() to implement the actual testing code. 7. Optional: override tearDown() to clean up the system after the test (for example, to close files and other external connections). The default implementation is empty. If subclassing another test, tearDown() may adapt the result of a super.tearDown() call or just reuse the inherited method.
Discussion	■ Add each test case to a test suite as described in step 4 of recipe 'JUnit 1: How to create automated tests in JUnit'. ■ To allow reuse of setUp() through subclassing, we recommend defining test attributes with protected access. ■ On some occasions one might reuse the runTest() method on different fixtures through inheritance. This happens, for example, if the test checks an invariant (constraint of the object structure) that should be valid on all object structures.

Table 6.3 Cookbook recipe for defining a test case

As described in the recipe, overriding the runTest(), setUp(), and tearDown() methods is optional. Figure 6.8 illustrates five common adaptation scenarios. TestA, TestB, and TestC are the most common adaptations. TestD reuses the runTest() method of TestB and applies it to different setUp() and tearDown() methods, whereas TestE reuses the setUp() and tearDown() code of its superclass TestC but redefines the runTest() method.

In practice, the existing adaptation variants are so manifold that the guidelines given in the recipe can often only discuss major variants. In addition to the adaptation options shown in Figure 6.8, a number of less likely variants of adaptations exist.

Earlier we identified some tests to be conducted on instances of class ComplexNumber. Example 6.5 shows the source code of one of these tests – it defines three attributes to hold the fixtures, a setUp() method and the appropriate runTest() method. Figure 6.9 shows the corresponding UML-F class diagram.

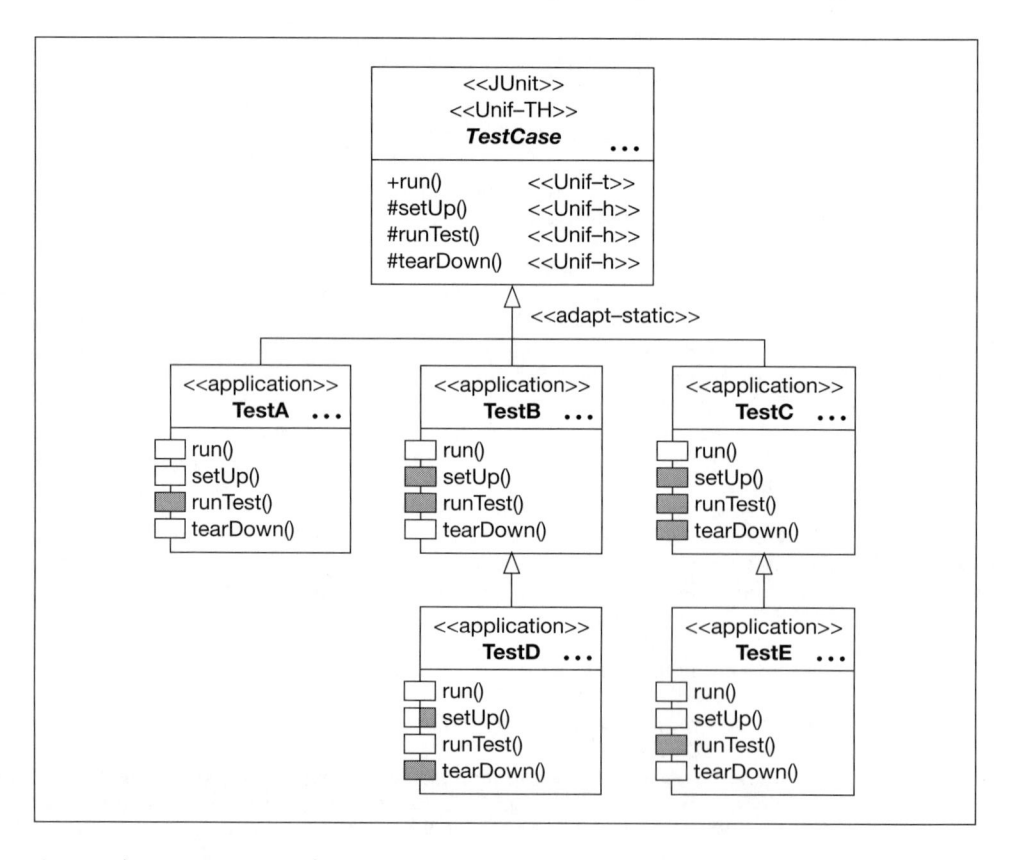

Figure 6.8 Some adaptation options for TestCase subclasses

```java
public class ComplexTestAdd extends TestCase {
      private ComplexNumber fOneZero;
      private ComplexNumber fZeroOne;
      private ComplexNumber fOneOne;
      protected void setUp() {
          fOneZero = new ComplexNumber(1, 0);
          fZeroOne = new ComplexNumber(0, 1);
          fOneOne = new ComplexNumber(1, 1);
      }
      public void runTest() {
          ComplexNumber result =
                              fOneZero.add(fZeroOne);
          /* assert is provided by JUnit in the
          Assert class, which is the super class of
                                          TestCase */
          assert(fOneOne.equals(result));
      }
}
```

Example 6.5 Sample test case for class ComplexNumber

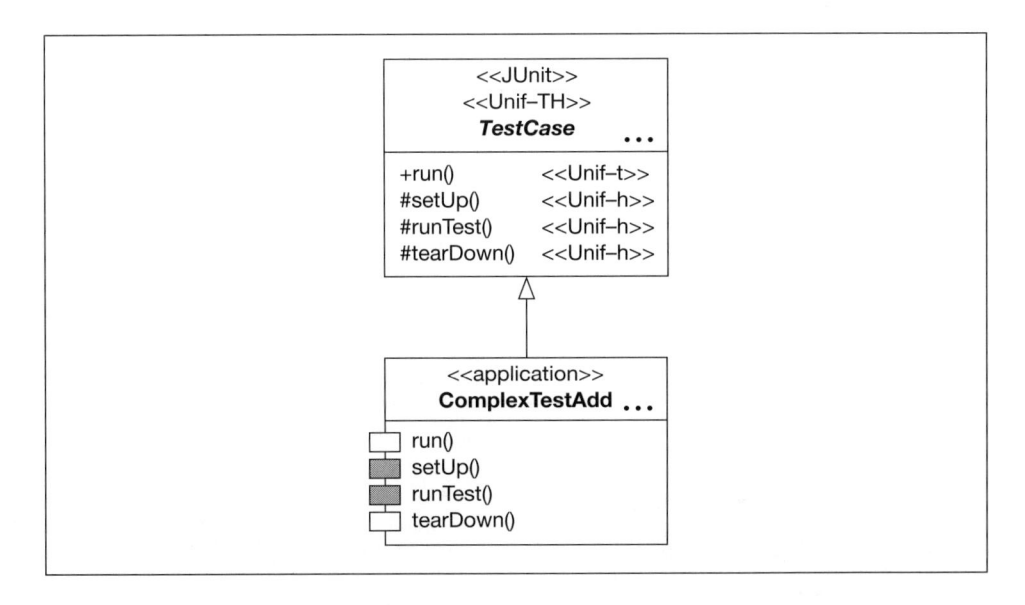

Figure 6.9 ComplexTestAdd class structure

6.2.3 Definition of several test cases in one source code file

The previous recipe requires the definition of each test in a separate class. To keep the number of classes, and thus the number of source code files, small it would be useful to define each test case in an individual method, but several of them within one class. However, all these methods need different names, whereas the JUnit framework as introduced so far accepts test case implementations only with the name runTest().

JUnit allows the definition of several test cases within one class by applying the GoF Adapter design pattern (Gamma et al., 1995) to match the actual method name containing the test with the name runTest() and by relying on so-called anonymous inner classes. Java provides the concept of anonymous inner classes for defining anonymous subclasses and overriding specific methods, without having to provide explicit class names. From a modeling viewpoint, such an anonymous inner class is like a normal class except that the name is missing. We define the tag «anonymous» to mark inner classes. Table 6.4 introduces that tag.

Tag	«anonymous».
Applies to	Class.
Type	Boolean.
	<<anonymous>> ... <<anonymous>> VirtualName ...
Motivation and purpose	Mark Java anonymous inner classes, to denote that they do not have a name.
Explanation of effect	The tag is used to describe that a class is anonymous. Normally each class in a class diagram must have an explicit name. This tag allows an exception to that rule. If desired, a class marked with the «anonymous» tag can still have a name given in the diagram.
Expansion	Does not apply.
Discussion	If concrete object structures are to be denoted, then it is useful to use a virtual classname in the diagram to refer to them. This virtual name can also be used in explanations.

Table 6.4 The «anonymous» tag

Figure 6.10 illustrates how the Adapter design pattern accomplishes the match between the methods testAddZeroZero() and runTest(). The use of anonymous inner subclasses allows the repeated definition of test case methods within one class.

Table 6.5 provides a variant of the JUnit 1.1 recipe. The recipe 'JUnit 1.1A: How to define test cases as inner classes' uses the technique of anonymous inner subclasses to define multiple test cases within one class. The basic idea is to override the method runTest() in each inner class individually, whereas the setUp() and tearDown() methods are typically not overridden in these inner classes.

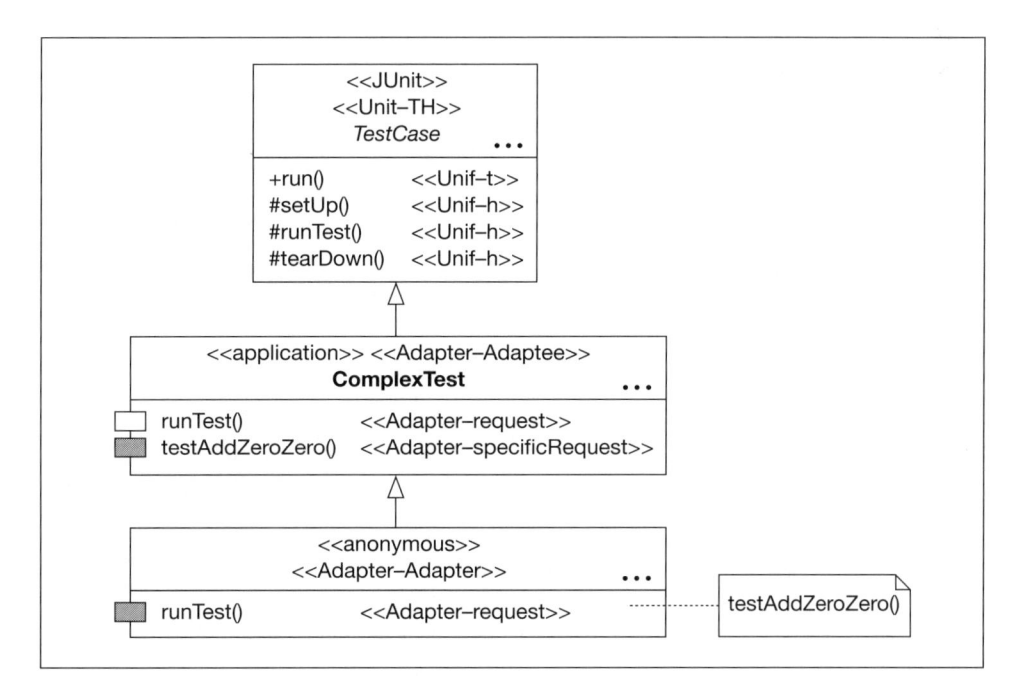

Figure 6.10 Applying the Adapter design pattern to the runTest() method

Recipe 'JUnit 1.1A: How to define test cases as inner classes'	
Intent	A given piece of code needs a set of tests that should not be defined in separate regular classes.
Classes	TestCase.
Steps to Apply	1. Decide what is to be tested, and on the appropriate setting for the tests to be defined. The following questions may help. ■ Which functionality is to be tested? A method call or an interaction between several related components? ■ What are the important test data (fixtures) to operate on? ■ What is the expected outcome? 2. Is there similar code in the test cases that can be reused? In particular, take a look at the setUp(), runTest(), and tearDown() methods. 3. Build a new explicit subclass, either of TestCase or of a previously defined subclass. 4. Define/add the attributes necessary to hold the object structures (fixtures) needed for the test. 5. Optional: override setUp(). The default implementation in TestCase is empty. If subclassing another test, setUp() may adapt the result of a super.setUp() call or just reuse the inherited method. If changing an existing test class, do not override setUp() directly, but in the anonymous subclass only. By analogy with the runTest() adaptation, you can provide a new method that can be adapted to setUp(). 6. Define appropriate testing methods which must be invoked by runTest() in the inner subclasses. 7. Optional: override tearDown() to clean up the system after the test. The same considerations/restrictions apply as for method setUp().
Discussion	■ See also the discussion and explanation of the recipe 'JUnit 1.1: How to define a test case'. ■ Adding new tests to an existing test class is suitable if the test class follows the policy of defining tests through inner subclasses already. Tests grouped in one test class should not only test related functionality, but also be structured similarly. ■ Due to the enforcement of strict test separation, setUp() is called for each test individually. This allows the tests to modify the fixture each time, but leads to time consuming overheads if many tests are defined in the same suite that operate on many different parts of the fixture defined by setUp(). Then it is useful to define a part of the used fixture in setUp(), and a less common part individually by test methods.

Table 6.5 Cookbook recipe for defining test cases by means of inner classes

Although the above recipe is still straightforward, it illustrates that several aspects have to be considered. In particular, the existence of adaptation paths different from the standard pathway increase the length and content of a recipe considerably. If a recipe becomes too complex, it is useful to extract parts into subrecipes. In particular, a presentation of unlikely alternatives can then be discussed in separate recipes without cluttering the main recipe too much.

Example 6.6 shows parts of the code that results from an application of the above recipe to the ComplexNumber example. (The missing part – the inner classes – are presented in Section 6.3 where test suites are considered). As the construction of complex numbers is cheap, two objects are instantiated in the setUp() code. These complex numbers are used in several tests. Additional objects are created in the individual tests on demand. Figure 6.11 shows the UML-F class diagram that illustrates this adaptation.

```
public class ComplexTest extends TestCase {
    private ComplexNumber fZeroZero;
    private ComplexNumber fZeroOne;
    public ComplexTest (String name) {
            super(name);
    }
    protected void setUp() {
        fZeroZero = new ComplexNumber(0, 0);
        fZeroOne = new ComplexNumber(0, 1);
    }
    public void testAddZeroZero() {
        ComplexNumber num = new ComplexNumber(3, 7);
        ComplexNumber result = num.add(fZeroZero);
        assert(num.equals(result));
    }
    public void testAddCommuting() {
        ComplexNumber num1 = new ComplexNumber(25,-9);
        ComplexNumber num2 = new ComplexNumber(17, 45);
        ComplexNumber result1 = num1.add(num2);
        ComplexNumber result2 = num2.add(num1);
        assert(result1.equals(result2));
    }
    public void testEquals() {
        /* assert is provided by JUnit in the Assert
           class, which is the super class of TestCase */
        assert(!fZeroOne.equals(fZeroZero));
    }
    // add more tests here
}
```

Example 6.6 Some test case definitions for the ComplexNumber class

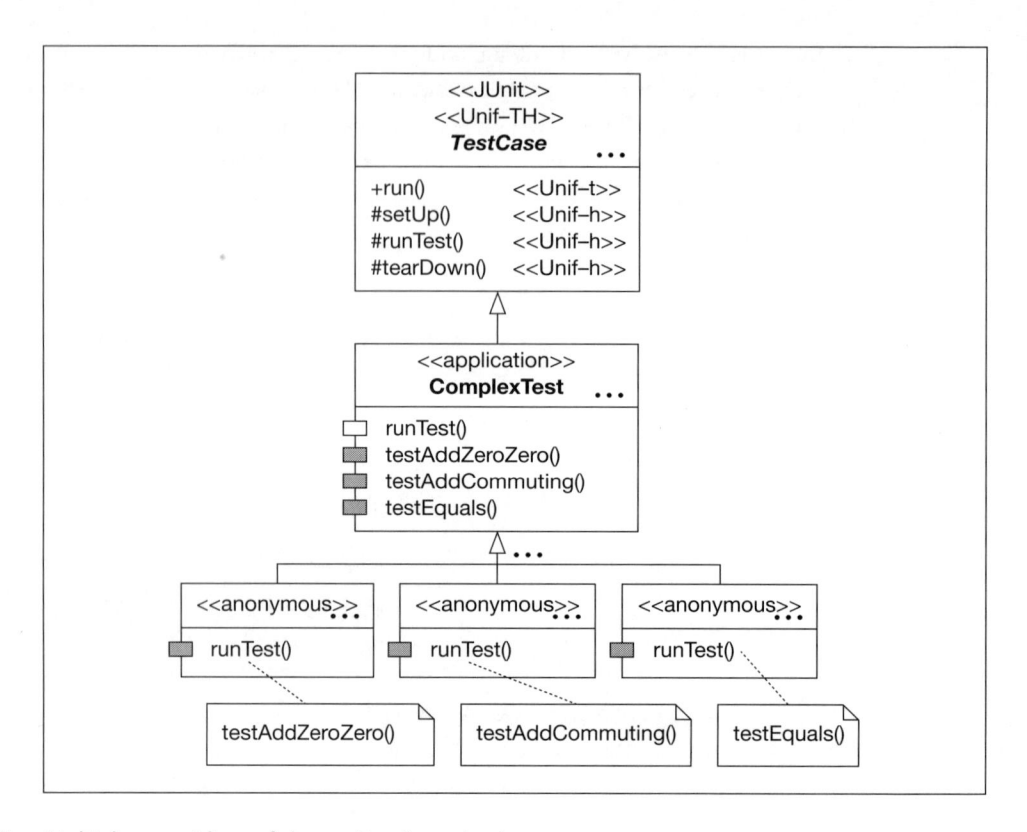

Figure 6.11 Multiple overriding of the runTest() method

6.3 Organizing test cases into test suites

The previous section shows how to define new tests. This section describes how to organize test cases into test suites.

6.3.1 A cookbook recipe for composing a test suite

The recipe 'JUnit 1.2: How to compose a test suite' completes the set of recipes that guide the principal adaptation of JUnit. The TestSuite class applies the Composite construction principle, except that the generalization is «fixed» (see Figure 6.3). This means that no additional direct subclass of Test shall be defined in the application.[1] For that reason, a JUnit adaptation only defines subclasses of TestCase.

Chapter 6 UML-F based documentation and adaptation of the JUnit testing framework

A method suite() is used to define new test suites. For convenience, it can be defined as a static method in a TestCase subclass. Figure 6.12 shows a sequence diagram which illustrates how a test suite is created. The method suite() creates a TestSuite object and adds the set of test cases by invoking addTest() for each test case or test suite object that should be part of the test suite.

Table 6.6 describes the steps for defining a JUnit test suite. If inner classes have been used to define test cases, then the instances of inner subclasses of a test case have to be composed in a test suite. Thus, the previous recipe 'JUnit 1.1A' and the presented 'JUnit 1.2' are to some extent intertwined.

When JUnit is launched, for example through a Java command line interface, it takes the name of a TestCase subclass as parameter, invokes its suite() method getting a test suite object as result, and invokes the run() method on that test suite.

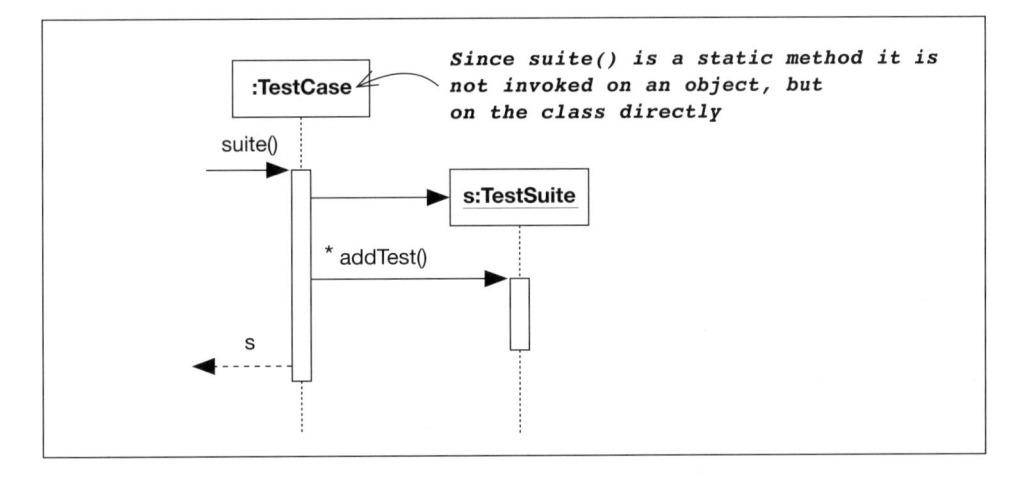

Figure 6.12 Creating test suites

---

[1] Since Test is an interface, this means that no additional direct implementations of the interface should be defined. In this case, the only valid implementations for Test are TestCase and TestSuite.

Recipe 'JUnit 1.2: How to compose a test suite'	
Intent	A number of tests have been defined and shall be composed to a single test suite. A new test suite shall combine a number of already existing tests and test suites.
Classes	TestSuite and TestCase.
Steps to Apply	1. Identify the tests and test suites to be grouped together. What common characteristics or purpose do they have? 2. Should the new tests be added to an existing test suite definition? If so, then include appropriate code for adding them in that suite by extending its suite() method. 3. Otherwise, introduce a static method called "suite()" returning a Test object and locate it in an appropriate TestCase class. In the following the code for method suite() is discussed. 4. Create a new TestSuite object. 5. If each test case is defined using recipe JUnit 1.1 (therefore in a single class), then just instantiate each of the classes and add these objects to the test suite. 6. Otherwise, we assume the new tests are located as methods in the same class. Then use the Adapter technique of anonymous inner subclasses to map each method to runTest() and add the resulting objects to the test suite. 7. If the new test suite is to contain other test suites as well, add those in the same way as the other tests.
Discussion	In addition to creating class-wide test suites, it is often useful to compose package, subsystem and finally system-wide test suites. Their possibly overlapping contents of tests make them less manageable over time. However, it might be worthwhile to define short life test suites that focus on particular features of the system if the overall runtime of a complete test suite is considerable.

Table 6.6 Cookbook recipe for composing a test suite

6.3.2 Adaptation of a sample test suite

Based on the recipe 'JUnit 1.2: How to compose a test suite', we derive a compact suite() implementation as shown in Example 6.7.

```
public static Test suite() {
    TestSuite suite = new TestSuite();
    suite.addTest(new ComplexTest
    ("testAddZeroZero") {
        protected void runTest()
        { this.testAddZeroZero(); }
    } );
    suite.addTest(new
    ComplexTest("testAddCommuting"){
        protected void runTest()
        { this.testAddCommuting(); }
    } );
    suite.addTest(new ComplexTest("testEquals"){
    protected void runTest()
    { this.test Equals();}
    });
    return suite;
}
```

Example 6.7 Creating a test suite in the suite() method of class ComplexTest

6.4 Reporting test results

To complete the JUnit cookbook, the recipe 'JUnit 2: How to report test results' describes how to modify the default mechanism of collecting and presenting test results. The design of the TestResult class relies on the Separation construction principle. Bear in mind the abstractly coupled JUnit classes TestCase and TestResult (see Figure 6.6). JUnit provides several subclasses of TestResult featuring textual or graphical output. However, other variants might be required, for example to save results to a database.

The definition of another TestResult variant is probably only done once in a JUnit adaptation. As this chapter concentrates mainly on demonstrating the feasibility of the cookbook approach in combination with the UML-F profile, we keep this recipe short and refer the interested reader to a more detailed description (Beck and Gamma, 1998a). Table 6.7 describes this recipe – it reuses the generic recipe for the Separation construction principle given in Chapter 5.

Recipe 'JUnit 2: How to report test results'	
Intent	Providing addtional mechanisms for reporting tests.
Classes	TestResult.

Steps to Apply	1. Understand how the test reporting structure works.
	2. Determine whether there is already a subclass that provides the desired or a similar reporting mechanism. Can an existing subclass be used 'as is' or used as a base class for inheritance?
	3. Build a new subclass of the TestResult class.
	  ■ Implement the hook methods startTest(), addFailure(), addError(), and/or endTest().
	  ■ Determine whether you can, or should, reuse the provided default implementation, e.g. through calling the inherited method.

Discussion	This recipe should be applied rarely. In most cases the default features provided by JUnit are sufficient.

Table 6.7 TestResult adaptation recipe

Figure 6.13 shows the UML-F class diagram of a TestResult adaptation for the generation of HTML files. If an error or a failure occurs, a line is added to the HTML file. The notes attached to the hook methods describe the method behavior.

Figure 6.14 shows a browser that displays an HTML file that reports a failure when testing the ComplexNumber class with an assertion that (0, 1) added to (1, 1) would wrongly sum up to (1, 1).

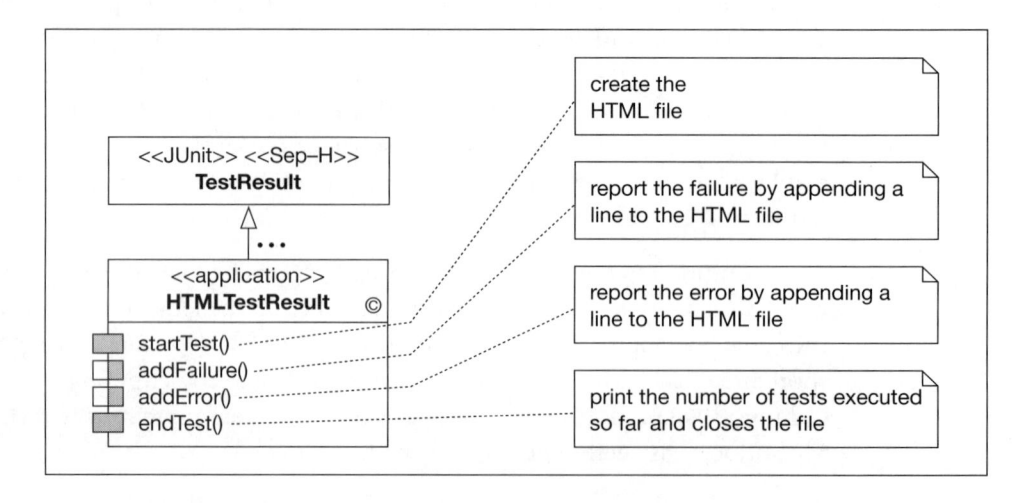

Figure 6.13 Generating HTML files for the presentation of test results

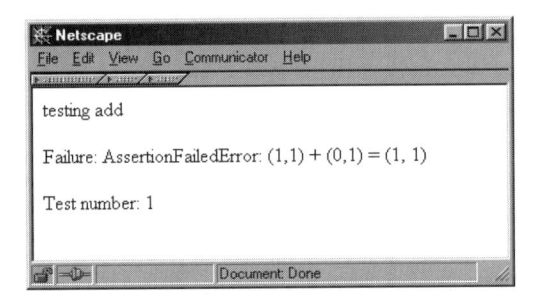

Figure 6.14 Display of a sample HTML file that reports a failure

6.5 Summary

The case study in this chapter applies UML-F to describe the JUnit framework. It also presents cookbook recipes which document the adaptation of the framework. This demonstrates that UML-F tags are useful in pinpointing framework variation points. The case study further illustrates how UML-F and cookbooks can be integrated to support framework adaptation.

Chapter 7

Hints and guidelines for the framework development and adaptation process[1]

This chapter focuses on the framework development and adaptation process and presents a number of methodological concepts that are intended to assist in the design, development, and adaptation of frameworks. One objective of the chapter is to show that, although they can certainly benefit from the use of traditional concepts, frameworks have new needs that require the introduction of new methodological tools and concepts.

The chapter starts with the presentation of the *cluster cycle process model* (Meyer, 1990) which captures the overall flavor of framework development. Based on that model, the following steps are envisaged in developing a framework in a more systematic and efficient way:

- identification of the domain area's key abstractions
- definition of the flexibility requirements (variation points)
- definition of the framework design
- refinement of the design and its transformation into an architecture
- adaptation of the framework.

The chapter then proceeds to review the concepts of *class families* and *class teams*. Although proposed almost a decade ago, we will argue that they anticipate and cover many of the needs of a framework-based development process. The argument will be

---

[1] Chapter written with Timothy B. Brown and Alessandro Pasetti of the Software Research Laboratory (headed by Wolfgang Pree) at the University of Constance, Germany.

illustrated with a case study from a real-life framework (designed by the authors for the European Space Agency) to model spacecraft control systems. The case study will also serve to introduce two innovative concepts – *framelets* and *implementation cases* – which were devised to aid the design and development of frameworks, and which complement and extend the concepts of class families and class teams. Implementation cases form the basis of what we call *eXtreme design* (XD).

Finally, the chapter considers the framework adaptation problem and in particular it focuses on *adaptation cases* and *adaptation reports*. Adaptation cases are an aid to the actual process of creating an individual application from a framework. Adaptation reports are a means of formalizing the experience gained from the development of individual applications and make it available to all projects using the same framework. Both augment framework cookbooks which describe the mature, standard adaptations of a framework.

Note that the presentation of the process, along with the various hints and methodological guidelines, does not take organizational and management aspects (such as team structures and incentive models) into account. These aspects are at least as important as the techniques presented in this chapter for a successful framework project. Goldberg and Rubin (1995) discuss these issues in an excellent manner by providing a project management framework instead of one-size-fits-all recommendations. They identify the various project parameters that influence the organization and management of a framework project.

7.1 The cluster cycle process model of framework development and adaptation

Object-oriented development techniques rely on the same activities as those described in conventional process models – that is, analysis, specification, design, implementation, test, and maintenance. Unfortunately, methods such as the Unified Process (Jacobson et al. 1999) suggest slightly different but synonymous terms. In the following material, note that we deliberately use references dating back more than a decade to corroborate that the coarse-grained characteristics of reuse-centered development have been well known for some years.

Classical software development strategies do not focus on the reusability of software components. Meyer (1989) remarks that 'object-orientedness is not just a programming style but the implementation of a certain view of what software should be – this view implies profound rethinking of the software process.' Thus, Meyer discerns two views or cultures:

- The conventional culture is *project-based*: the classical software lifecycle or some of its variations, such as the waterfall model with certain possible iterations (Boehm, 1976), or a prototype-oriented software development methodology (Pomberger et al., 1991), have the aim of solving *one* particular problem. The recommended strategy, which is inherent in the usual software lifecycle models, is top-down. The primary question addressed in the analysis and design phases is 'What must the system do?', followed by a stepwise refinement of a system's functions. Henderson-Sellers and Edwards (1990) summarize the flaws of top-down system development – 'Top-down decomposition does not promote reusability.' The data structure aspect is often neglected. Finally, top-down designed systems are too rigid and impede evolutionary change.
- The preconditions of a new culture – called *product culture* by Meyer (1989) – are object-oriented development techniques. This culture produces not only software systems that solve *one* particular problem, but also reusable software components that are useful for a potentially large number of applications. So the lifecycle of a piece of software is generally extended.

The object-oriented, long term view implies a new activity in the software lifecycle, called *generalization*, and a modification of the specification activity:

- The use of object-oriented languages does not automatically mean that the software produced is reusable; the additional lifecycle activity of generalization is necessary to achieve this goal. This activity is, in most cases, part of an iterative process since the need for more general software components is often not realized until they are reused.
- A set of ready-made reusable/adaptable software components also influences the system specification. In contrast to the project-based culture, where a software system is developed to satisfy specific needs, good frameworks typically capture the existing 'best practices' in a domain. For example, the SAP system represents a framework that – although developed with a non-object-oriented language – standardizes significant portions of how companies conduct business covering areas such as accounting, human resource management, production planning, and manufacturing. The SAP framework can be adapted and fine tuned to the specific needs of companies. Nevertheless, several aspects cannot be changed.

In other words, instead of slavishly adhering to the user's or customer's requests in the realm of a conventional custom-made system construction process, the system specification inherent in a framework most likely provides a somewhat different functionality (for example, without some nice-to-have features) which can be created by means of existing framework components. The customer has the choice between a custom-made system implemented (almost) from scratch with significantly more effort and cost, and a system built out of ready-made components by adapting a framework. The framework has the additional advantage that the quality of the resulting system in terms of reliability will probably be higher than the custom-made system. This is particularly true if the framework has been thoroughly tested and/or has already been reused several times. Some offers might be hard to refuse.

Which process model captures the framework development and adaptation process? Though the answer to that question is controversial, we have found that the cluster model – Meyer (1990) coined the term in the early 1990s – describes the flavor of the process quite well on a coarse-grained level (see Figure 7.1). A cluster, in this context, is a group of related classes and/or interfaces. The design, development and adaptation of classes/interfaces belonging to one cluster constitutes *one* lifecycle. Note that the model also comprises the adaptation process of a framework. The following changes to the usual arrangement of the activities in the software lifecycle become necessary in this model.

- Activities of the software lifecycle are not applied to the system as a whole. Instead, system development is split into several sub-lifecycles overlapping in time. A sub-lifecycle is associated with one cluster. The clusters are typically at different stages in the lifecycle, regardless of whether the framework is in the development or adaptation stage. This reflects the fact that the iterative design of abstract classes/interfaces requires that some subsystems be located in the implementation activity. If the implementation effort reveals that certain abstractions are not suitable, the redesign of the abstractions has to go on in parallel with the implementation of the particular subsystems.

- Though Meyer (1990) merged design and implementation activities within one cluster, we suggest keeping them separate even though these activities might sometimes overlap within one cluster. The concept of implementation cases (introduced in Section 7.8) provides more fine-grained methodological insights into that aspect of framework development. In order to not clutter the cluster cycle model in Figure 7.1, it does not show lines between the activities within a cluster and between clusters. Analogous with enhanced waterfall cycle models, the cluster cycle model allows moving back and forth between the activities.

A framework adaptation also takes place in one or more clusters. The characteristics of an adaptation are that the importance of the specification and design activities is diminished while the focus shifts to the implementation and test activities. The implementation activity could involve black-box compositional configurations and/or white-box inheritance-based adaptations.

- The additional activity of generalization is introduced with the aim of producing reusable software components. Meyer (1990) also merged that activity with the test activity. Nevertheless, we again regard generalization and testing as separate activities. Framework adaptations might lead to generalization activities in various clusters.

Regarding the sequencing of the cluster lifecycle, we recommend working first on the most general clusters (providing some utility features) and then proceeding to those that are application specific. The following sections discuss that aspect in more detail. The case study illustrates how the clusters manifest in a sample framework.

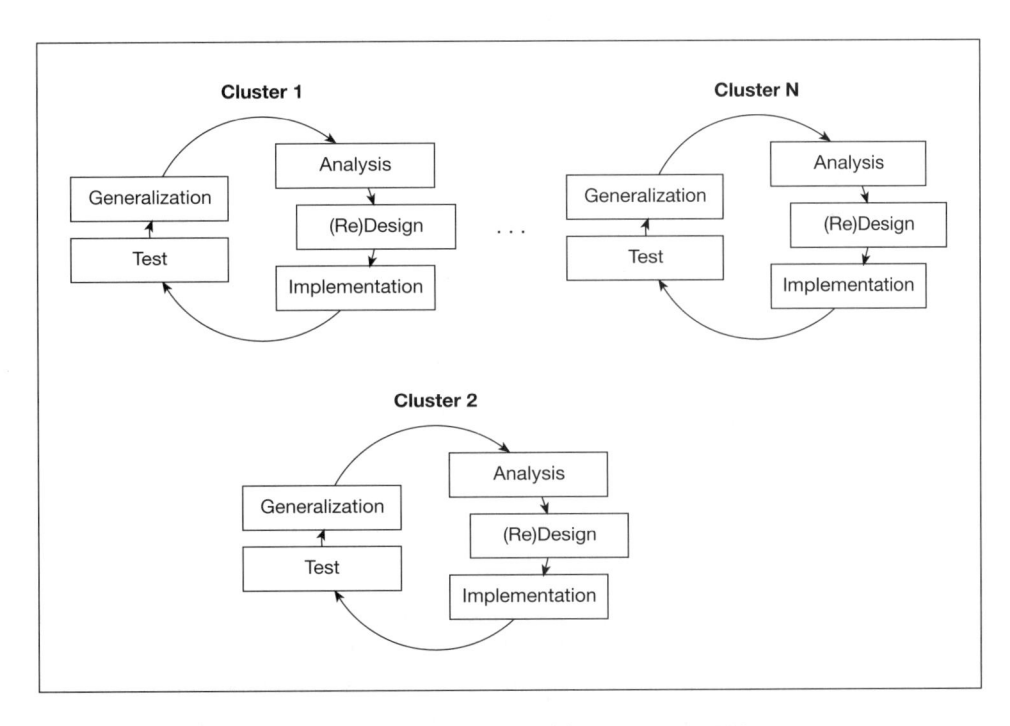

Figure 7.1 Cluster model of the software lifecycle (adapted from Meyer, 1990)

7.2 Defining the key abstractions as an initial step

Experience gained in numerous framework projects has proven that framework development requires sound domain knowledge. This is especially true in the initial steps of framework development. Of course, no methodology can provide the domain knowledge or the resulting domain language – what *can* be expected from methodological guidelines are the priorities and the order in which to accomplish certain steps.

If a framework is developed from scratch, the critical first step is the identification and coarse-grained design of a domain's key abstractions. Class-Responsibility-Collaboration (CRC) cards can support that effort. The CRC card approach was presented by Beck and Cunningham (1989) at the OOPSLA'89 conference. CRC cards are helpful in finding objects/classes in general. Their value stems from the fact that they enforce a coarse-grained view on the domain's principal entities. Basically, they capture the class/interface name, its handful of responsibilities (not the methods, which represent a more detailed view) and whether there is a close relationship between the entities without having to specify the kind of relationship. Figure 7.2 shows the CRC cards of the abstract classes Component and Container in Java's Swing framework library. The overlapping of the two cards provides a visual clue that the two abstractions are closely related. That is also indicated in the Collaborations sections of the two cards. Note that CRC cards are plain US index cards as used in offices. Real paper cards are considered to be better suited for this purpose than computerized versions that are manipulated on screen by means of a software tool. Beck and Cunningham (1989) stress the value of physically moving the paper cards around – for example, on a pin wall: 'When learners/designers pick up an object, they seem to more readily identify with it, and are prepared to deal with the remainder of the design from its perspective.'

We suggest creating a separate CRC design that comprises only the abstract entities of the framework under development. We refer to that as the aCiRC cards (abstract Class/interface Responsibility Collaboration cards). The two aCiRC cards of the Java Swing framework are the one for Component and the one for Container – and just those!

This leads us to a hint regarding the typical number of aCiRC cards in a framework design. The interesting conclusion from studying frameworks in various domains and of varying complexity regarding the overall number of classes and interfaces is that, first, the number of domain abstractions is not directly proportional to the number of classes and, second, the absolute number of domain abstractions is

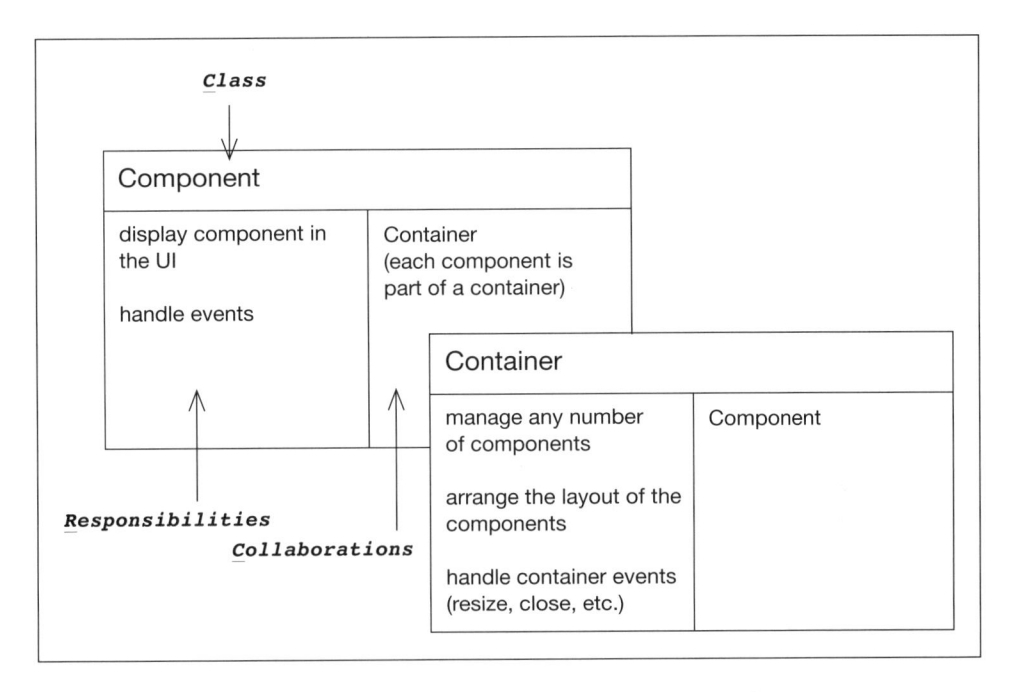

Figure 7.2 Sample CRC cards for the Java Swing abstractions Component and Container

rather small. The typical number is between two and seven abstractions. Though this is only a rough rule of thumb, it gives a clue regarding the number of aCiRC cards you should expect.

aCiRC cards as basis for framework adaptations

If a framework already exists and is to be adapted, aCiRC cards are a valuable means of understanding the principal structure and interactions of the framework. If no aCiRC cards are available, we recommend writing them up in retrospect.

7.3 Class families, class teams, and subsystems

Erich Gamma coined the terms class teams, class families, and (specifically in this context) subsystems in his Ph.D. thesis (1991).

Class families evolve around the principal abstractions of a framework. The members of a class family adhere to the interface defined by the corresponding abstract class or interface. For example, the Component family in the Java Swing framework contains around 50 members – they are subclasses of the abstract class Component. The Container family is a subfamily of the Component family and has about 10 members.

If the family crystallization point – that is, the abstract class or interface – is already identified in the set of aCiRC cards, the families will evolve in a top-down manner. The abstraction is there first; the specific family members follow later. Quite often, families evolve in a bottom-up process when framework developers recognize similarities between several concrete classes. Thus, the abstract class or interface is defined based on the experience incorporated in the specific classes. Thus an aCiRC card should be added if families arise in a bottom-up manner.

Consider an important design hint for class families – the root of class families should be lightweight. For example, excessive data representations should be avoided in abstract classes that correspond to key abstractions in the framework domain.

Class teams consist of cooperating families. Thus the relationship between aCiRC cards might provide useful hints as to which class families could form teams. Class teams rely on abstract coupling and are reused as a whole. For example, the two class families in the Java Swing framework form a team. In the ET++ framework (Weinand and Gamma, 1994) the class families Text, TextView, and TextFormatter form a team. The specific text representations (abstract class Text) can be displayed by various views (subclasses of the abstract class TextView). The Text and TextView combination cooperate with any text-formatting algorithm through the abstract coupling of the Text abstraction with the TextFormatter abstraction.

Subsystems explicitly encapsulate a class team by offering an adequate interface. Thus, a subsystem corresponds to the definition of a software component in Chapter 1. The Façade pattern (Gamma et al., 1995) also discusses this modularization aspect (see Figure 7.3). In general, the definition of an additional abstraction makes reuse easier for clients and reduces the coupling between specific classes of teams.

The concepts of class families, class teams, and subsystems also help in redesigning framework hierarchies. Gamma (1991) distinguishes between vertical and horizontal reorganizations. The following reorganization steps should be regarded as triggers of framework evolutions:

- Vertical reorganizations of framework class hierarchies

   The following operations represent vertical reorganizations.

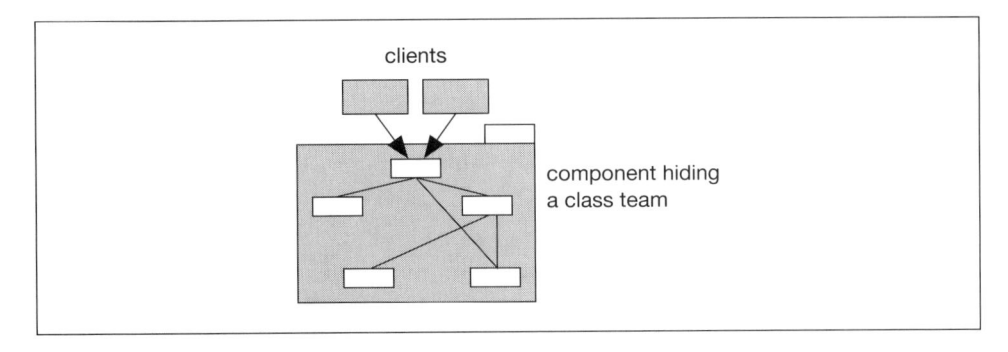

Figure 7.3   Packaging a class team in a component (= subsystem, = Façade)

   1 Moving common properties/protocols/parameters of classes up the class hierarchy. This usually happens within a class family. Check whether commonalities exist.
   2 Splitting up an overly complex class into a class family. This creates a class family. Check whether a class is too complex in terms of number of methods, conditional statements in the methods, and/or data structures.
   3 Avoiding the overriding of too many specific methods by adding abstract classes. This also creates a class family. Check whether specific methods are often overridden in adaptations.
- Horizontal reorganizations of framework class hierarchies

   The following operations represent horizontal reorganizations.
   1 Splitting up a class with too many responsibilities into a class team. The class team might be packaged into a component. Check whether a class has too many responsibilities (in terms of CRC responsibilities). Consider ten or more responsibilities as a rule of thumb limit for discovering classes with too many responsibilities.
   2 Moving features into strategy classes (according to the Strategy/Bridge patterns, which rely on the Separation construction principle). Check whether compositional adaptation of certain features is required. (See also next section.)
- Framelets

   There is a close relationship between class families and class teams/subsystems on the one side and what we call framelets on the other. Essentially, they represent views at different levels of abstractions of a framework. The class families and teams look at the framework as a concrete architecture, whereas the framelets describe it as an abstract design. Framelets are discussed in Section 7.6.

7.4 Identification of a framework's variation points

What makes a 'good' framework? Actually, this provocative and probably oversimplified question cannot be answered without understanding the relevant domain and its inherent flexibility requirements. In other words, striving for flexibility for flexibility's sake, achieved by incorporating as many design patterns as possible, does not result in a good framework. On the contrary, unnecessary flexibility leads to significantly more complexity. Frameworks must be adaptable in an adequate way depending on domain-specific requirements.

Overall, flexibility has to be injected into a framework in appropriate doses.[2] As the quality of a framework depends directly on the appropriateness of its variation points,[3] the identification of those variation points must be an explicit activity in the framework development process. Means of documenting variation points and of communicating them among domain experts and software developers become crucial.

This section first sketches a variation point driven framework development process and shows how that fits into the cluster cycle model. So-called variation point cards, as described by Pree (1995), represent another variant of CRC cards. They capture flexibility requirements. Variation point cards form the basis of transforming an object model into a domain-specific framework. They also correspond to domain-specific design patterns. Variation point cards are analogous to CRC cards, which help to define an initial object model. They document the flexibility requirements and form the basis of framework (re)design, whereas CRC cards comprise the principal entities of an object-oriented design and form the basis of a class design.

7.4.1 Variation point driven framework development

The pain of designing a framework is described by Wirfs-Brock and Johnson (1990): 'Good frameworks are usually the result of many design iterations and a lot of hard

---

[2] Parnas (1976) and Coplien (1999) discuss this issue in general, using the terms 'software family' and 'commonality/variability analysis'.

[3] Pree (1995) uses the term 'hot-spot' as a synonym for variation point. As the term hot-spot has recently been used in the different context of an optimization technique for the execution of Java, we prefer to use variation point. Furthermore, the term 'variation point' triggers an association to the commonality/variability analysis originally proposed by Parnas (1976). In fact, the concepts of commonality/variability analysis and variation points are closely related.

Chapter 7 Hints and guidelines for the development and adaptation process

work.' So don't expect a panacea, for no framework will be ideal from the beginning. More realistically, there should be a means of reducing the number of design iterations. Figure 7.4 gives an overview of the variation point driven framework development process, which includes the identification of flexibility requirements as an explicit activity. One simple but effective means of documenting and communicating variation points are variation point cards.

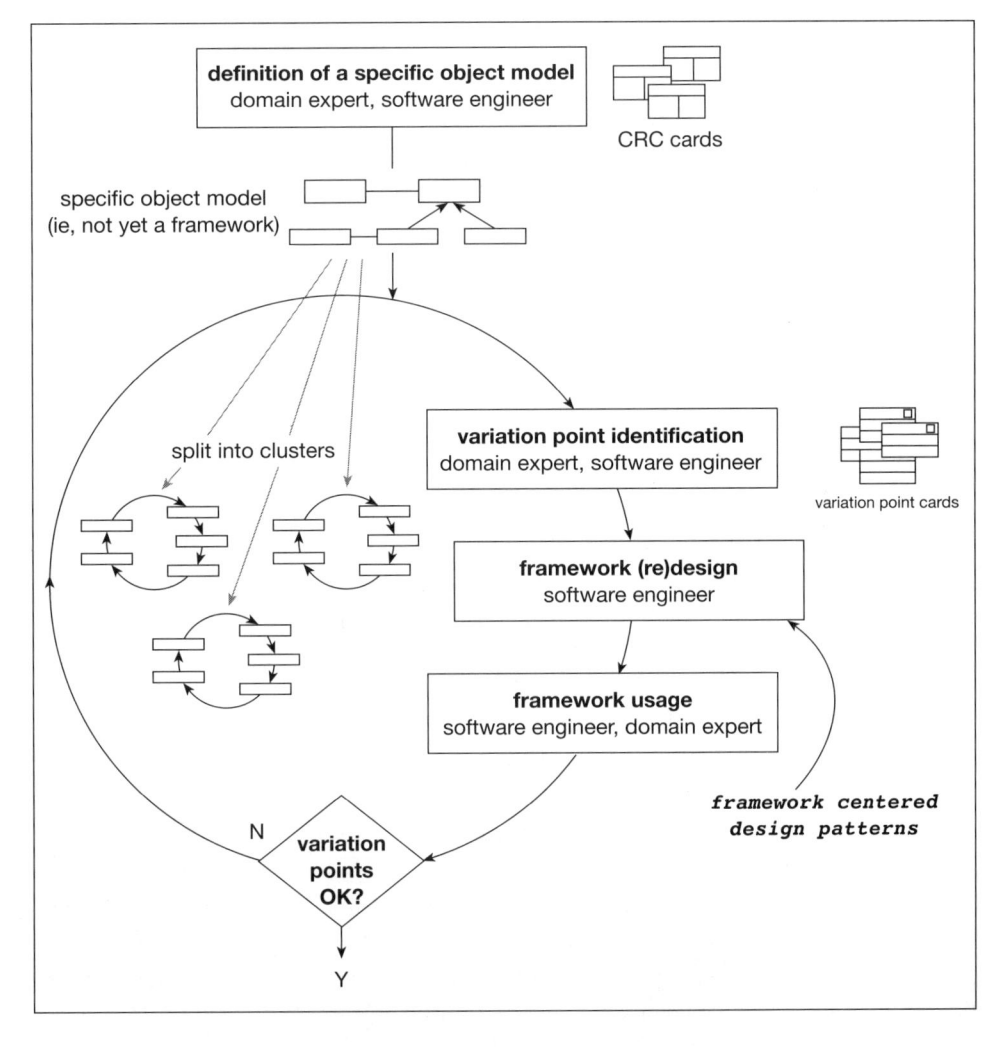

Figure 7.4 Variation point driven framework development process

7.4.2 Definition of a specific object model

State of the art object-oriented analysis and design (OOAD) methodologies support the initial identification of objects/classes, and thus a modularization of an overall software system. As mentioned earlier, CRC cards are commonly used during an initial design. Overall, object modeling is as challenging as any software development. Methodologies can only provide vague guidelines – object modeling requires primarily domain-specific knowledge.

Software engineers assist domain experts in this activity. The distinction between a domain expert and a software engineer is a rather hypothetical one. It should just express the kind of knowledge needed. Of course, software developers will also acquire deep domain knowledge the longer they work in a particular domain.

Modeling a specific solution is itself a complex and iterative activity in which object models must be refined until they meet the domain-specific requirements. This comprises object/class identification and probably the complete development of a specific, custom-made software system. Before starting the framework development cycle, it would, of course, help considerably to have two or more object models of similar applications at hand – identifying commonalities would be easier. Unfortunately, this is often not the case.

Note that the actual framework development process builds on top of a specific yet mature object model. Based on the identification of the key abstractions (see Section 7.2), the object model is split into clusters. The variation point driven development process takes place around the cluster cycle model. That is, the incorporation of flexibility requirements affects one or several clusters.

7.4.3 Variation point identification

The main problem of variation point identification is that domain experts are not used to generalizing or abstracting from a specific system. They usually lack an understanding of object-oriented concepts such as classes, objects, inheritance, design patterns, and frameworks. As a consequence, the communication between domain experts and software engineers should be reduced to a common denominator. That common denominator is functionality, not in which class/interface the functionality is placed. Variation point cards (Pree, 1995) represent one possibly suitable communication vehicle. They were inspired by the few essential construction principles of frameworks.

A variation point card captures the following information: a one line description of the functionality that has to be kept flexible; whether runtime adaptation is required; a brief description of the functionality; and at least two examples of its variability. The case study in Section 7.5 provides examples of variation points and how they manifest themselves in the framework design. In general, software developers transform variation point cards into a framework design by defining a hook for the variation point described on each card. Depending on the requirement to change the variation point at runtime, the Unification or Separation construction principle is applied to place the hook. Software engineers also determine where to place the hooks based on the existing class hierarchy.

7.4.4 Framework (re)design

After domain experts have initially identified and documented the variation points, software engineers have to modify the object model in order to gain the desired flexibility expressed in the variation point cards. After this activity, UML-F and the associated framework construction principles and patterns presented in the previous chapters assist the software engineer. In other words, patterns describing how to achieve more flexibility in a framework do not lead to satisfactory frameworks if software engineers do not know where flexibility is actually required. Variation point identification is a precondition for exploiting the full potential of framework construction principles and patterns.

7.4.5 Framework usage

A framework needs to be specialized several times in order to detect its weaknesses – that is, any inappropriate or missing variation points. The cycle in Figure 7.4 expresses the framework evolution process. Explicit variation point identification, as supported by UML-F, can contribute to a significant reduction of the number of iteration cycles.

7.5 The AOCS framework: a case study

The previous sections have described the conceptual steps in the framework development process. We now illustrate them through the concrete case of the Attitude and Orbit Control System (AOCS) framework which we developed under a research and development contract with the European Space Agency. Its architecture is fully documented in Pasetti (2001), where there is also a description of the AOCS domain. The framework source code can be obtained from the project web site[4] which also provides a guided tour through the framework together with the complete set of cookbook recipes for adapting the AOCS framework. The AOCS framework is implemented in C++. So the following description relies on C++ code fragments.

AOCS is usually the most complex subsystem on board a satellite. Its task is to ensure that the satellite attitude and orbit remain stable and follow profiles prespecified by ground control. In the case of geostationary telecommunication satellites, for instance, AOCS is responsible for ensuring that each particular satellite retains its position over the Earth's equator at a given longitude, and that it keeps its antennas pointed toward the ground station.

The conceptual structure of an AOCS is shown in Figure 7.5. AOCS is a typical embedded hard real-time control system. Its chief task is to periodically collect measurements from a set of sensors and convert them into commands for a set of actuators. AOCS interacts with a ground control station from which it receives commands (*telecommands*), and to which it forwards housekeeping data (*telemetry*).

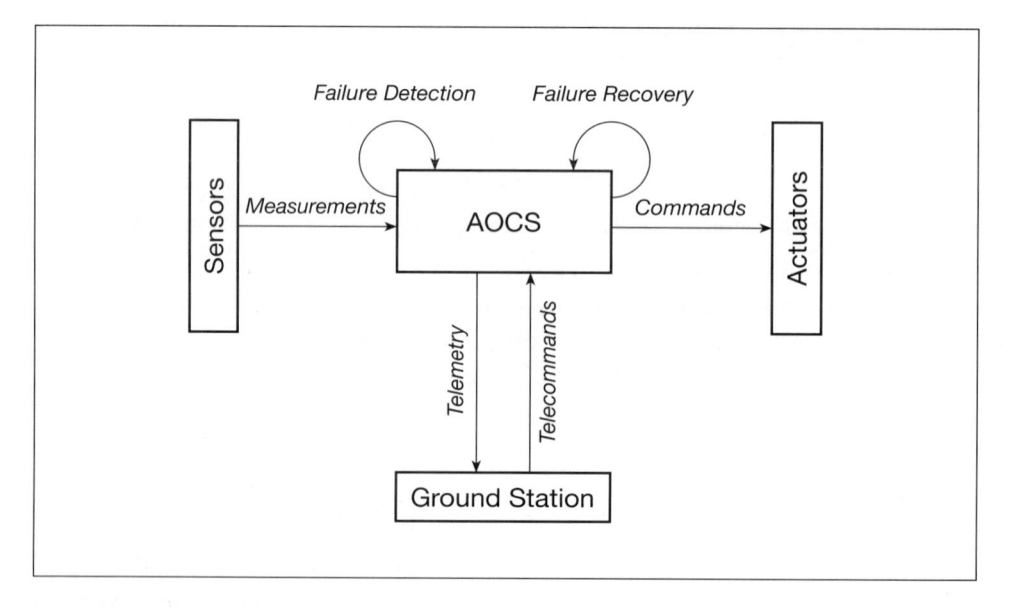

Figure 7.5 Conceptual structure of an AOCS

---

[4] http://www.SoftwareResearch.net/AOCSFrameworkProject/ProjectHomePage.html

Like all satellite systems, AOCS must remain fully operational in the event of any single failure and must survive prolonged periods of ground station outage. Robustness to faults and autonomy require AOCS to perform failure detection and failure recovery actions.

It is clearly not possible to cover all the aspects of the AOCS framework in this chapter. The following subsections concentrate on two AOCS functionalities (out of thirteen overall) and on how they were modeled by the framework. The emphasis is on showing how the methodological concepts presented in the first part of this chapter can help the framework design process.

7.5.1 Controller functionality

An AOCS typically contains several control loops serving such diverse purposes as stabilizing the attitude of the satellite, stabilizing its orbital position, controlling the execution of slews for turning around a satellite, and managing the satellite internal angular momentum.

The objects implementing these control loops are called *controllers*. They tend to implement the same flow of activities starting with the acquisition and filtering of measurements from sensors, continuing with a computation, and ending with the application of commands to actuators designed to counteract any deviation of the variable under control (e.g. the satellite attitude) from its desired value. Despite the ubiquity of closed-loop controllers and the similarities in their structure, existing AOCS applications have not developed any abstractions to represent them. Controllers are normally implemented by one-of-a-kind objects that hardcode the control algorithm. The management of controllers is not recognized as an explicit and separate activity. This lack of domain-wide abstractions is a good example of the project-oriented design that was criticized by Meyer (1989).

The first step in the design of a solution for the controller functionality in the AOCS framework therefore lies in the realization that a *controller abstraction* is needed. This abstraction must be characterized with the help of a domain expert who defines the generic operations that can be performed on a controller. The aCiRC cards can be used for this purpose. Initially, the controller abstraction can be represented by an abstract interface (see Figure 7.6).

All objects representing closed-loop controllers must implement the interface Controllable. It recognizes two methods. The doControl method directs the object to acquire the sensor measurements, to detect discrepancies from the desired value,

```
┌─────────────────────────────────────────────────┐
│                  *Controllable*                 │
│                                                 │
│           ▱ doControl(): void                   │
│           ▱ isStable(): bool                    │
└─────────────────────────────────────────────────┘
```

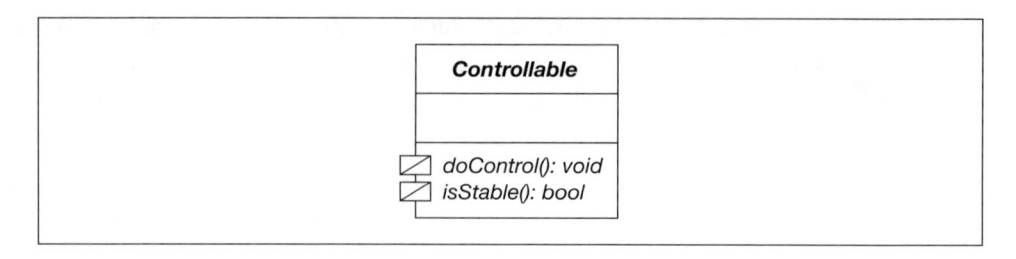

Figure 7.6   Controllable interface

and to compute and apply the commands for the actuators. Since closed-loop controllers can become unstable, an additional method, isStable, is provided to ask a controller to check its own stability.

Although the implementation of the control algorithms is application-specific (each controller on each satellite has its own control algorithm), there are some types of control algorithms that recur often. It therefore makes sense for the framework to provide default implementations of interface Controllable that can be configured to provide those common control algorithms. Application developers will then have the choice of providing their own entirely new implementation, of using a default implementation, or of modifying a default implementation by subclassing it and overriding selected methods. The framework will offer a set of objects implementing the same interface Controllable thus forming a *class family*.

Variation points

The next step in the design of the controller part of the AOCS framework is the identification and analysis of the variation points. One such variation point was implicitly identified by the controller abstraction – the control algorithm, as encapsulated by an object implementing the interface Controllable, is a point where flexibility is required because different AOCS applications use different control algorithms.

A second variation point arises from the observation that, for the same control loop, an AOCS may need different control algorithms at different stages of a mission. Consider, for instance, the control of a satellite's attitude. Immediately after the satellite has been ejected from its launcher, control algorithms are required that are capable of stabilizing the satellite even in the presence of the high angular rates that are typically induced by the ejection mechanism. Later in the mission, after the satellite has been brought to a near standstill, the emphasis is on very fine control (sometimes to an accuracy of fractions of an arcsecond) and more sensitive control algorithms are required. Therefore an AOCS controller typically operates in different *modes* corresponding to different operational conditions. Each mode has its own set of control algorithms. Switching from one mode to the next is often done autonomously by the satellite, according to criteria that vary from mission to mission. The set of modes and the mode-switching logic together represent another framework variation point.

After the variation points have been fully characterized and documented with the help of domain experts, it is necessary to identify architectural solutions to implement the flexibility that they require. This is where domain-specific design patterns, which are created to model adaptability, are introduced. Our experience suggests that the designer should start by analyzing the design patterns in a standard catalog, such as the GoF catalog (Gamma et al., 1995), and then proceed to refine them so as to tailor them to a specific domain. The objective is to build a repository of domain-specific design patterns. Good design patterns are hard to find and we believe that, just as software engineers have long been in the habit of maintaining libraries of subroutines and components, they should learn to do the same for design patterns. Frameworks are one vehicle through which such repositories can be built and made available across projects and design teams.

Let us now apply this procedure to the first controller variation point. An analysis of its characteristics points us to a modified form of the Separation construction principle. A *controller manager* object is introduced that is responsible for all the controllers in an application. It holds a list of objects of type Controllable and, when it is activated, it asks them to check their stability and, if the stability is confirmed, to perform their allotted control action. This results in the UML-F diagram shown in Figure 7.7.

Consider now the second variation point, namely the dependency on operational mode. To each operational mode, a list of controllable objects is associated. The controller manager should switch from one list to another depending on operational conditions. The mode-switching logic, however, is a point of variation and therefore should be abstracted out of the controller manager to make it possible for applications to modify it easily. One solution is to define a mode-manager interface (see Figure 7.8).

A controller mode manager holds multiple lists of controllable objects – one list for each operational mode. At any given time, there is one active list, which is returned by getList. The active list is updated by calling updateList.

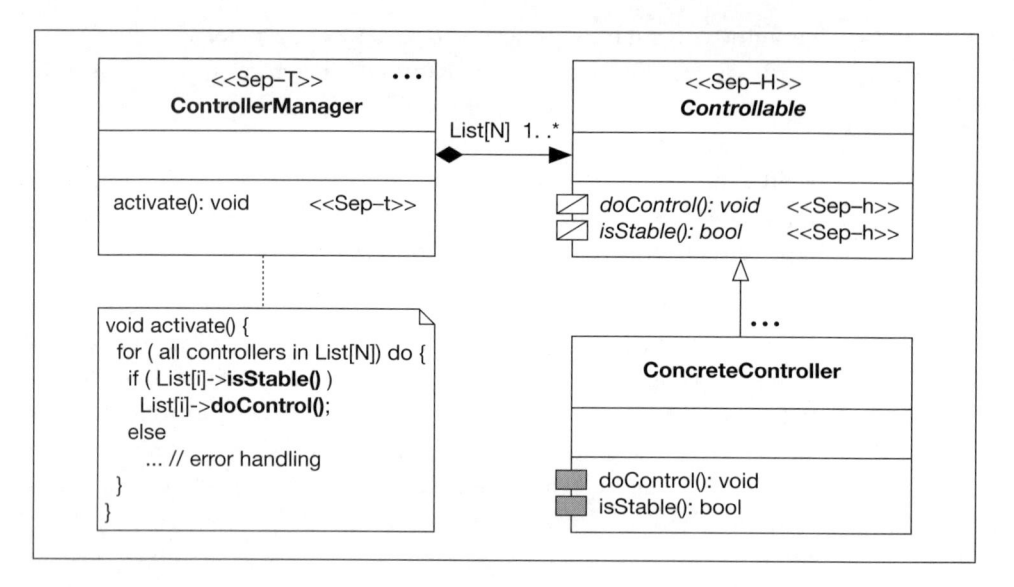

```
                    <<Sep-T>>            ...                      <<Sep-H>>
                 ControllerManager                              Controllable
                                            List[N] 1..*
                                        
            activate(): void   <<Sep-t>>               doControl(): void    <<Sep-h>>
                                                      isStable(): bool     <<Sep-h>>

         void activate() {                                          ...
           for ( all controllers in List[N]) do {
             if ( List[i]->isStable() )                      ConcreteController
               List[i]->doControl();
             else
               ... // error handling                      doControl(): void
           }                                              isStable(): bool
         }
```

Figure 7.7   Controller manager and interface Controllable

The latter method implements the mode-switching logic and represents the mode variation point.[5]

Concrete mode managers implementing concrete mode-switching logic are implemented as subclasses of ControllerModeManager. The resulting solution for the controller functionality is shown in Figure 7.9.

```
                    ControllerModeManager


              getList(): ControllableList
              updateList(): void
```

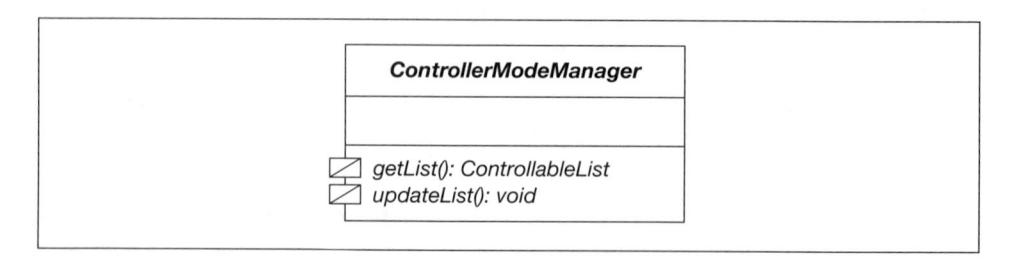

Figure 7.8   ControllerModeManager interface

---

[5] If the ControllerModeManager is to change controller modes autonomously, then each time the getList method is invoked, it can call the updateList method to determine which list is active, based on some external conditions prior to returning the ControllableList. Another option would be for the updateList method to be called by some external object to trigger a change in controller mode.

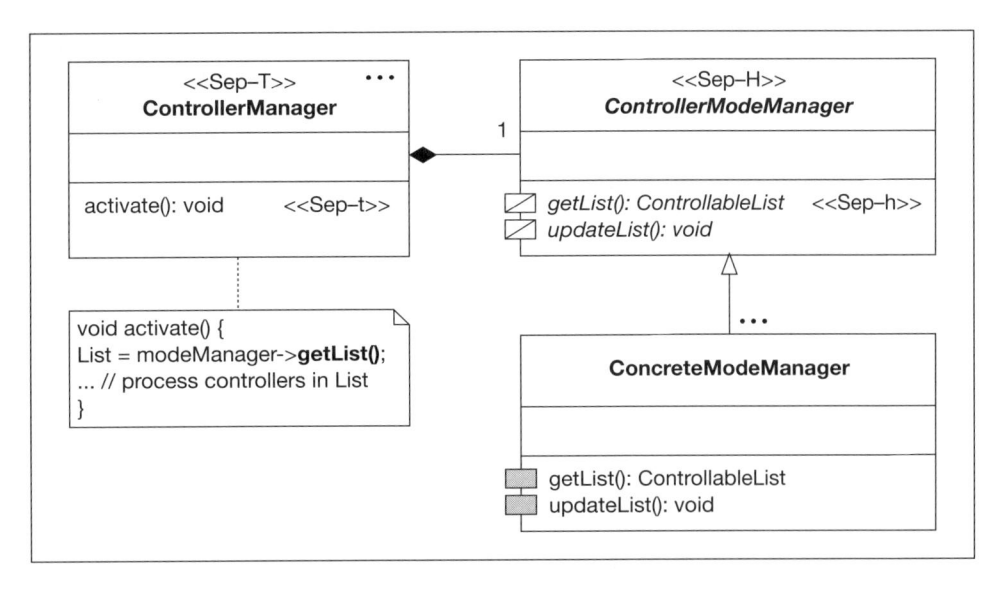

Figure 7.9 Abstract coupling of ControllerManager and ControllerModeManager

This solution to the mode-dependency problem is loosely based on the Abstract Factory design pattern (Gamma et. al., 1995) (the mode manager acts as an abstract factory) with the important differences that the controller manager interrogates the mode manager every time it is activated, not just at initialization, and that the mode manager dynamically decides which list of controllers to supply on the basis of current operational conditions. Note that although the mode-switching logic is application-dependent, here too, as in the case of the controllable objects, it is possible to recognize some standard implementations that the framework can provide as predefined implementations of interface ControllerModeManager, thus giving rise to a second class family.

The proposed solution separates the implementation of the control algorithms (in the controllable objects) from their management (in the controller manager), and from the mode-switching logic (in the mode manager). The controller manager is an application-independent component, whereas the controller and the controller mode-manager abstractions generate two class families. These two families, together with the controller manager, form a *class team*. As it stands, our solution requires other parts of the AOCS framework to interact with several different objects – the mode manager, the controller objects, and the controller manager. This interaction can be simplified by embedding all the controller-related objects in an enclosing object that becomes the only interface between them and the rest of the AOCS application. This solution is based on the Façade design pattern (Gamma et. al., 1995) and is shown in an informal notation in Figure 7.10. The dashed lines with arrowheads represent references that the common interface has to its contained components. When the components are packaged as indicated by the dashed rounded rectangle in the diagram, the class team becomes a subsystem.

Thus, it is possible to recognize in the design solution for the controller functionality all the elements presented in the first part of this chapter. The solution is based on two abstractions, namely the controller and mode-manager abstractions, to which there correspond two major variation points. The objects modeling the controller functionality in an AOCS application can be encapsulated in a subsystem. Their classes form a class team containing two class families.

The design process is iterative, with a first iteration performed on the controller variation point and a second performed on the mode-management variation point. The design problem is attacked in the first instance by making use of standard design patterns. These patterns are then continually refined until a domain-specific design pattern is produced. This domain pattern acts as the conceptual glue that holds together the class families in the class team.

7.5.2 The telemetry functionality

As a second example of framework design, we consider the development of a design solution to the problem of telemetry management. Telemetry data are the housekeeping data that a satellite must periodically send to its ground station to allow those on the ground to verify the correct functioning of the satellite. The data represent a subset of the state of the objects making up the AOCS software.

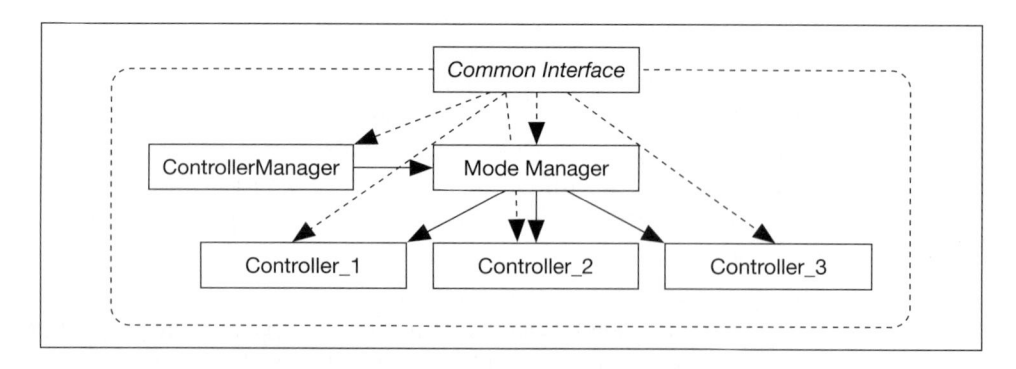

Figure 7.10 Subsystem encapsulation for controller

In current AOCS systems, telemetry processing is controlled by a so-called telemetry handler that collects telemetry data directly, formats and stores the data in a dedicated buffer, and then has the data transferred to the ground. To accomplish its task, the telemetry handler needs an intimate knowledge of the type and format of the telemetry data. It has to know which objects to collect data from, which data to collect from those objects, and how the collected data is to be formatted for transmission to the ground. It is this coupling between telemetry handler and telemetry data that makes the former application-specific and hinders its reuse. A symptom of this tight coupling is the lack, in conventional AOCS applications, of an abstraction for 'telemeterable' objects – the software treats objects that need to send data to the telemetry stream on an individual basis, not as members of a group of like entities. This is another illustration of the project-oriented design style of conventional software.

As in the case of controller functionality, a framework-based solution for the telemetry problem begins with the identification of the basic domain abstraction. The first obvious abstraction is the *telemetry stream*, representing the data sink to which telemetry data are written. A telemetry stream acts as a proxy, within the AOCS software, for the channel through which telemetry data are forwarded to the ground station. It can be represented by the abstract class in Figure 7.11.

The TmStream interface provides a write method for each of the main data types used in the framework. For simplicity, the figure only shows two such methods. The UML-F tag '...' is used to signify that not all methods are shown. Additionally, a flush method is provided for data streams where data are first buffered and then forwarded in chunks.

The second abstraction is perhaps more interesting because it introduces the concept of a *telemeterable* object, namely an object whose state can potentially be included in telemetry. To this abstraction is associated the abstract interface

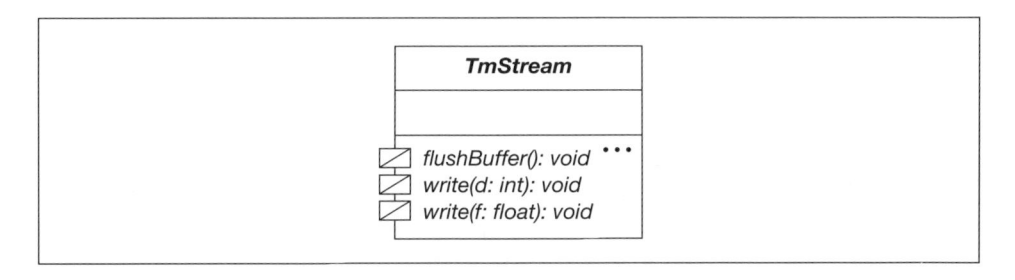

Figure 7.11   The abstract class TmStream

Telemeterable (see Figure 7.12) which defines the methods that may be performed on a telemeterable object.

The fundamental method is writeToTm(). Calling it causes an object to write its internal state to the telemetry stream. The method takes a telemetry stream as an argument because the object needs to know *where* the telemetry data should be written. The object will use the write methods provided by the telemetry stream interface to write selected portions of its internal state to the telemetry stream.

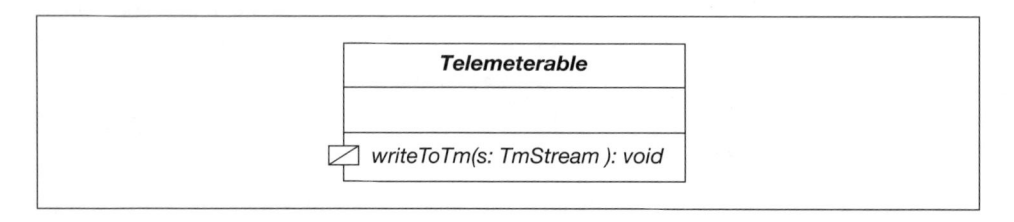

Figure 7.12 Telemeterable interface

Variation points

The next step in the design process is again the identification of the variation points. One obvious variation point is the telemetry stream itself – different AOCS use different mechanisms for sending telemetry data to the ground. The second variation point is given by the format and content of the telemetry data that varies from mission to mission. A domain-specific design pattern is again needed to cope with these elements of variation. Figure 7.13 illustrates the pattern as a UML-F diagram.

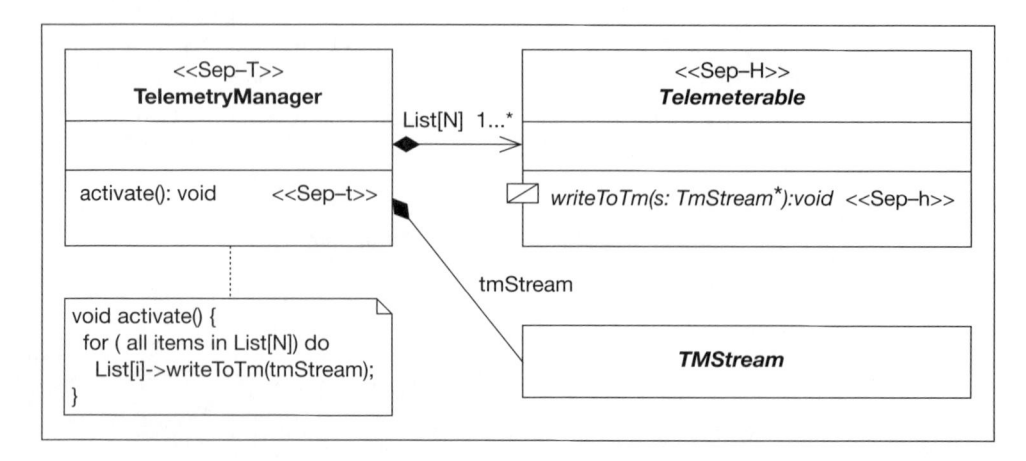

Figure 7.13 Telemetry Manager and Telemeterable

A telemetry manager is introduced that holds a reference to the telemetry stream and to the list of telemeterable objects. When it is activated, it goes through the items in the list calling their writeToTm method and passing to them the currently valid telemetry stream.

The TmStream interface gives rise to a class family because the framework provides a handful of concrete implementations corresponding to commonly used telemetry streams. The telemeterable interface is more problematic – this interface is typically implemented by objects that participate in other parts of the framework. The controller objects of the previous subsection, for instance, would normally be telemeterable objects since the state of the controllers is the kind of information that should be included in the telemetry data. Telemeterable is therefore a pure interface for which no implementation can be defined at framework level. A class family cannot be defined for it because, at the level of design defined so far, it is not possible to say which classes will implement it. This will become clear only when the design solution for the telemetry problem is merged with the design solutions for the other AOCS functionalities to produce a full framework architecture. At that point it might, for instance, be decided that controllers should be telemeterable objects, and this allows their inclusion in the telemeterable class family.

This difficulty in associating a class family to the Telemeterable interface will be taken up in Section 7.7 where we introduce the concept of framelets. For the time being, it is important to stress that this second example has again shown how a framework design solution can be articulated along the steps identified in the cluster cycle model.

7.6 The AOCS manager pattern

There is noticeable similarity between the Controller and Telemetry design patterns. Both rely on a 'manager' which maintains (or has access to) a list of objects. The manager does not know the exact type of each of the objects in its managed list. Instead, the manager only knows that each of the objects is an implementation of a particular interface. The interaction between the manager and each managed object is solely through this 'manageable' interface. The manager has a method (in both cases called activate) which serves as a template method in an application of the Separation construction principle. The activate method cycles through all the managed objects and performs an operation on each by calling one or more of the hook methods defined in the manageable interface. Figure 7.14 shows this Manager pattern in a more generic manner. Note that the Manager pattern is a sort of higher level pattern that captures a similarity among the more specific patterns that are defined by the framework.

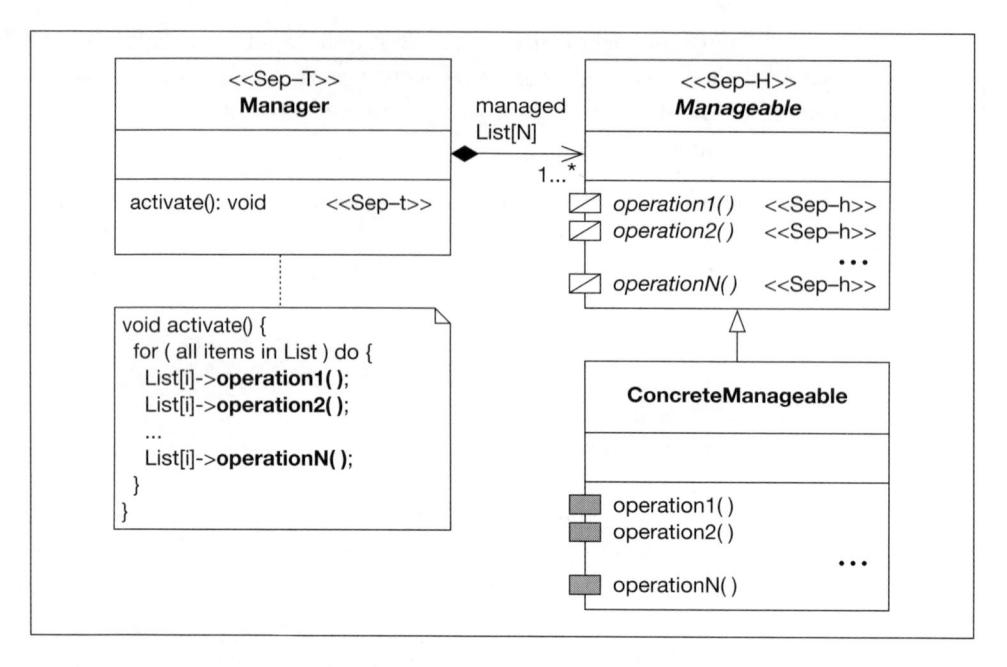

Figure 7.14 The Manager pattern relying on the Separation construction principle

This pattern has proven to be useful in the AOCS framework for separating the management of a set of objects with similar functionality from the actual implementations of that functionality. Therefore, following the template of Chapter 4, we introduce this pattern as an AOCS-specific pattern and create a set of domain-specific tags.

The UML-F tags for the Manager pattern are:

- «Mngr–Manager»
- «Mngr–activate»
- «Mngr–managed»
- «Mngr–*Manageable*»
- «Mngr–*operationN*»
- «Mngr–ConcreteManageable»
- «Mngr–operationN».

Table 7.1 summarizes the UML-F tags for the Manager pattern.

Names	«Mngr–Manager», «Mngr–activate», «Mngr–managed», «Mngr–*Manageable*», «Mngr–*operationN*», «Mngr–ConcreteManageable» and «Mngr–operationN».
Apply to	class («Mngr–Manager», «Mngr–*Manageable*», «Mngr–ConcreteManageable»); method («Mngr–activate», «Mngr–*operationN*», «Mngr–operationN»); interface («Mngr–*Manageable*») association («Mngr–managed»).
Type	default: String; «Mngr-operationN»: Int
Motivation and Purpose	The tags highlight the application of the Manager pattern in a framework by marking the classes, interfaces, methods, and associations belonging to that pattern.
Informal explanation of effect	The Manager pattern separates the management of a set of objects which have similar functionality from the implementation of the functionality. This allows the management aspect to be implemented as a generic, reusable part of the framework. Specific behaviors are built into concrete implementations of the *Manageable* interface. They implement the various operationN methods.
Expansion	The Manager pattern tags expand to tags for the Separation construction principle.
Discussion	The pattern tags «Mngr–Manager», «Mngr–activate», «Mngr–*Manageable*», and «Mngr–*operationN*» must always be used together. The other tags for this pattern are optional, but can only be used in conjunction with the former list of tags. Several different methods within the same class/interface can be tagged with the «Mngr–*operationN*» and «Mngr–operationN». A specific number can be added as value of these tags.

Table 7.1 Definition of the UML-F Manager pattern tags

Applying these newly introduced tags, the design pattern underlying the Controller framework can be redrawn as shown in Figure 7.15.

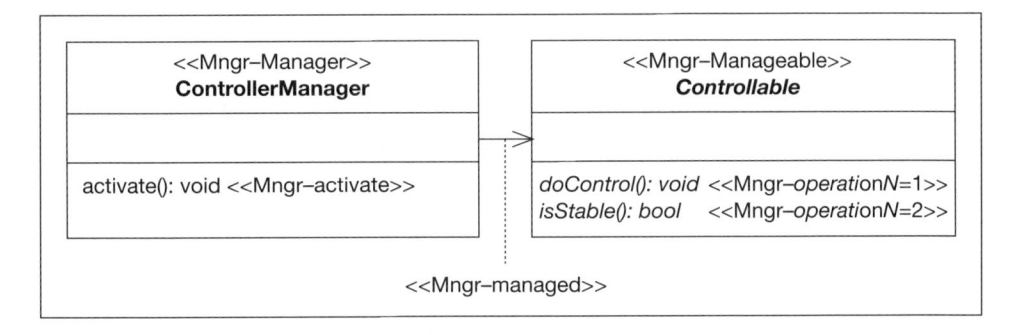

Figure 7.15 Controller Manager and Controller annotated by the Manager pattern tags

7.7 Framelets as an aid to framework design

Before introducing the concept of framelets, it is useful to make a distinction between *architecture* and *design*. There is general agreement in the software engineering community that an architecture is a description of the set of objects in a software system in terms of their external signatures (usually, their interfaces) and their mutual relationships (Bass et al., 1998). There is less agreement over what constitutes a design. Sometimes design is simply seen as the process that results in an architecture; sometimes it is regarded as identical to the architecture. Here, we will use the term 'design' to signify the organization of the software at the purely abstract level, where the focus of attention is on finding abstract solutions that offer the degree of adaptability required by the variation points, rather than on defining objects and their relationships.

The difference between design and architecture is the same as the difference between a design pattern and its instantiation. An example may help clarify this distinction. Consider the Factory Method pattern for instance. By itself, the pattern represents a pure design solution to a design problem. Pattern instantiation takes place when the pattern is applied to a concrete architectural situation and results in the classes of the pattern being mapped to specific classes and in other non-essential changes – for instance, having more than one factory method. At this point, the design pattern is instantiated and it represents an *architectural* solution.

A similar distinction between design and architecture can apply to an entire system. Indeed, analysis of the thought processes that result in the definition of an architecture shows that the designer passes through a design stage before arriving at the architectural stage. The design stage becomes especially evident in the case of frameworks whose architecture is often considerably more sophisticated than that of individual applications and where designers make a correspondingly larger investment in its definition.

The solutions presented in the previous section for the AOCS framework case study are clearly at the design level. There are at least three characteristic features of the design level that can be evinced from them.

First, the abstract interfaces and classes are defined in an incomplete manner. Consider for instance, the Telemeterable interface. It features only one method (writeToTm) but a realistic implementation has to include other methods to control the telemetry format (telemetry data usually have several formats), or to ask an object to give the size of its telemetry image (and this is important to verify compatibility with the capacity of the telemetry stream channel). These methods are not important at the design level, where the emphasis is on identifying a solution to the abstract problem of flexibly collecting housekeeping data from the AOCS objects; but they definitely need to be defined at the architectural level where, by definition, all interfaces must be fully specified.

Second, no effort is made at the design level to integrate solutions to different design problems. Our case study addresses the problem of telemetry data management and controller management, but nothing is said about their mutual interaction – for instance, the question of whether controller objects should be telemeterable is not even considered. This type of interaction is obviously important at the architectural level, where a map of all the objects in the framework with their base classes is provided.

The third characteristic feature of the design level is its emphasis on design patterns. The search for solutions at this level is essentially a search for design patterns to model the variation points identified during the domain analysis. This search may start from standard patterns but it normally progresses to the definition of new patterns that are optimized for the particular domain of interest. In the case study, the solutions to the controller and telemetry problems can be seen as AOCS-specific design patterns. The Manager pattern provides a generalized version of these two patterns.

It is possible to argue that what we call 'design stage' is no more than what others see as the first iteration in the architectural definition phase. Nevertheless, we believe that the explicit identification of a design stage is worthwhile because it draws attention to the multistage character of the process through which a software architecture is constructed. When dealing with project-oriented development, this character is not strongly in evidence because the various iterations in the architectural definition phase are conceptually similar – they are all aimed at identifying objects and their relationships, and successive iterations differ merely in the degree of granularity of the description they offer. In the case of product-oriented development, however, the development process clearly breaks up into separate phases. The task of identifying variation points and their matching design patterns is conceptually different from that of defining object architectures – hence the value of giving different names to the associated development stages.

In the case of a large framework, the design process can be quite complex. For instance, AOCS applications are not large, typically consisting of between 10,000 and 20,000 lines of compact code. Yet, their domain analysis led to the recognition of 23 major variation points. In such cases, it is clearly desirable to have some means of simplifying the design process. *Framelets* were introduced in response to this need.

Framelets simplify the framework design process by applying to it the traditional 'divide and conquer' approach. At design level, the framework consists chiefly of a set of variation points and design patterns. Framelets partition this set into smaller subsets of related variation points and design patterns that are then handled, as far as possible, separately from each other.

Object-based methodologies conceptualize a software system as a set of objects. They accordingly recommend that simplification be achieved by breaking up this set of objects into smaller subsets of objects that are tightly integrated with each other but only loosely coupled with those of other subsets. Framelets transpose this approach to the case of frameworks. The only difference is that attention is focused not on objects, but on the variation points and design patterns used in the design of the framework. Hence, partitioning is performed not on the set of objects that make up a system, but on the set of variation points and design patterns used in the design of the framework. Figure 7.16 illustrates the difference.

It is worth noting that framelets do not partition the space of concrete classes in a system, because the same class may be involved in different design patterns. The telemeterable interface is a case in point. Although it is proposed as part of a design pattern to address the telemetry problem, it may be implemented by objects, such as the controller objects, that participate in other design patterns and that are introduced to address completely different design problems. Thus the question 'To which framelet do the controller objects belong?' does not really make sense. The

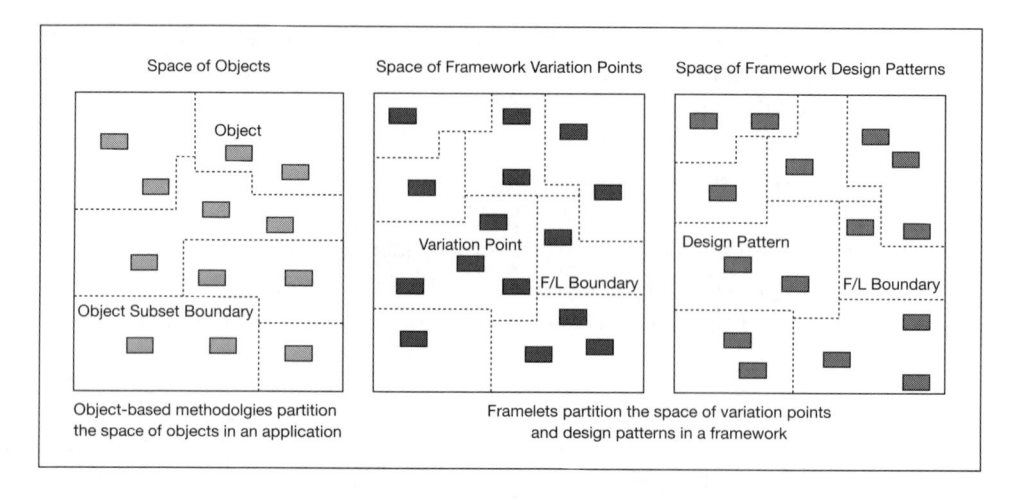

Figure 7.16 Framelets and object subsets

questions that *do* make sense are 'To what framelet does the controller design pattern belong?', and 'To what framelet does the controller mode variation point belong?'

The AOCS framework was designed as a set of framelets. The initial domain analysis led to the definition of 23 variation points. These were then divided into 13 framelets that happened to contain between one and three related variation points. The controller and telemetry functionalities described in the previous section, for instance, gave rise to two dedicated framelets. Design solutions were then developed for each framelet by developing design patterns that could address the adaptability and flexibility requirements intrinsic to the variation points. At a later stage, this multiplicity of design solutions gave way to a single architecture in which all classes – both concrete and abstract – were fully defined, together with their mutual interactions.

What then is the relationship between the class family and class team concepts, and the framelet concept? The two are closely linked, but they exist at different levels of abstraction. Framelets are useful at the design level, where they simplify the design process by breaking it up into smaller and independent design units. Framelets are no longer very useful after the transition to the architectural phase because, at that stage, the attention shifts to concrete classes and cannot be mapped onto framelets. At this stage, simplification is best achieved by organizing the system along class families and class teams. Note that sometimes framelets and class families/class teams can be homologous. This is the case, for instance, in the controller framelet where, even at the design stage, it is possible to distinguish class families and class teams. However, this is by no means always the case, as shown by the telemetry example where it turns out to be impossible at the design stage to associate a well-defined class family to the Telemeterable interface. The telemeterable class family only emerges at the architectural level, when all the framelets are merged together. Framelets, class families, and class teams, therefore, are means of simplifying the software development process by subdividing the framework into simpler units. In this sense, they realize the cluster-based lifecycle.

The relationship between framelets and class families, and the distinction between the design and architectural levels is graphically illustrated in Figure 7.17 for the case of the AOCS framework case study. The top half of the figure shows the framework design level containing the telemetry and controller framelets. The framelets are essentially made up of the respective design patterns without showing the variation points. The bottom half of the figure shows the framework architectural level populated with the class families that are generated by the base classes and abstract interfaces induced by the design patterns. Note how the class

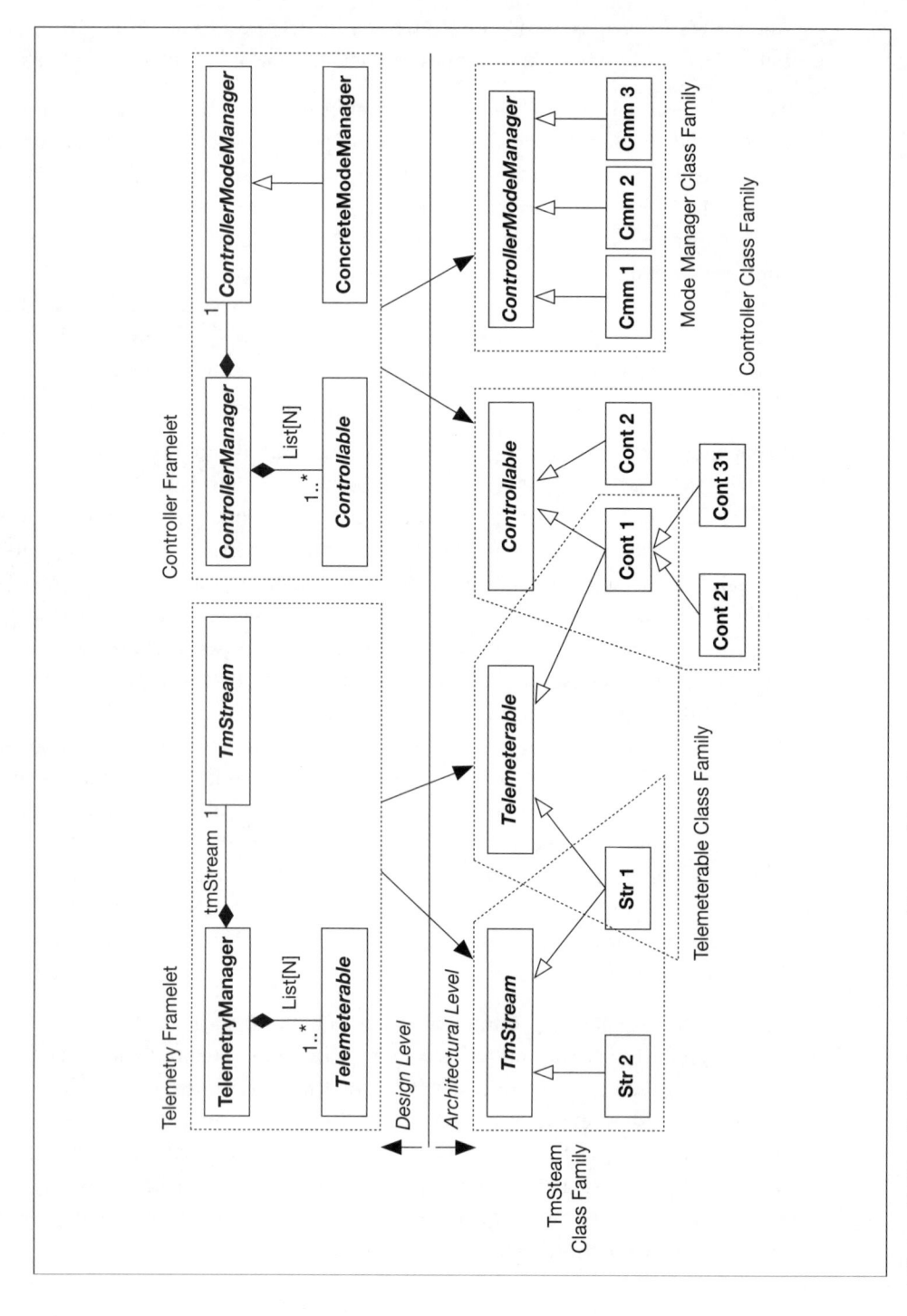

Figure 7.17 Design level versus architectural level

families do not partition the space of framework classes, because some classes implement multiple interfaces from several framelets.

Before concluding this section, it is perhaps useful to summarize its main points:

- A distinction should be made between design and architecture.
- This distinction is especially important in the case of software frameworks, where the distance between analysis and architectural definition is much greater than for single applications and where, consequently, there is a greater need for the recognition of an intermediate stage.
- At design level, the focus of attention is on variation points and design patterns; at architectural level, it is on classes and objects.
- At design level, simplification is best achieved by partitioning the set of design patterns and variation points into subsets called framelets; at architectural level, simplification is best achieved by organizing the set of classes in the framework into class families and class teams.

7.8 eXtreme Design (XD), with implementation cases

As already mentioned, class families, class teams, and framelets help tackle the complexity inherent in the framework development process. The kind of complexity that they address is *quantitative*, namely the result of the large number of artifacts – classes, variation points, design patterns – that go into the construction of a framework. Framework complexity has another, *qualitative*, aspect that stems from its high level of abstraction. A framework must model an entire domain and is therefore qualitatively more complex than an individual application that only models a single point within this domain. Implementation cases are proposed as a means of addressing this second type of framework complexity.

The AOCS case study has shown so far how the framework design process begins by identifying domain abstractions and variation points, and progresses through successive refinements of design solutions to implement them. These design solutions are typically localized, in that they address individual variation points (or small clusters of related variation points). After several such solutions have been devised, the need naturally arises to test their effectiveness and, above all, their mutual compatibility. The need to verify the adequacy of design abstractions arises also in the context of single-product development – but it is especially acute in the case of frameworks where the gap between design and code is much wider and where there is a correspondingly greater risk of mistaken or suboptimal design choices.

The simple, if not simplistic, approach of addressing this need is to wait until the design is implemented in code – perhaps in a prototype – and then test its suitability directly. This approach may work when developing single applications but it would be too time consuming in developing frameworks because testing a framework means using it to instantiate several applications in the framework domain and then separately testing the applications thus instantiated for their correctness. A more direct means of testing the design, as opposed to testing the code, is needed. So-called 'implementation cases' answer this need precisely.

A framework is a tool to help developers build an application rapidly within a framework domain. An implementation case describes an aspect of this application instantiation process by specifying how a component, an architectural feature, or a functionality for an application in the framework domain can be implemented using the constructs offered by the framework.

An example may help illustrate this definition in relation to the design solution for the controller functionality in the AOCS framework. Among other aspects, the proposed solution addresses the problem of the dependency of the attitude control algorithms on a satellite's operational conditions. In a typical situation, an AOCS application might have two control algorithms: a low accuracy algorithm, and one for high accuracy adjustments. An implementation case could then be formulated whereby a controller could be built that switches between high and low accuracy control depending on the size of the control error. This implementation case can then be worked out by showing how the constructs offered by the framework can be combined to achieve this effect. This would probably be done by developing a skeleton controller mode manager that has access to the control error and supplies the appropriate control algorithm to the controller manager depending on the size of the control error.

Implementation cases define an objective for a localized adaptation action. They are said to be 'worked out' when they are accompanied by a description of how their adaptation objective can be achieved using the framework. Implementation cases address the qualitative aspect of framework complexity because they force designers to think about the reification of the abstractions they are creating, while at the same time giving them the opportunity to test the adequacy of these abstractions.

The term 'implementation case' was coined by analogy with the term 'use case' as employed by some methodologies for application development. A use case describes the way an application is intended to be used. Use cases cannot be defined for a framework because a framework is not a working application, and it is not used in the same sense in which an application is used. An implementation case is its equivalent in the sense that a framework is a tool to help implement applications, and implementation cases describe how a feature of an application can be implemented.

In the AOCS framework project, implementation cases were defined early in the design phase and were then gradually worked out as the design advanced. Typically, whenever a new major construct was introduced, its effectiveness was tested by working out an implementation case that used it. When necessary, new implementation cases were introduced to cover the functionalities introduced by the newly defined construct. Initially, implementation cases were defined at a very high level by simply describing the objective of the adaptation action they represented. They were then periodically revisited and progressively refined to reflect the advancing state of the framework definition. At the end of the architectural design phase, they can be described at the pseudocode level. Typically, the pseudocode is intended to demonstrate how predefined framework constructs, components, interfaces, and design patterns could be used to achieve the objective prescribed by the implementation case. It is worth stressing that this process of refinement of implementation cases was *the single most important source of changes in the AOCS framelet design*, and it is believed that it replaced at least one iteration cycle in the framework design.

7.8.1 Implementation cases as a vehicle for framework specification

Implementation cases were introduced as a way of continually monitoring the adequacy of a framework design during a design process. However, they can serve at least two other purposes. Like use cases for single applications, implementation cases can be used as a specification vehicle for frameworks. A sufficient number of them can cover all the functionalities of a framework and can thus be used as a way of specifying it.

The acceptance test for the framework then becomes its ability to implement all the components and architectural features described in the implementation cases. The ease with which this can be done is a measure of the quality of the framework – a well-designed framework should offer abstractions and components that let users quickly and naturally implement the constructs required by the implementation cases.

7.8.2 From implementation cases to cookbook recipes

Implementation cases can play a third role. At the end of the framework development process, they are a kind of commented pseudocode. They could thus be included in the framework user manual, where they can represent cookbook recipes showing how framework constructs can be used to develop small applications or fragments of applications. (See Chapters 5 and 6 for further discussion of cookbooks and cookbook recipes.)

How many implementation cases should be generated for a given framework? The discussion in the previous sections of this chapter should have made clear that the primary entities making up a framework are: the domain abstractions; the variation points and their associated design patterns; and the class families and class teams, possibly grouped together in subsystems. A useful heuristic is that each one of these entities should participate in two or three implementation cases. In a formal project setting, traceability matrices can be used to measure coverage. However, this is just a rule of thumb. The question asked above has no straightforward answer and the experience of the designer will be paramount, as in so many other software engineering issues.

Because of the novelty of the concept, no more concise formalism has yet been defined to represent and model implementation cases. In the AOCS project, implementation cases are mostly described in a mixture of informal language, pseudocode, and UML-F. It is recommended that implementation cases be described in an informal but systematic manner. For each implementation case, the following information should be provided:

- implementation case objective
- objective description
- framelets involved in the implementation case
- framework constructs involved in the implementation case
- description of how the implementation case is worked out.

Note that, in the approach proposed here, implementation cases are defined incrementally during the design process. Hence, the information items listed above are not all supplied at the same time. Initially, only the objective and its description are provided. Other fields are filled in gradually as the framework design is refined. The implementation description section, in particular, is expanded and made more detailed as the constructs for working out the implementation case become available. Eventually, the implementation description section will probably contain commented pseudocode showing how the implementation case objective can be met by combining and adapting framework components. The degree of maturity of the implementation case descriptions and their stability can thus be used as a measure of the maturity of the framework design.

As a concrete example, let us consider again the implementation case presented at the beginning of this section. As defined in Table 7.2, the implementation case corresponds to the beginning of the design definition phase. As the design progresses, more details can be provided as to how the control algorithms are to be encapsulated, how the control error is to be monitored, how the controller is to be loaded into the controller mode manager, etc. After the transition to the architectural phase, the implementation description is gradually translated into pseudocode until, at the end of the framework development process, the implementation case has become a cookbook recipe.

Objective
Build an attitude controller with two control modes (high and low accuracy).

Objective description
This implementation case shows how to build an attitude controller that can switch between two control algorithms ('high accuracy' and 'low accuracy' algorithms) depending on the size of a satellite's attitude control error.

Affected framelets
Controller framelet.

Affected constructs
Controllable interface.
ControllerModeManager interface.

Affected variation points
Control algorithm variation point.
Controller mode variation point.

Implementation description
- Build two subclasses of Controllable to encapsulate the low and high accuracy algorithms.
- Build a subclass of ControllerModeManager that can manage two controllers and that monitors the attitude error and uses it to switch between the two controllers.
- Load the two controllers into the controller mode manager.
- Load the controller mode manager into the controller manager.

Table 7.2   Sample implementation case

As indicated by the section title, a connection may also be established between implementation cases and eXtreme Programming (XP) (Beck, 1999). The framework approach is obviously alien to the philosophy of XP with its rejection of reuse as a legitimate objective of the software development process, and its minimalist attitude to design. However, adoption of implementation cases furthers some of the key principles advocated by XP, such as rapid feedback (since they allow very short turnaround times between design and implementation), and concrete experiments (since they make design experiments possible at an early stage in the development process). To the extent that implementation cases resemble minimal self-contained implementations, their use promotes practices such as small releases and continuous integration that are key to XP paradigms. Finally – and again in line with the XP philosophy – implementation cases shift the emphasis from design to testing (or, more precisely, to the testing of the design).

The relationship between implementation cases and the XP style is, however, analogous only because XP is concerned with the rapid prototyping of applications, whereas implementation cases are concerned with the rapid design of frameworks. One could perhaps describe implementation cases as an 'eXtreme Design (XD)' approach to framework development.

7.9 Framework adaptations through cookbook recipes, adaptation cases, and adaptation reports

The previous sections of this chapter have given hints and guidelines for the process of developing frameworks. We now shift focus and discuss the novel techniques called 'adaptation cases' and 'adaptation reports' that have proven useful in the creation of applications from a framework. Before launching into this, it is worthwhile briefly discussing how these concepts relate to each other and to cookbook recipes as presented in Chapter 5 and Chapter 6.

Remember that implementation cases are a means of 'test-driving' a framework design as it evolves. When the framework is ready for use by application developers, the implementation cases used during framework development will have themselves evolved into cookbook recipes. The framework user need not know or care whether a particular cookbook recipe comes from an implementation case or was generated independently. This observation allows us to eliminate the distinction between implementation cases and cookbook recipes. We refer only to cookbook recipes, with the understanding that we are, by implication, also referring to any implementation cases that have generated the recipes.

Adaptation cases are used during the process of creating an application through adapting a framework. They build on cookbook recipes and make the relationship between application requirements and cookbook recipes explicit. They might lead to the definition of composite recipes (see Chapter 5). *Adaptation reports* are used during application creation. They are a means of reporting a developer's experiences while trying to create an application from a framework.

7.9.1 Adaptation cases

The users of a framework adapt the framework to create an application that meets a set of application requirements. Following the common terminology of object-oriented design, in which an object is said to be instantiated from a class and the object is referred to as an instance of the class, we refer to an application created by adapting a framework as an *instance* or *instantiation* of the framework. The process of creating the application is referred to as *instantiating* or *adapting* the framework.

As a design tool, each implementation case provides the framework developer with an opportunity to answer a question of the form, 'If a user of my framework needs to create an application that does X, how would the user need to adapt my framework to achieve that goal?' For example, in our earlier sample implementation case, the question the framework developer was asking can be stated as, 'If a user of the AOCS framework needed to create an application that includes an attitude controller with both a high accuracy and a low accuracy control mode, and have the control mode change based on the size of the attitude control error, how would the framework user need to adapt the AOCS framework?' The answer to that question can be found primarily in the Implementation Description section of the implementation case.

At the point at which an application developer is actually instantiating an application from the framework, the question is no longer the theoretical, '*If* a user needs to ....' The question then becomes the related, but more concrete, 'I need to create an application from this framework that does X; what do I need to do?' This is where adaptation cases are helpful.

In order to even ask such questions, the application developer must have a set of requirements for the application to be developed. Use cases are a common technique of capturing, representing, and discussing application requirements. Thus, we start our discussion of adaptation cases with the assumption that our application requirements are represented as use cases.[6]

---

[6] There is very little in the adaptation case concept that ties it directly to use cases. Application requirements presented in some other form, even as just a simple requirements list, can also be used as a starting point for the creation of adaptation cases with only slight modifications to what is presented here.

An example use case provides a starting point for our discussion. Table 7.3 sketches an example use case for an AOCS application to be instantiated from the AOCS framework.

Use case
Stabilization of the attitude of an astronomical observation satellite during ejection from launch vehicle.

Actors (external entities)
Launch vehicle (initiator), ground station, astronomical object (object to be observed).

Pre-conditions
1. Launch vehicle has arrived at the appropriate altitude and location for ejection of satellite.
2. Satellite pre-ejection self-test routine has been performed and all tests in the routine have been successful.

Post-conditions (objectives)
1. Satellite attitude is correct and stable. 'Correct and stable' is defined as having its telescope pointed at the astronomical object to within 0.5 arcseconds along the yaw and pitch axes, with an angular rate on the roll axis below 0.1 deg/sec.
2. The ground station will have data available about the control of the satellite, including measurements used as input to the controller and commands sent to actuators by the controller.

Basic flow
1. The launch vehicle ejects the satellite.
2. Immediately upon ejection, the AOCS initiates attitude control in low accuracy control mode. Low accuracy control mode is defined such that the satellite's telescope is pointing to within 5 degrees of the astronomical object along both its yaw and pitch axes.
3. Immediately upon ejection, the AOCS will begin collecting data about the state of attitude control as reflected by control errors and commands sent to actuators to correct the errors. This data will be collected at a rate of 4 Hz (250 millisecond intervals). Since the satellite may not yet be stable enough to communicate this information to the ground station, this data will be collected and saved for transmission later.
4. Once the control error along both axes is within 5 degrees, the AOCS will switch over to high accuracy control mode. High accuracy control mode is defined such that the satellite's telescope is pointing to within 0.5 arcseconds of the astronomical object along both its yaw and pitch axes.
5. After switching to high-accuracy control mode, the AOCS will send the previously collected data about the state of attitude control to the ground station.
6. Also after switching to high accuracy control mode, the AOCS will change the rate at which it collects attitude control state data to 2Hz (500 millisecond intervals).

Table 7.3   Example use case

Note that this use case is somewhat less detailed and precise than what might be available in reality. Such details as which exact control algorithms are to be used in the low and high accuracy modes, whether or not there is a limit on the time that should be spent in low accuracy mode, and what actions should be taken if that time limit is exceeded (an alternative flow) are missing from this use case. It is also possible that this particular use case might, in reality, be broken up into a number of smaller use cases.[7] However, the point here is not to understand the requirements of an AOCS for a particular satellite in detail. This examplar use case is adequate for our current purpose.

Our next step is to find the set of cookbook recipes that provide us with the steps needed to adapt the framework to create an application that will behave as the use case dictates.

We can define an adaptation case as a relation between the subset of application requirements expressed by a use case and the set of cookbook recipes for the framework we are instantiating. This relation is such that each requirement is related to the cookbook recipes that provide the steps for meeting that requirement.[8] This is illustrated in Figure 7.18.

It is worth noting that we have carefully defined the adaptation case as a relation and not as a mapping. If we had defined it as a mapping, we would be dictating that each requirement maps to a single recipe. As Figure 7.18 shows, we allow for

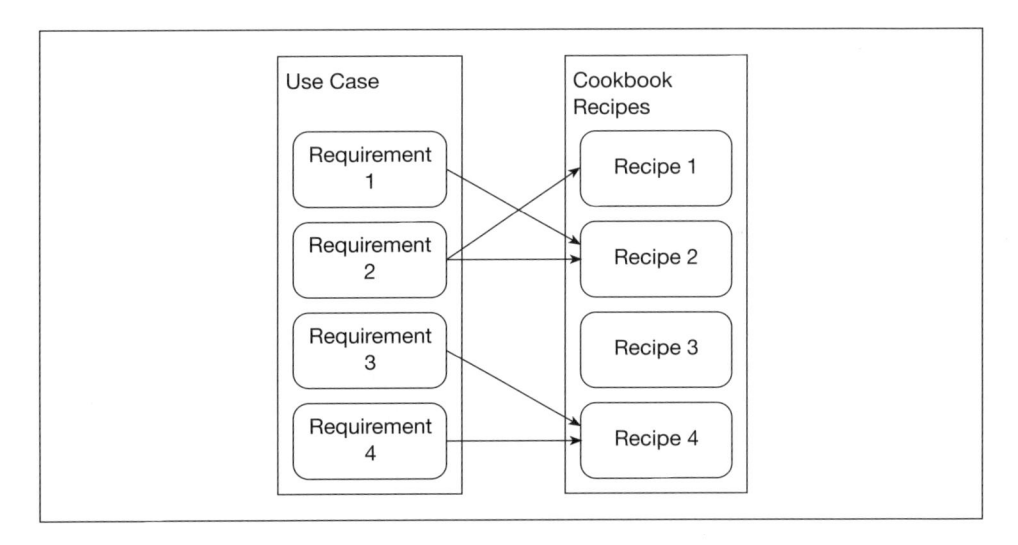

Figure 7.18 Conceptual illustration of an adaptation case

---

[7] It should be noted that the objective of the post-ejection phase for a satellite is usually more modest than acquiring an astronomical object with full accuracy, as in the given objective of the use case.

[8] As was mentioned in a previous footnote, we are not tied to requirements that are presented in the form of use cases. The important thing to note is that an adaptation case is a relation between a subset of application requirements and the set of cookbook recipes. As presented, the use case is the organizing unit for our requirements. If requirements are organized differently, then adaptation cases can also be organized differently.

the possibility that a requirement can only be met by performing the adaptations called for in multiple recipes.

Just as an individual use case does not show all the possible uses of an application, an individual adaptation case does not show all the necessary adaptations of a framework to create the desired application. A set of use cases is essential to fully specify an application, and a set of adaptation cases is essential to fully specify a framework instance. Once we have defined an adaptation case for each use case, which specifies our application, then we have discovered the set of adaptations necessary to create our desired application from the framework.

Returning to our example use case, let us begin to create its corresponding adaptation case. Within a use case, the requirements can most often be found by examining the flow section(s). Sometimes, to get a complete picture of the requirements we need to look in the Post-conditions section also, but requirements found here generally overlap with those found in the flow section(s).

In our examplar use case, step 1 of the Basic Flow shows the external entity (Launch vehicle) initiating the use case. Step 2 begins to show what our system is supposed to do in response. From steps 2 and 4 we see that there is a need for an attitude controller that can switch between two control algorithms ('high accuracy' and 'low accuracy') depending on the size of the attitude control error. The examplar implementation case presented in Section 7.8 provides us with a recipe to meet this requirement. Thus we see that steps 2 and 4 of this use case are related to that implementation case/recipe. Let us call the recipe *Recipe 1: Implementing Multi-mode Controllers*.

From steps 3 and 5, we see that there is a need for a telemetry system that can buffer telemetry data and send it to the ground station at some later time. To meet this requirement, we would look for a recipe in our cookbook that shows us how we can create an implementation of the TmStream interface that stores data written to it using its write() methods and then transmits that data to the ground when its flushBuffer() method is called.

In searching for such a recipe, we may indeed find that there is an existing component, provided as part of the framework, that meets our need. In this case, the recipe should show us how to 'plug in' that existing component. Let us suppose we have such an existing component and a recipe showing how to make use of that component. We'll call that recipe *Recipe 2: Configuring and Using the Provided Buffered Telemetry Stream*.

From steps 3 and 6, we see that there is a need for a telemetry system that supports changing the rate of collection of telemetry data. Again, to meet this requirement, we would look for a recipe in our cookbook that shows the adaptations we need to make. It is not obvious from the presentation of the AOCS framework in the previous sections how the framework would be adapted to meet this requirement. However, let us assume for now that we have a recipe that provides us with the necessary steps. We'll call that recipe *Recipe 3: Implementing Multi-rate Telemetry*.

From step 3, we see that telemetry data must be provided about attitude controllers. Therefore, we note that the framework calls for making an object implement the telemeterable interface and adding that object to the list of telemeterable objects held by the telemetry manager. We'll call the recipe providing these steps *Recipe 4: How to Collect and Send Telemetry Data for an Object*.

Given this use case, set of requirements, and set of recipes, a textual representation of the adaptation case would look like Table 7.4. This is very likely incomplete. Other requirements and recipes may also be associated with this use case. For example, the need for objects that interact with and read data from particular types of sensors (perhaps star sensors) could be inferred from this use case. Similarly, the need for objects that interact with and send commands to actuators in order to apply forces or torques to a satellite could also be inferred from this use case. Each of these requirements will also be related within the adaptation case to a cookbook recipe.

The inevitable question arises, 'What if we encounter a requirement for which we cannot find a related recipe for guiding us as to how to adapt the framework?' There are three foreseeable situations in which this will occur:

1. The adaptation is possible, but is deemed too easy or trivial to rise to the level of deserving its own recipe.
2. The adaptation is possible and somewhat complicated, but no recipe has been written for it.
3. The adaptation is not possible because the framework was not designed around the variation point or behavior required.

In the first situation, we can simply embed the adaptation instructions (a 'minirecipe') into the adaptation case in the table where we would normally have referenced a separate recipe.

In the second situation, we can investigate the necessary adaptations and create our own recipe. Alternatively, depending on our level of access to the framework developer(s), we can report the situation to them and request that a recipe be

Adaptation Case 1

Associated use case
Stabilization of the attitude of an astronomical observation satellite during ejection from launch vehicle.

Framework: AOCS framework

Requirement–recipe relation
Requirement
(Flow steps, post-conditions, etc.)
Related recipes
(used to meet requirement)

Flow steps 2 and 4: multi-mode attitude controller

Recipe 1: Implementing Multi-mode Controllers

Adaptation notes:
- High accuracy mode and low accuracy mode are as defined in the use case

Flow steps 3 and 5: buffering telemetry data

Recipe 2: Configuring and Using the Provided Buffered Telemetry Stream

Flow step 3: Collection of telemetry data for attitude controllers

Recipe 4: How to Collect and Send Telemetry Data for an Object

Adaptation notes:
- Telemetry data for an attitude controller includes last measurement used for determining control error, last control error calculated, and last command sent to actuator

Flow steps 3 and 6: collection of telemetry data at various rates

Recipe 3: Implementing Multi-rate Telemetry

Adaptation notes:
- Collection rates: 4Hz and 2Hz

Table 7.4 Example adaptation case

provided. In either case, if a new recipe is created it should be added to the cookbook for the framework.

In the third situation, we should report the situation to the framework developer(s) and to other developers who may want to adapt the framework in a similar way. If the adaptation is deemed appropriate, the framework developer(s) might change the framework to allow for the new adaptation.

The second and third of these situations call for us to report our findings. How should we do this reporting? That is one of the areas in which the technique presented in the next section can be helpful.

7.9.2 Adaptation reports

Adaptation reports are inspired by a type of report used by airplane pilots to help each other avoid weather-related surprises and other difficulties while flying. Called pilot reports (or sometimes PIREPS), these are brief reports, given in flight, by a pilot about weather conditions actually being experienced. Observations of weather conditions made by ground stations give an incomplete picture of the actual conditions aloft. Thus, pilot reports supplement the weather information from ground stations and are a valuable source of information for other pilots in the vicinity.

Predictions about the feasibility and practicality of a certain framework adaptation are analogous with the weather reports from a ground station. They cannot always give the whole picture and need to be supplemented by reports from developers trying to adapt the framework. These developers are like the pilots flying through and experiencing specific weather conditions. Adaptation reports provide a mechanism for these developers to report on their experience so that other developers needing to make similar framework adaptations can benefit.

A pilot report that essentially indicates that conditions in the air are exactly as the ground station predicted is of less value to other pilots than a report that indicates how conditions aloft are different from those expected. This is particularly true when conditions aloft are worse than predicted from the ground. Similarly, an adaptation report which indicates that the developer's adaptation experience was just as expected (based on the existing framework documentation) is of less value to future adapters of the framework than one pointing out how the developer's experience differs from that expected. Again, this is particularly true when the experience was somehow worse than expected.

Thus, adaptation reports focus primarily (although not solely) on problems that occur during framework adaptation. A developer should create an adaptation report in situations such as when a necessary adaptation could not be made, when no recipe was found for an adaptation, or when an adaptation (or set of interacting adaptations) had an unforeseen side effect. Another case in which an adaptation report should be created is when the developer has successfully implemented a difficult or tricky adaptation so that other developers can save time and effort by mimicking or reusing his adaptation. Table 7.5 describes a proposed template for adaptation reports.

Adaptation report title	
Framework	The framework being adapted.
Application	Brief description or name of application being developed.
Requirements	■ Description of, or reference to, the requirements that were to be met by this adaptation. ■ Reference to use case from which the requirements were drawn, if applicable.
Recipes involved	■ Cookbook recipes that were used, attempted, or are closely related to the requirements. ■ If no recipe was found, then this section could be left blank, or state that no recipe was found.
Framework classes/ interfaces	Details of which, if any, framework classes or interfaces were used or adapted.
Application classes	■ List of which classes, if any, were developed specifically for meeting the above requirements. ■ Include subclasses of framework classes listed above, implementations of interfaces listed above, and any completely new classes created.
Adaptation Success?	Was the adaptation successful?
Reason for report	Choose one of the following: ■ recipe not found – adaptation successful (nclude proposed new recipe or a reference to it in the Discussion section below) ■ proposed recipe not found – adaptation not possible (?) ■ recipe not found – request recipe generation ■ recipe(s) found – unforeseen side effects of recipe, or interaction of recipes (e.g. performance problems) ■ recipe(s) found – incorrect recipe ■ successful difficult or tricky adaptation ■ other.
Discussion	General discussion of the reason for the report. This may include, but is not limited to, such things as: ■ recipes reviewed ■ alternatives considered ■ problems encountered ■ proposed new recipe if applicable ■ workarounds discovered and used ■ performance characteristics of adaptation used.

Table 7.5 Adaptation report template

Returning to our example use case and adaptation case, let us suppose that we discover, while trying to create an adaptation case, that there is no recipe available that provides steps for the collection of telemetry data at various rates. On further investigation, we eliminate the possibility that this adaptation is so trivial that no recipe is required – in fact, as far as we can tell, such an adaptation is simply not possible given the existing framework. This is an occasion that calls for generating an adaptation report. Table 7.6 provides an example of such a report.

Collecting Controller Telemetry Data at Multiple Rates	
Framework	AOCS Framework.
Application	AOCS for astronomical observation satellite.
Requirements	■ See use case: stabilization of the attitude of an astronomical observation satellite during ejection from launch vehicle. ■ Flow steps 3 and 6 specify a requirement that the AOCS support changing the rate of collection of telemetry data for attitude controllers.
Recipes	No recipe found.
Framework classes/interfaces	Not applicable.
Application classes	Not applicable.
Adaptation success?	No.
Reason for report	Recipe not found – adaptation not possible (?)
Discussion	■ No recipe could be found that provides steps to adapt the collection of telemetry data for attitude controllers to allow for two different collection rates. Further investigation leads us to believe that there is no variation point in the framework that supports such an adaptation. Perhaps one should be added. ■ One proposed workaround is collecting telemetry data at the higher rate (4 Hz) and creating a controller class such that when in high accuracy control mode the controller only reports telemetry data on every other request – thus giving an effective rate of (2 Hz). ■ This proposed workaround is not currently deemed to be a good choice. Adding a new variation point to the framework is preferable.

Table 7.6 Example adaptation report

Ideally, such a report would be forwarded to the framework developers. The framework developers could either respond that the adaptation is indeed possible and provide a recipe for it, or that the adaptation is not possible and that a variation point will be added to the framework to allow such an adaptation, or that the adaptation is not possible and will not be added.[9]

7.10 Summary

We have provided a set of hints and guidelines for the development and adaptation processes of frameworks. The cluster cycle model sketches the flavor of these processes. The various hints and guidelines are not a complete solution to the problems of developing and using frameworks. They have, however, proven useful in the realm of various framework projects in leading to a more rapid production of higher-quality frameworks and applications derived from frameworks. So-called aCiRC cards support the identification and documentation of domain abstractions. Variation point analysis helps to inject the right doses of flexibility into a framework. Framelets help in structuring a framework at the design level. Class families, class teams, and subsystems provide an architectural view of the modularization of frameworks. Implementation cases test drive the framework design and result in cookbook recipes. Finally, cookbooks, adaptation cases, and adaptation reports support the adaptation of frameworks.

7.11 UML-F outlook

The book has laid the ground for the UML-F profile, presented its notational elements and demonstrated its application in the realm of the framework development and adaptation process. We recommend that you regularly check the UML-F Web site www.UML-F.net which gives the latest news on this profile.

We invite you to provide feedback on the various aspects of UML-F, suggest improvements, and let us know your opinion of the UML-F profile.

---

[9] Recall the discussion at the beginning of the chapter, which pointed out that adding unneccessary variability to a framework does not result in a better framework.

Appendix A

UML-F tag quick reference

This appendix provides a quick reference to the UML-F tags defined in this book. Section A.1 gives a quick overview of the notation used. The following sections then summarize UML-F.

A.1 Tag notations

UML-F unifies standard UML's *stereotypes* and *tagged values* into the UML-F *tag*. See Section 3.2 for further information.

The following are equivalent forms in UML-F:

«stereotype–name» ≡ {stereotype–name}

For Boolean tags, the following forms are equivalent:

«name» ≡ «name = True» ≡ {name = True}

For non-Boolean tags, the following forms are equivalent:

«name = value» ≡ {name = value}

Multiple tags can be combined into one pair of double guillemets, « », or one pair of curly brackets, { }, using a semicolon as the separator:

«name1=value1; name2=value2» ≡ {name1=value1; name2=value2}

The following abbreviations are allowed for string tags:

«name» ≡ «name = ""»
«name:value» ≡ «name = value»
«name1, name2: value» ≡ «name1 = value; name2 = value»

A.2 Presentation tags

The following UML-F tags deal with the visual representation of elements. They do not define or add any properties to the annotated modeling elements. See Section 3.4.1 for further information.

A.2.1 Completeness and hierarchy tags

Tag form	Summary
©	*Completeness marker* The graphical representation is complete – e.g. the class methods or attributes are all shown, all generalizations of the class are shown, all information about an association is shown, etc.
...	*Incompleteness marker* Inverse of ©. The graphical representation is possibly incomplete – e.g. not all class methods or attributes are shown, not all generalizations of the class are shown, not all association information is shown, etc. This is also the default.
δ	*Hierarchical representation* The graphical representation shows only members that are introduced or redefined at the current level. Inherited members are not shown.
Λ	*Flat representation* The graphical representation shows inherited members as well as newly introduced or redefined members. The full hierarchy is shown.

A.2.2 Enhanced graphical inheritance indicators

The following graphical elements convey information about methods or attributes in class or object diagrams. They are attached to the side of the class or object box beside the method or attribute to which they apply. If they are contained inside the box, they also indicate that the method or attribute is inaccessible by other elements in the diagram. If they cross the boundary of the class or object box, they indicate that the method or attribute is accessible by other elements in the diagram. See Section 3.4.2 for further information.

Appendix A UML-F tag quick reference 199

Tag form	Summary
▭	*Unfilled rectangle* The method or attribute is inherited and not redefined.
▬	*Gray rectangle* The method or attribute is either newly defined, or it is inherited but completely redefined.
▭▬	*Half-gray/half-unfilled rectangle* The method is redefined but uses the inherited method through a super()-call.
◿	*Unfilled rectangle with diagonal line* The method is abstract and must be overridden in subclasses.

A.2.3 Sequence diagram tags

Through the following graphical elements, sequence diagrams become more expressive. It is possible to describe repeated messages, alternatives, etc. See Section 3.4.4 for further information.

Tag form	Summary
*	*Unbound repetition* For a message: the message can be repeated as often as desired – zero occurrences are allowed. For an object: there can be multiple instantiations of the object's class (including zero).
+	*Optional* The message is optional, occurring at most once.
|	*Alternatives* The sequence diagram is subdivided into alternative diagrams.
(A–B)	*Bound repetition* A concise way to describe multiple occurrence of a message or an object (between A and B times).
«trigger»	*Trigger* Marks the message in a sequence diagram that causes the subsequent interaction to occur.

A.3 Basic framework modeling tags

The following UML-F tags show properties of the annotated modeling elements and are particularly useful in the context of designing and documenting a framework. See Section 3.5 for further information.

Tag form	Summary
«application»	The element belongs to an application, not to the framework.
«framework»	The element belongs to the framework.
«utility»	The element belongs to a utility library or to the runtime environment.
«fixed»	The element is fixed – no changes (alteration of a method, addition of new methods to a class, addition of new subclasses, etc.) may be made.
«adapt–static»	The element can be adapted during design-time through subclassing – during runtime, the element is fixed.
«adapt–dyn»	The element can be changed at runtime.

A.4 Essential tags for the framework construction principles

A.4.1 Template and hook tags

See Chapter 4 for further information.

Tag form	Summary
«template»	The method is a template method or the class contains a template method.
«hook»	The method is a hook method or the class/interface contains a hook method.

A template–hook tag group can be formed by giving the tag group a name. This would result in the tags taking the form «template: *group-name*» and «hook: *group-name*».

A.4.2 Tags for the Unification and Separation construction principles

See Chapter 4 for further information.

Tag form	Summary
«Unification–TH» or «Unif–TH»	The class is an application of the unification construction principle and thus contains both a template and hook method.
«Unification–t» or «Unif–t»	The method is a template method in an application of the Unification construction principle.
«Unification–h» or «Unif–h»	The method is a hook method in an application of the Unification construction principle.
«Separation–T» or «Sep–T»	The class contains the template method in an application of the Separation construction principle.
«Separation–H» or «Sep–H»	The class contains the hook method in an application of the Separation construction principle.
«Separation–t» or «Sep–t»	The method is a template method in an application of the Separation construction principle.
«Separation–h» or «Sep–h»	The method is a hook method in an application of the separation construction principle.

A Unification principle tag group can be formed by giving the tag group a name. This would result in the tags taking the form «Unif–TH: *group-name*», «Unif–t: *group-name*», and «Unif–h: *group-name*». A Separation principle tag group can be formed using an analogous technique. This would result in the tags taking the form «Sep–T: *group-name*», «Sep–H: *group-name*», «Sep–t: *group-name*», and «Sep–h: *group-name*».

A.4.3 Tags for Composite, Decorator, and Chain of Responsibility

The three construction principles with a recursive flavor are identical to the patterns Composite, Decorator, and Chain of Responsibility in the GoF catalog shown in Appendix B. Chapter 4 and Section A.5 provide guidelines on how to derive the corresponding tags from the particular pattern structure.

A.5 Framework pattern tags

When a pattern is presented, it is given a pattern name. The structure section of the GoF pattern catalog provides a class diagram that shows the pattern's participating classes, interfaces, methods, associations, and attributes. The class, interface, method, association, and attribute names given in such a diagram, together with the pattern name, form a set of UML-F tags for the pattern. This is true regardless of whether we are discussing a pattern out of a pattern catalog or an application-specific pattern. The UML-F tags for a pattern take the form shown in the following table.

See Chapter 4 for further information.

Tag form	Summary
«PatternName–ClassName»	The annotated class plays the role of the class given the name ClassName in the pattern named PatternName.
«PatternName–*InterfaceName*»	The annotated interface plays the role of the interface given the name *InterfaceName* in the pattern named PatternName.
«PatternName–methodName»	The annotated method plays the role of the method given the name methodName in the pattern named PatternName.
«PatternName–associationLabel»	The annotated association plays the role of the association given the label associationLabel in the pattern named PatternName.
«PatternName–attributeName»	The annotated attribute plays the role of the attribute given the name attributeName in the pattern named PatternName.

Note that class and interface names start with an uppercase letter, while method names, association labels, and attribute names start with a lowercase letter. Also note that interface names are presented in italics. Abstract classes and abstract methods would also be presented in italics.

Appendix B presents the tags for the framework-related design patterns of the pattern catalog (Gamma et. al., 1995).

Appendix B

UML-F tags for the GoF framework patterns

For the sake of completness, this appendix lists the UML-F tags of all GoF framework patterns (Gamma et al., 1995). As discussed in Chapter 4, these tags are derived from the structure of each pattern in the GoF pattern catalog. We refrain from a complete presentation of the tag sets according to the tag definition template, as the patterns are discussed in detail in the pattern catalog. Thus, we restrict the presentation to the sections Tags, Apply to, Type, and Expansion and leave out the sections Motivation and purpose, Informal explanation of effect, and Discussion. Chapter 4 provides a complete presentation of the tags for the Factory Method, Strategy, and Composite patterns.

The appendix first presents the Unification-based patterns Factory Method and Template Method, goes on to the Separation-based patterns Abstract Factory, Bridge, Builder, Command, Interpreter, Observer, Prototype, State, and Strategy followed by the recursive patterns Composite, Decorator, and Chain of Responsibility.

B.1 Factory Method pattern tags

Figure B.1 shows the static structure of the Factory Method pattern (Gamma et al., 1995) annotated with UML-F tags. Table B.1 summarizes the Factory Method pattern UML-F tags. Factory Method is based on the Unification construction principle.

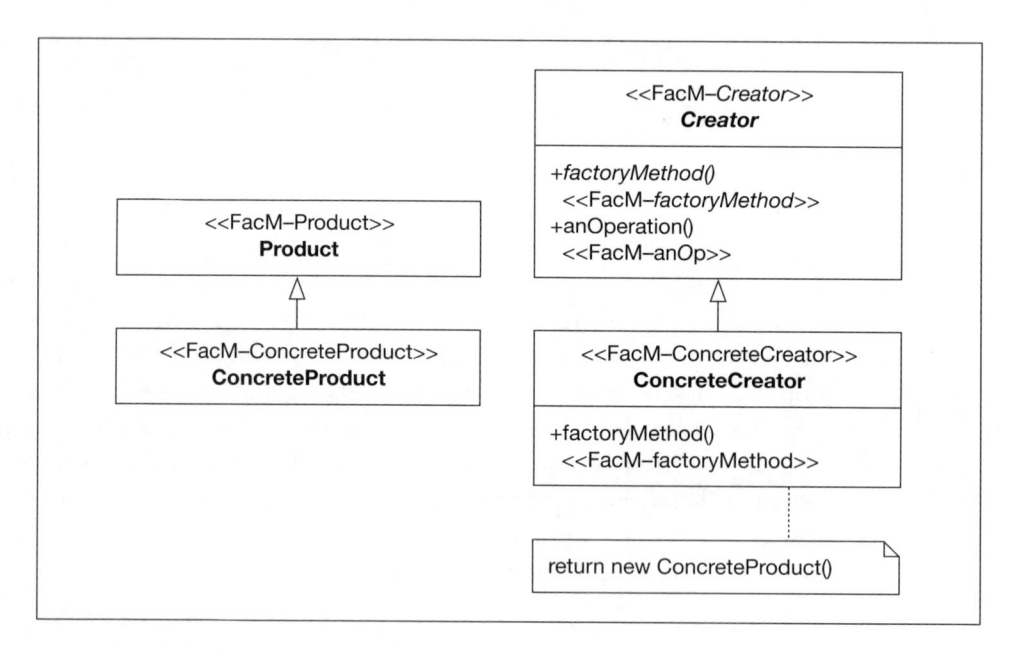

Figure B.1 Structure of the Factory Method pattern annotated with UML-F tags

Tags	«FacM–*Creator*», «FacM–*facM*», «FacM–anOp», «FacM–Product», «FacM–ConcreteProduct», «FacM–ConcreteCreator» and «FacM–facM».
Apply to	As shown in Fig. B.2: Class («FacM–*Creator*», «FacM–Product», «FacM–ConcreteProduct», «FacM–ConcreteCreator»); Method («FacM–*facM*», «FacM–anOp», «FacM–facM»); Interface («FacM–Product»).
Type	String.
Expansion	The Factory Method pattern is based on the Unification principle and therefore its tags expand as follows: «FacM–*Creator*» to «Unif–TH», «FacM–*facM*» to «Unif–h», and «FacM–anOp» to «Unif–t».

Table B.1   Definition of the UML-F Factory Method pattern tags

B.2 Template Method pattern tags

Figure B.2 shows the static structure of the Template Method pattern (Gamma et al., 1995) annotated with UML-F tags. Table B.2 summarizes the Template Method pattern UML-F tags. Template Method is based on the Unification construction principle.

```
                ┌─────────────────────────────────┐
                │  <<TemplateM–AbstractClass>>    │
                │         AbstractClass           │
                ├─────────────────────────────────┤
                │ +templateMethod()               │
                │   <<TemplateM–templateMethod>>  │
                │ +primitiveOperation()           │
                │   <<templateM–primitiveOp>>     │
                └─────────────────────────────────┘
                              △
                              │
                ┌─────────────────────────────────┐
                │  <<TemplateM–ConcreteClass>>    │
                │         ConcreteClass           │
                ├─────────────────────────────────┤
                │ +primitiveOperation()           │
                │   <<templateM–primitiveOp>>     │
                └─────────────────────────────────┘
```

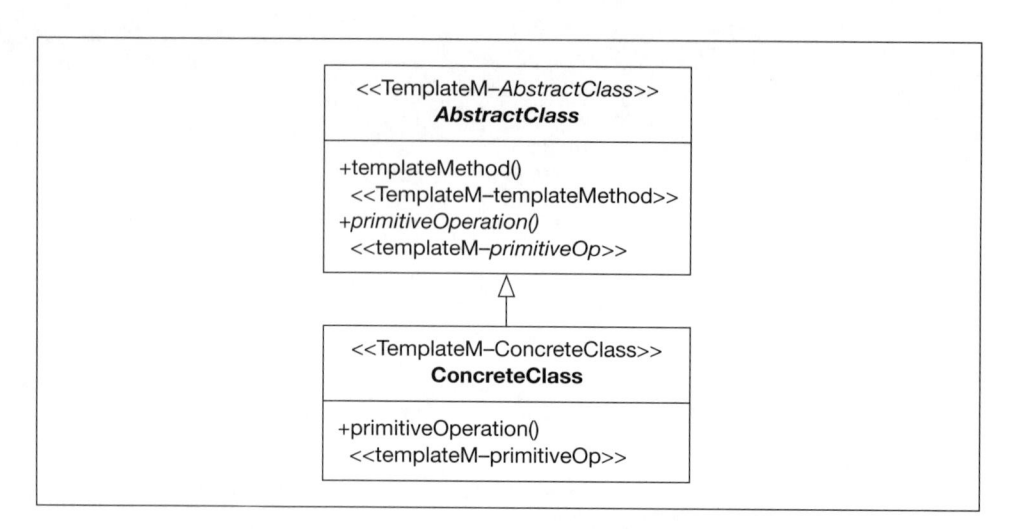

Figure B.2 Structure of the Template Method pattern annotated with UML-F tags

Tags	«TemplateM–*AbstractClass*», «TemplateM–*ConcreteClass*», «TemplateM–templateM», «TemplateM–*primitiveOp*», and «TemplateM–*primitiveOp*».
Apply to	As shown in Fig. B.1: Class («TemplateM–*AbstractClass*», «TemplateM–*ConcreteClass*»); Method («TemplateM–templateM», «TemplateM–*primitiveOp*», «TemplateM–*primitiveOp*»).
Type	String
Expansion	The Template Method pattern is based on the Unification principle and therefore its tags expand as follows: «TemplateM–*AbstractClass*» to «Unif–TH», «TemplateMethod–templateM» to «Unif–t», and «TemplateM–*primitiveOp*» to «Unif–h».

Table B.2 Definition of the UML-F Template Method pattern tags

B.3 Abstract Factory pattern tags

Figure B.3 shows the static structure of the Abstract Factory pattern (Gamma et al., 1995) annotated with UML-F tags. Table B.3 summarizes the Abstract Factory pattern UML-F tags. Abstract Factory is based on the Separation construction principle.

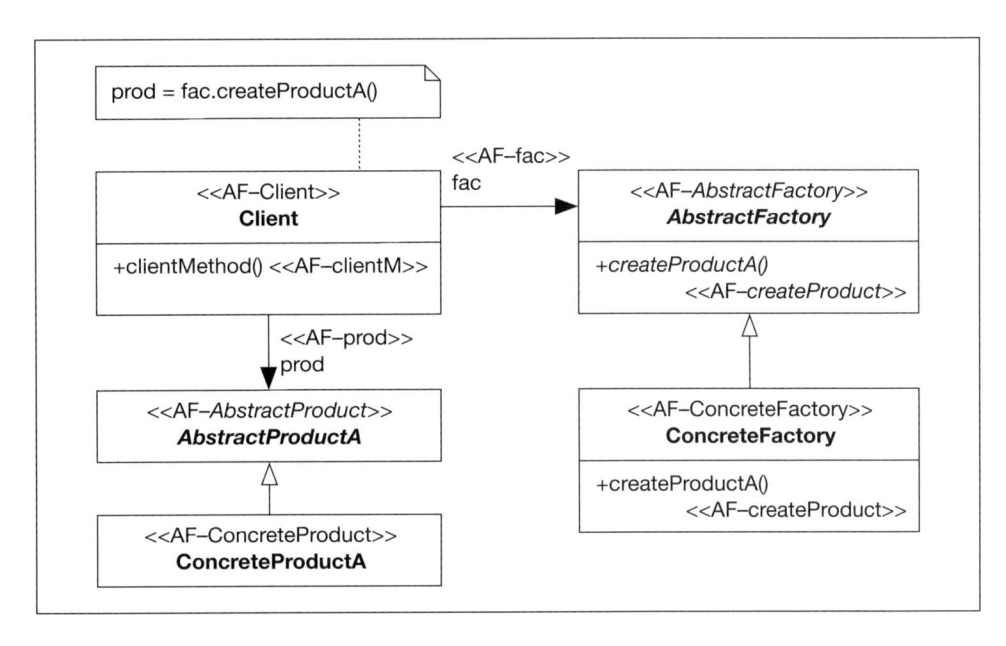

Appendix B UML-F tags of the GoF framework patterns

Figure B.3 Structure of the Abstract Factory pattern annotated with UML-F tags

Tags	«AbstractFactory–Client», «AbstractFactory–*AbstractFactory*», «AbstractFactory–ConcreteFactory», «AbstractFactory–*AbstractProduct*», «AbstractFactory–ConcreteProduct», «AbstractFactory–clientM», «AbstractFactory–*createProduct*», «AbstractFactory–createProduct», «AbstractFactory–fac», and «AbstractFactory–prod». [or their short forms «AF–...»]
Apply to	As shown in Fig. B6: Class («AF–Client», «AF–*AbstractFactory*», «AF–ConcreteFactory», «AF–*AbstractProduct*», «AF–ConcreteProduct»); Method («AF–clientM», «AF–*createProductA*», «AF-createProductA»); Interface («AF–Client», «AF–*AbstractFactory*», «AF–*AbstractProduct*»); Association («AF–fac» , «AF–prod»).
Type	String.
Expansion	The Abstract Factory pattern is based on the Separation principle and therefore its tags expand as follows: «AF–Client» to «Sep–T», «AF–clientM» to «Sep–t», «AF–*AbstractFactory*» to «Sep–H», and «AF–*createProduct*» to «Sep–h».

Table B.3 Definition of the UML-F Abstract Factory pattern tags

B.4 Bridge pattern tags

Figure B.4 shows the static structure of the Bridge pattern (Gamma et al., 1995) annotated with UML-F tags. Table B.4 summarizes the Bridge pattern UML-F tags. Bridge is based on the Separation construction principle

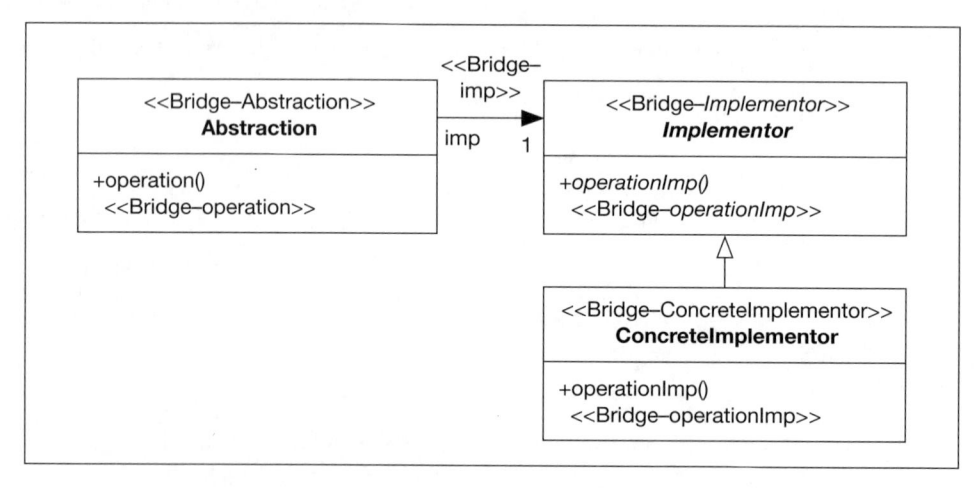

Figure B.4   Structure of the Bridge pattern annotated with UML-F tags

Tags	«Bridge–Abstraction», «Bridge–*Implementor*», «Bridge–ConcreteImplementor», «Bridge–operation», «Bridge–*operationImp*», «Bridge–operationImp», and «Bridge–imp».
Apply to	As shown in Fig. B.3: Class («Bridge–Abstraction», «Bridge–*Implementor*», «Bridge–ConcreteImplementor»); Method («Bridge–operation», «Bridge–*operationImp*», «Bridge–operationImp»); Interface («Bridge–Abstraction», «Bridge–*Implementor*»); Association («Bridge–imp»).
Type	String.
Expansion	The Bridge pattern is based on the Separation principle and therefore its tags expand as follows: «Bridge–Abstraction» to «Sep–T», «Bridge–operation» to «Sep–t», «Bridge–*Implementor*» to «Sep–H», and «Bridge–*operationImp*» to «Sep–h».

Table B.4   Definition of the UML-F Bridge pattern tags

B.5 Builder pattern tags

Figure B.5 shows the static structure of the Builder pattern (Gamma et al., 1995) annotated with UML-F tags. Table B.5 summarizes the Builder pattern UML-F tags. Builder is based on the Separation construction principle.

```
<<Builder-Director>>                <<Builder-builder>>      <<Builder-Builder>>
Director                            builder                  Builder
+construct()                                                 +buildPart()
  <<Builder-construct>>                                        <<Builder-buildPart>>
                                                                     △
                                                                     │
                                                         <<Builder-ConcreteBuilder>>
                                                         ConcreteBuilder
                                                         +buildPart()
                                                           <<Builder-buildPart>>
```

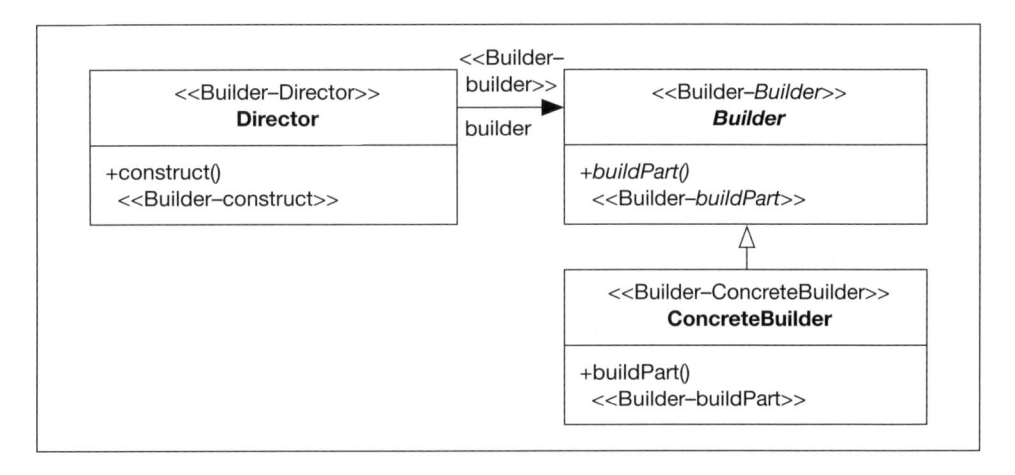

Figure B.5 Structure of the Builder pattern annotated with UML-F tags

Tags	«Builder–Director», «Builder–*Builder*», «Builder–ConcreteBuilder», «Builder–construct», «Builder–*buildPart*», «Builder–buildPart», and «Builder–builder».
Apply to	As shown in Fig. B4: Class («Builder–Director», «Builder–*Builder*», «Builder–ConcreteBuilder»); Method («Builder–construct», «Builder–*buildPart*», «Builder–buildPart»); Interface («Builder–Director», «Builder–*Builder*»); Association («Builder–builder»).
Type	String.
Expansion	The Builder pattern is based on the Separation principle and therefore its tags expand as follows: «Builder–Director» to «Sep–T», «Builder–construct» to «Sep–t», «Builder–*Builder*» to «Sep–H», and «Builder–*buildPart*» to «Sep–h».

Table B.5 Definition of the UML-F Builder pattern tags

B.6 Command pattern tags

Figure B.6 shows the static structure of the Command pattern (Gamma et al., 1995) annotated with UML-F tags. Table B.6 summarizes the Command pattern UML-F tags. Command is based on the Separation construction principle.

Appendix B UML-F tags of the GoF framework patterns

```
┌─────────────────────────────────────────────────────────────────────┐
│                           <<Command–                                │
│   <<Command–Invoker>>    command>>    <<Command–Command>>           │
│        Invoker          ───────────→        Command                 │
│                          command  1                                 │
│   +clientMethod()                     +execute()                    │
│   <<Command–clientM>>                 <<Command–execute>>           │
│                                              △                      │
│                                              │                      │
│                                   <<Command–ConcreteCommand>>       │
│                                        ConcreteCommand              │
│                                       +execute()                    │
│                                       <<Command–execute>>           │
└─────────────────────────────────────────────────────────────────────┘
```

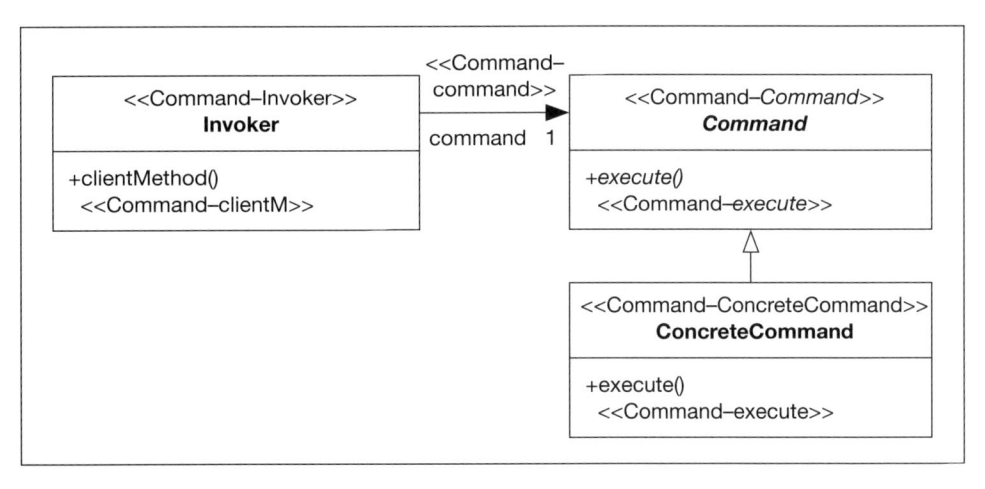

Figure B.6 Structure of the Command pattern annotated with UML-F tags

Tags	«Command–Invoker», «Command–*Command*», «Command–ConcreteCommand», «Command–clientM», «Command–*execute*», «Command–execute», and «Command–command».
Apply to	As shown in Fig. B.7: Class («Command–Invoker», «Command–*Command*», «Command–ConcreteCommand»); Method («Command–clientM», «Command–*execute*», «Command–execute»); Interface («Command–Invoker», «Command–*Command*»); Association («Command-command»).
Type	String.
Expansion	The Command pattern is based on the Separation principle and therefore its tags expand as follows: «Command–Invoker» to «Sep–T», «Command–clientM» to «Sep–t», «Command–*Command*» to «Sep–H», and «Command–*execute*» to «Sep–h».

Table B.6 Definition of the UML-F Command pattern tags

B.7 Interpreter pattern tags

Figure B.7 shows the static structure of the Interpreter pattern (Gamma et al., 1995) annotated with UML-F tags. Table B.7 summarizes the Interpreter pattern UML-F tags. Interpreter is based on the Separation construction principle.

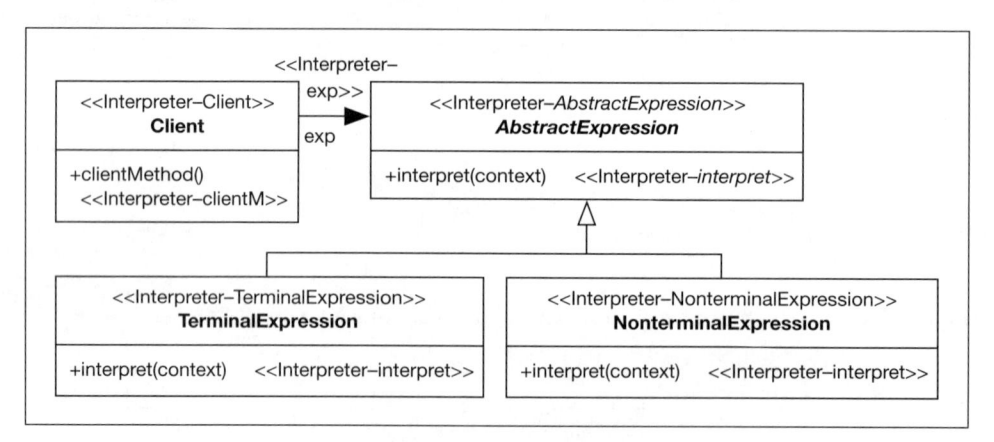

Figure B.7 Structure of the Interpreter pattern annotated with UML-F tags

Tags	«Interpreter–Client», «Interpreter–*AbstractExpression*», «Interpreter–TerminalExpression», «Interpreter–NonterminalExpression», «Interpreter–clientM», «Interpreter–*interpret*», «Interpreter–interpret», and «Interpreter–exp».
Apply to	As shown in Fig B.5: Class («Interpreter–Client», «Interpreter–*AbstractExpression*», «Interpreter–TerminalExpression», «Interpreter–NonterminalExpression»); Method («Interpreter–clientM», «Interpreter–*interpret*», «Interpreter–interpret»); Interface («Interpreter-Client», «Interpreter–*AbstractExpression*»); Association («Interpreter–exp»).
Type	String.
Expansion	The Interpreter pattern is based on the Separation principle and therefore its tags expand as follows: «Interpreter–Client» to «Sep–T», «Interpreter–clientM» to «Sep–t», «Interpreter–*AbstractExpression*» to «Sep–H», and «Interpreter–*interpret*» to «Sep–h».

Table B.7 Definition of the UML-F Interpreter pattern tags

B.8 Observer pattern tags

Figure B.8 shows the static structure of the Observer pattern (Gamma et al., 1995) annotated with UML-F tags. Table B.8 summarizes the Observer pattern UML-F tags. Observer is based on the Separation construction principle.

```
                                  <<Observers–
                                  observers>>*
    <<Observer–Subject>>          ─────────────▶    <<Observer–Observer>>
         Subject                     observers            Observer
    +notify()<<Observer–notify>>                    +update()<<Observer–update>>
                                                              △
         ...                                                  │
         for each o in observers              <<Observer–ConcreteObserver>>
         o.update();                                 ConcreteObserver
         ...
                                                 +update()<<Observer–update>>
```

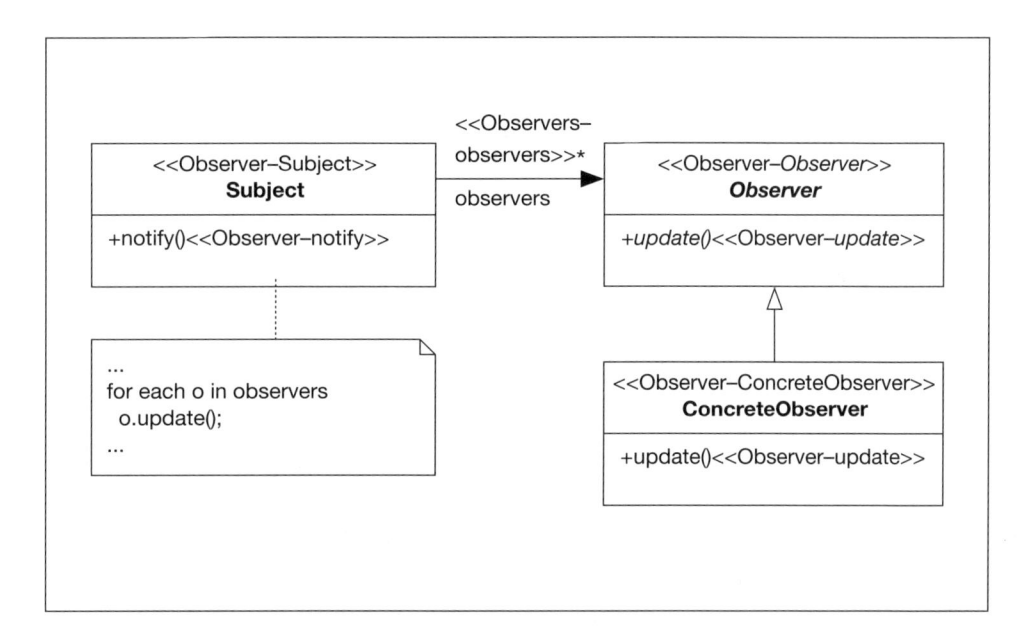

Figure B.8 Structure of the Observer pattern annotated with UML-F tags

Tags	«Observer–Subject», «Observer–*Observer*», «Observer–ConcreteObserver», «Observer–notify», «Observer–*update*», «Observer–update», and «Observer–observers».
Apply to	As shown in Fig B.8: Class («Observer–Subject», «Observer–*Observer*», «Observer–ConcreteObserver»); Method («Observer–notify», «Observer–*update*», «Observer–update»); Interface («Observer–Subject», «Observer–*Observer*»); Association («Observer–observers»).
Type	String.
Expansion	The Observer pattern is based on the Separation principle and therefore its tags expand as follows: «Observer–Subject» to «Sep–T», «Observer–notify» to «Sep–t», «Observer–*Observer*» to «Sep–H», and «Observer–*update*» to «Sep–h».

Table B.8 Definition of the UML-F Observer pattern tags

B.9 Prototype pattern tags

Figure B.9 shows the static structure of the Prototype pattern (Gamma et al., 1995) annotated with UML-F tags. Table B.9 summarizes the Prototype pattern UML-F tags. Prototype is based on the Separation construction principle.

Appendix B UML-F tags of the GoF framework patterns

```
┌──────────────────────────────────────────────────────────────────────┐
│                          <<Prototype–                                │
│   <<Prototype–Client>>   prototype>>    <<Prototype–Prototype>>     │
│         Client          ─────────────▶        Prototype              │
│   ──────────────────      prototype     ──────────────────           │
│   +clientMethod()                       +clone()<<Prototype–clone>>  │
│     <<Prototype–clientM>>                          △                 │
│                                                    │                 │
│                                         <<Prototype–ConcretePrototype>> │
│                                              ConcretePrototype       │
│                                         ──────────────────           │
│                                         +clone()<<Prototype–clone>>  │
└──────────────────────────────────────────────────────────────────────┘
```

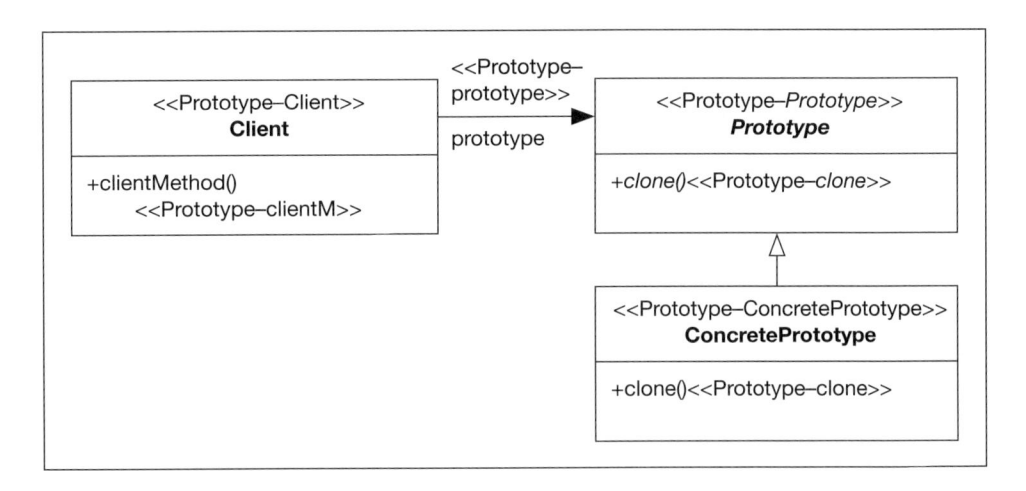

Figure B.9 Structure of the Prototype pattern annotated with UML-F tags

Tags	«Prototype–Client», «Prototype–*Prototype*», «Prototype–ConcretePrototype», «Prototype–clientM», «Prototype–*clone*», «Prototype–clone», and «Prototype–*prototype*».
Apply to	As shown in Fig. B.9: Class («Prototype–Client», «Prototype–*Prototype*», «Prototype–ConcretePrototype»); Method («Prototype–clientM», «Prototype–*clone*», «Prototype–clone»); Interface («Prototype–Client», «Prototype–*Prototype*»); Association («Prototype–*prototype*»).
Type	String.
Expansion	The Prototype pattern is based on the Separation principle and therefore its tags expand as follows: «Prototype-Client» to «Sep–T», «Prototype–clientM» to «Sep–t», «Prototype–*Prototype*» to «Sep–H», and «Prototype–*clone*» to «Sep–h».

Table B.9 Definition of the Prototype pattern tags

B.10 State pattern tags

Figure B.10 shows the static structure of the State pattern (Gamma et al., 1995) annotated with UML-F tags. Table B.10 summarizes the State pattern UML-F tags. State is based on the Separation construction principle.

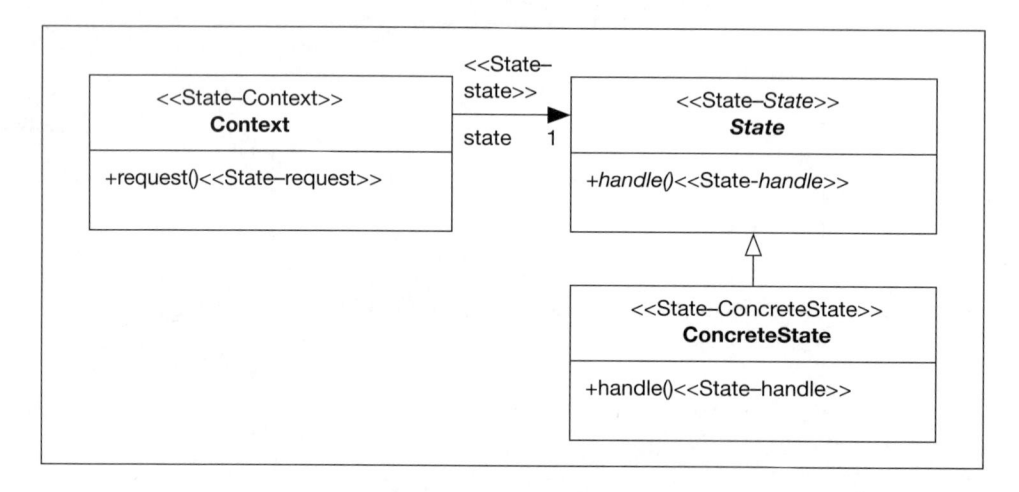

Figure B.10 Structure of the State pattern annotated with UML-F tags

Tags	«State–Context», «State–*State*», «State–ConcreteState», «State–request», «State–*handle*», «State–handle», and «State–state».
Apply to	As shown in Fig. B.10: Class («State–Context», «State–*State*», «State–ConcreteState»); Method («State–request», «State–*handle*», «State–handle»); Interface («State–Context», «State–*State*»); Association («State–state»).
Type	String.
Expansion	The State pattern is based on the Separation principle and, therefore, its tags expand as follows: «State–Context» to «Sep–T», «State–request» to «Sep–t», «State–*State*» to «Sep–H», and «State–*handle*» to «Sep–h».

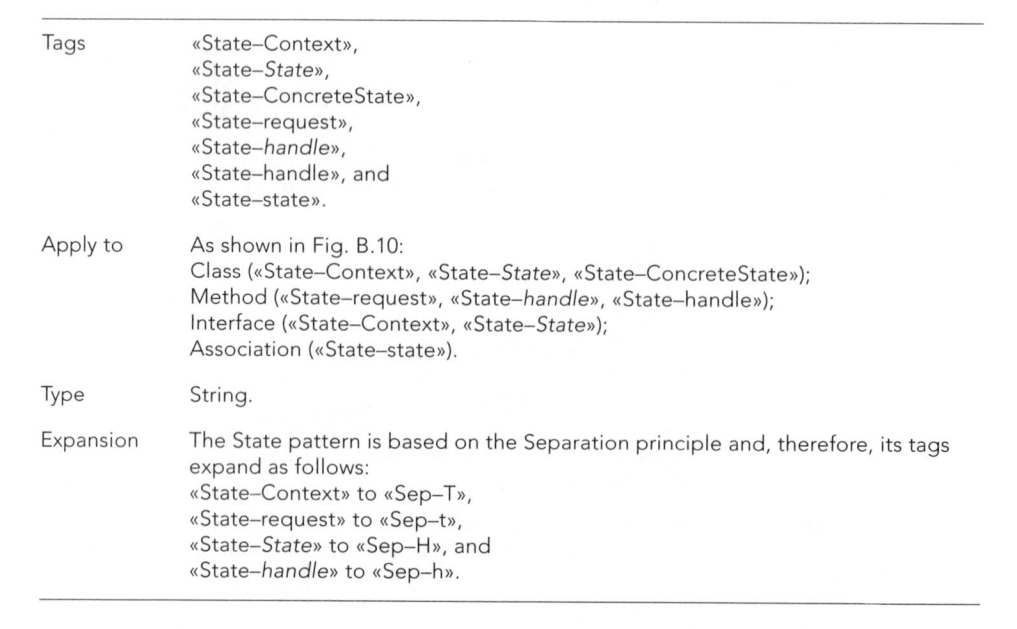

Table B.10 Definition of the UML-F State pattern tags

B.11 Strategy pattern tags

Figure B.11 shows the static structure of the Strategy pattern (Gamma et al., 1995) annotated with UML-F tags. Table B.11 summarizes the Strategy pattern UML-F tags. Strategy is based on the Separation construction principle.

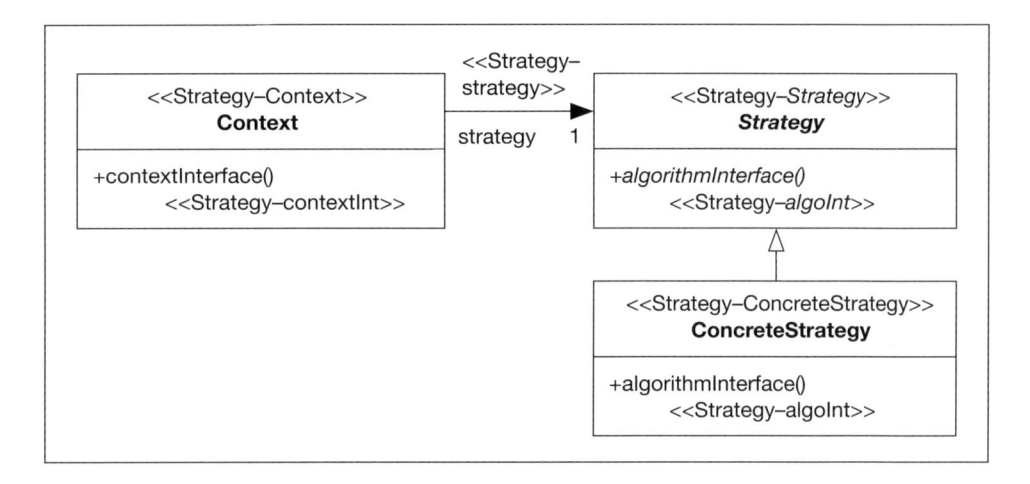

Figure B.11 Structure of the Strategy pattern annotated with UML-F tags

Tags	«Strategy–Context», «Strategy–contextInt», «Strategy–strategy», «Strategy–*Strategy*», «Strategy–*algInt*», «Strategy–ConcreteStrategy», and «Strategy–algInt»
Apply to	As shown in Fig. B.11: Class («Strategy–Context», «Strategy–*Strategy*», «Strategy–ConcreteStrategy»); Method («Strategy–contextInt», «Strategy–*algInt*», «Strategy–algInt»); Interface («Strategy–Context», «Strategy–*Strategy*»); Association («Strategy–strategy»).
Type	String.
Expansion	The Strategy pattern is based on the Separation principle and, therefore, its tags expand as follows: «Strategy–Context» to «Sep–T», «Strategy–contextInt» to «Sep–t», «Strategy–*Strategy*» to «Sep–H», and «Strategy–*algInt*» to «Sep–h».

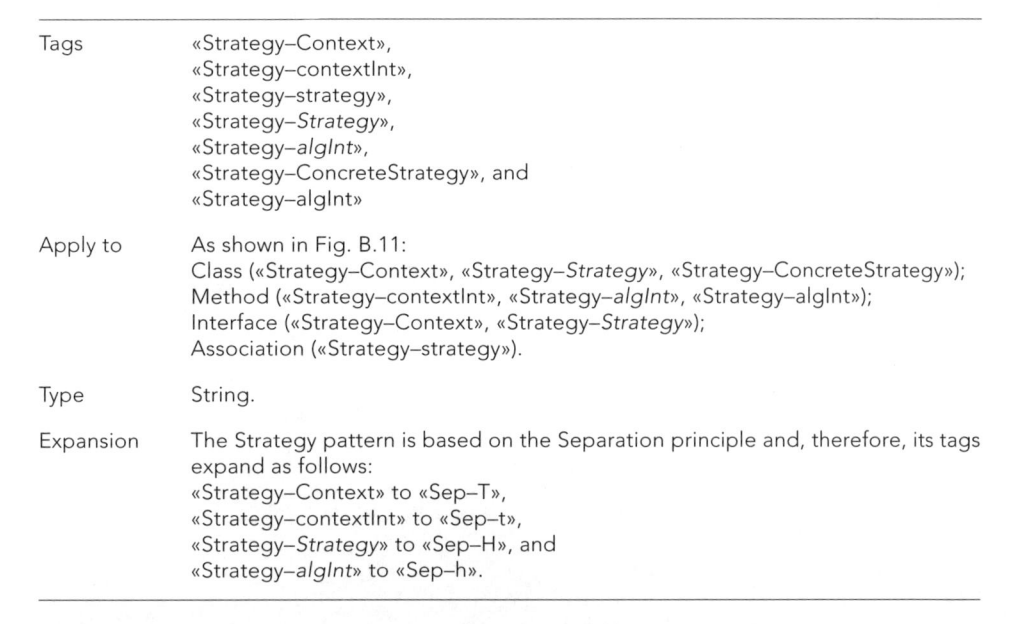

Table B.11 Definition of the UML-F Strategy pattern tags

B.12 Composite pattern tags

Figure B.12 shows the static structure of the Composite pattern (Gamma et al., 1995) annotated with UML-F tags. Table B.12 summarizes the Composite pattern UML-F tags. Composite corresponds to the Composite framework construction principle, which is a recursive combination of template and hook methods.

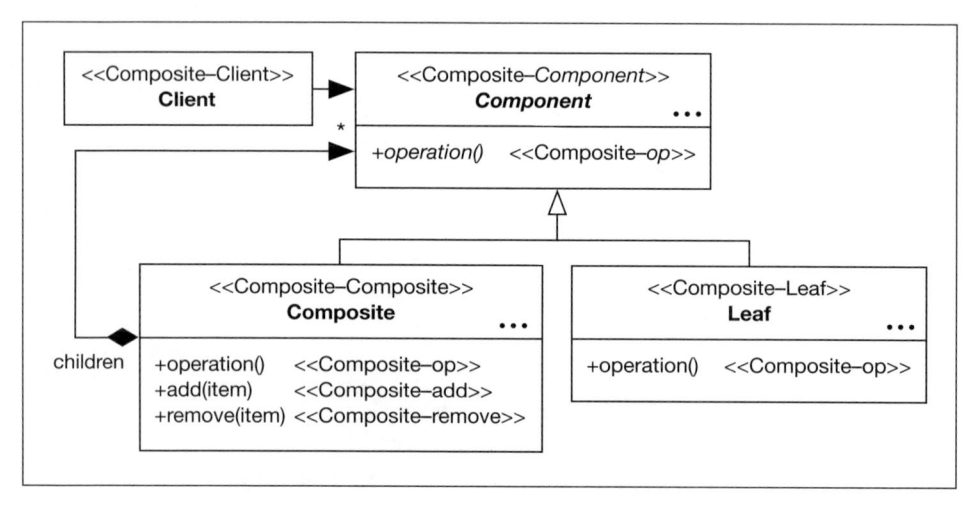

Figure B.12 Structure of the Composite pattern annotated with UML-F tags

Tags	«Composite–Client», «Composite–*Component*», «Composite–*op*», «Composite–Composite», «Composite–children», «Composite–op», «Composite–add», «Composite–remove», and «Composite–Leaf».
Apply to	As shown in Fig. B.12: Class («Composite–Client», «Composite–*Component*», «Composite–Composite», «Composite–Leaf»); Method («Composite–*op*», «Composite–op», «Composite–add», «Composite–remove»); Interface («Composite–Client», «Composite-*Component*»); Association («Composite–children»).
Type	String.
Expansion	Not applicable.

Figure B.12 Definition of the UML-F Composite pattern tags

B.13 Decorator pattern tags

Figure B.13 shows the static structure of the Decorator pattern (Gamma et al., 1995) annotated with UML-F tags. Table B.13 summarizes the Decorator pattern UML-F tags. Decorator corresponds to the Decorator framework construction principle, which is a recursive combination of template and hook methods in which each instance of the object containing the template method can only refer to zero or one instance of an object containing the hook method. This construction principle can be applied in order to selectively *add behavior by composition* without changing the hook directly.

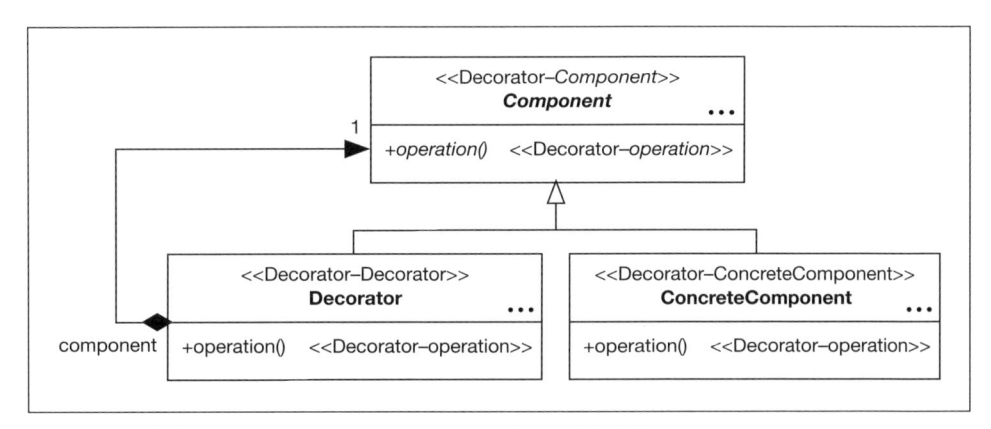

Figure B.13 Structure of the Decorator pattern annotated with UML-F tags

Tags	«Decorator–*Component*», «Decorator–Decorator», «Decorator–ConcreteComponent», «Decorator–*operation*», «Decorator–operation», and «Decorator–component».
Apply to	As shown in Fig. B.13: Class («Decorator–*Component*», «Decorator–Decorator», «Decorator–ConcreteComponent»); Method («Decorator–*operation*», «Decorator–operation»); Interface («Decorator–*Component*»); Association («Decorator–component»).
Type	String.
Expansion	Not applicable.

Figure B.13 Definiton of the UML-F Decorator pattern tags

B.14 Chain of Responsibility (COR) pattern tags

Figure B.14 shows the static structure of the Chain of Responsibility (COR) pattern (Gamma et al., 1995) annotated with UML-F tags. Table B.14 summarizes the COR pattern UML-F tags. COR corresponds to the COR framework construction principle, which is a recursive combination of template and hook methods in which the two methods are unified into a single method. A list (chain) of objects that implement this method is composed, and a request is forwarded through this list to be handled by each object in the chain.

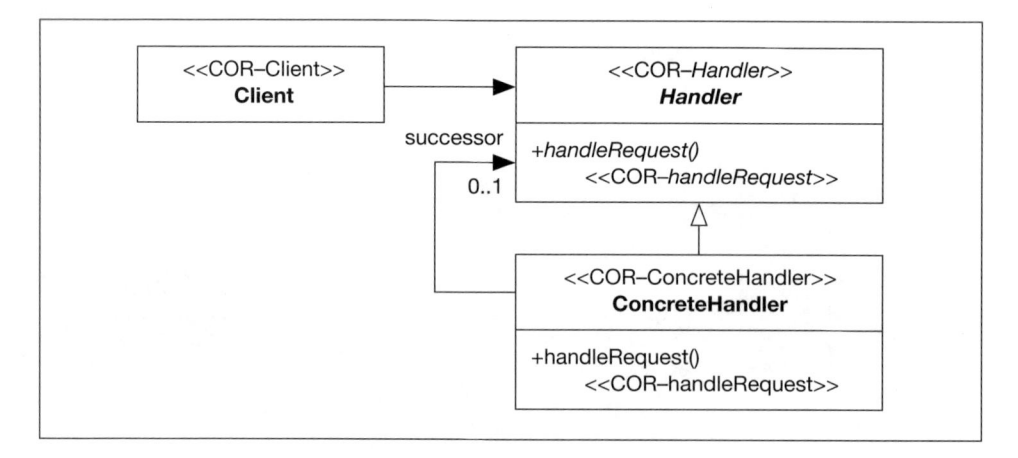

Figure B.14 Structure of the COR pattern annotated with UML-F

Tags	«COR–Client», «COR–Handler», «COR–ConcreteHandler», «COR–handleRequest», «COR–handleRequest», and «COR–successor».
Apply to	As shown in Fig B.14: Class («COR–Client», «COR–Handler», «COR–ConcreteHandler»); Method («COR–handleRequest», «COR–handleRequest»); Association («COR–successor»). Interface («COR-Client»)
Type	String.
Expansion	Not applicable.

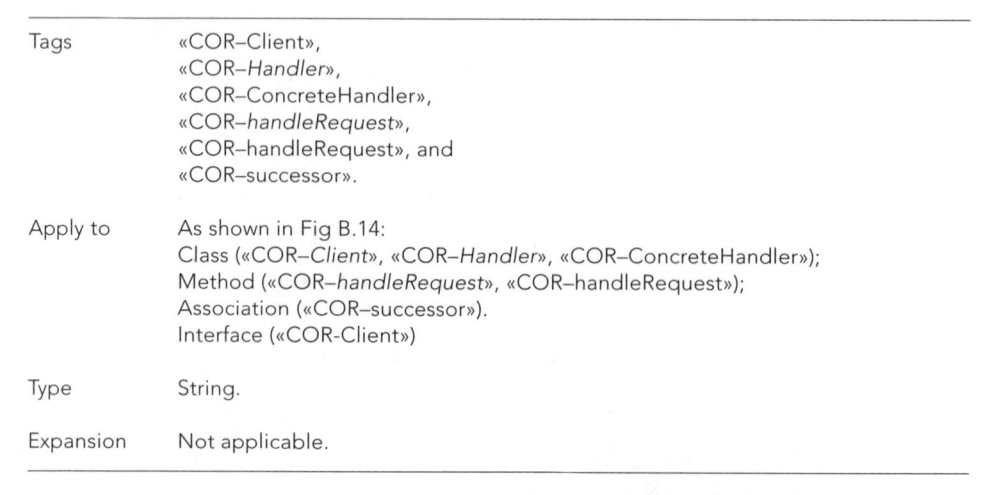

Table B.14 Definition of the UML-F COR pattern tags

Bibliography

Ambler, S., 1998. Process Patterns: Building Large-Scale Systems Using Object Technology. SIGS Books/Cambridge University Press.

Bass, L., Clements, P., Kazman, R., 1998. Software Architecture in Practice. Addison-Wesley.

Beck, K., 1999. eXtreme Programming Explained. Addison-Wesley.

Beck, K., Cunningham, W., 1989. A Laboratory for Object-Oriented Thinking. In: Proceedings of OOPSLA 89, New Orleans, Louisiana.

Beck, K., Gamma, E., 1998a. JUnit: A Cook's Tour (ftp://www.armaties.com/D/home/armaties/ftp/TestingFramework/Junit/).

Beck, K., Gamma, E., 1998b. Test Infected: Programmers Love Writing Tests. Java Report, 3(7).

Beck, K., Fowler, M., 2000. Planning eXtreme Programming. Addison-Wesley.

Bezivin, J., Muller, P. A., 1999. UML '98: Beyond the Notation – First International Workshop, Mulhouse, France, June 3–4. Springer Verlag.

Boehm, B., 1976. Software Engineering. IEEE Transactions on Computer C-25.

Booch, G. 1994. Object-Oriented Analysis and Design with Applications. Addison-Wesley.

Booch, G., Rumbaugh, J., Jacobson, I. 1998, The Unified Modeling Language User Guide. Reading, Massachusetts: Addison-Wesley.

Coleman, D., Arnold, P., Bodoff, S., Dollin, C., Filchrist, H., Haynes, F., Jeremaes, P., 1994. Object-Oriented Development: The Fusion Method, Prentice Hall.

Cook, S., Kleppe, A., Mitchell, R., Rumpe, B., Warmer, J., Wills, A., 1999 Defining UML Family Members Using Prefaces. In: TOOLS 32 Conference Proceedings, Eds Christine Mingins, Bertrand Meyer. IEEE Computer Society.

Coplien, J., 1999. Multi-Paradigm Design for C++. Reading, Massachusetts: Addison-Wesley.

D'Souza, D., Wills, A., 1998. Objects, Components, and Frameworks with UML. Reading, Massachusetts: Addison-Wesley.

Evans, A., Kent, S., Selic, B., 2000. UML 2000 – The Unified Modeling Language, Advancing the Standard. 3rd International Conference, Proceedings, Springer, LNCS 1939.

Fayad, M., Schmidt, D., Johnson, R., 1999a. Building Application Frameworks: Object-Oriented Foundations of Framework Design. Wiley & Sons.

Fayad, M., Johnson, R., 1999b. Domain-Specific Application Frameworks: Frameworks Experience by Industry. Wiley & Sons.

Fayad, M., Schmidt, D., Johnson, R., 1999c. Implementing Application Frameworks: Object-Oriented Frameworks at Work. Wiley & Sons.

Fontoura, M., 1999. A Systematic Approach for Framework Development, Ph.D. Thesis, Computer Science Department, Pontifical Catholic University of Rio de Janeiro, Brazil (available at http://www.almaden.ibm.com/cs/people/fontoura).

Fowler, M., 2000. Refactoring: Improving the Design of Existing Code. Addison Wesley.

France, R., Rumpe, B., 1999. UML '99 – The Unified Modeling Language, Beyond the Standard. 2nd International Conference, Proceedings, Springer, LNCS 1723.

Gamma, E., 1991. Objektorientierte Software-Entwicklung am Beispiel von ET++: Design-Muster, Klassenbibliothek, Werkzeuge. Doctoral Thesis, University of Zürich, 1991. Springer Verlag.

Gamma, E., Helm, R., Johnson, R., Vlissides, J., 1995. Design Patterns—Elements of Reusable Object-Oriented Software. Reading, Massachusetts: Addison-Wesley.

Goldberg, 1984. Smalltalk-80/The Interactive Programming Environment. Addison-Wesley.

Goldberg, A., Rubin, K., 1995. Succeeding with Objects: Decision Frameworks for Project Management. Reading, Massachusetts: Addison-Wesley.

Harel, D., 1987. Statecharts: A Visual Formulation for Complex Systems. Science of Computer Programming 8(3): 231–274.

Henderson-Sellers, B., Barbier, F., 1999. Black and White Diamonds. In: «UML»'99 – The Unified Modeling Language. Conference Proceedings. Eds: R. France, B. Rumpe. Springer Verlag. LNCS 1723.

Henderson-Sellers, B., Edwards, J.M., 1990. The Object-Oriented Systems Life Cycle. In Communications of the ACM, 33(9).

ITU-TS, 1999. Recommendation Z.120 (11/99): MSC 2000. Geneva.

Jacobson, I., 1993. Object-Oriented Software Engineering: A Use Case Driven Approach. Addison-Wesley.

Jacobson, I., Booch, G., Rumbaugh, J., 1998. The Unified Software Development Process. Reading, Massachusetts: Addison-Wesley.

Johnson, R., 1992. Documenting Frameworks Using Patterns. ACM Conference on Object-Oriented Programming, Systems, Languages and Applications, 1992.

Krasner, G., Pope, S., 1988. A Cookbook for Using the Model-View-Controller User Interface Paradigm in Smalltalk-80. Journal of Object-Oriented Programming, **1**(3).

Krüger, I., 2000 Distributed System Design with Message Sequence Charts. Ph.D. Thesis, Munich University of Technology (available at http://www.in.tum.de/~krüger/).

Meyer, B., 1989 The New Culture of Software Development: Reflections on the Practice of Object-Oriented Design. In Proceedings of Tools Œ89, Paris, France.

Meyer, B., 1990 Lessons from the Design of the Eiffel Libraries. Communications of the ACM, 33(9).

Microsoft Inc., 2001. Microsoft Visual C++ User's Guide.

Oestereich, B., 1999. Developing Software with UML. Addison-Wesley.

OMG, 2001. Unified Modeling Language Specification. Version 1.4. April.

Parnas, D.L., 1972. On the Criteria to be Used in Decomposing Systems into Modules. Communications of the ACM, **15**(12).

Parnas, D.L., 1976. On the Design and Development of Program Families. IEEE Transactions on Software Engineering.

Pasetti, A., 2001. Methodology, Design and Implementation of a Software Framework for Embedded Satellite Control Systems. Ph.D. Thesis, University of Constance (available at http://www.SoftwareResearch.net/AOCSFrameworkProject/ProjectHomePage.html)

Pomberger, G., Bischofberger, W., Kolb, D., Pree, W., Schlemm, H., 1991. Prototyping Oriented Software Development, Concepts and Tools. Structured Programming 12(1), Springer.

Powel Douglass, B., 2000. Real-Time UML: Developing Efficient Objects for Embedded Systems, Second Edition, Addison Wesley.

Pree, W., 1995. Design Patterns for Object-Oriented Software Development. Wokingham: Addison-Wesley/ACM Press.

Pree, W., Templ, J., 2000. Personal communications.

Rumbaugh, J., Blaha, M., Premerlani, W., Eddy, F., Lorensen, W., 1994. Object-Oriented Modeling and Design, Prentice Hall, Englewood Cliffs.

Rumbaugh, J., Jacobson, I., Booch, G., 1998. The Unified Modeling Language Reference Manual. Reading, Massachusetts: Addison-Wesley.

Szyperski, C., 1998. Component Software – Beyond Object-Oriented Programming. Addison-Wesley ACM Press

Warmer, J., Kleppe, A., 1999. The Object Constraint Language – Precise Modeling with UML. Addison-Wesley.

Weinand, A., Gamma, E., 1994. ET++ – a Portable, Homogenous Class Library and Application Framework. In Bischofberger, W.R., Frei H.P. (Eds), Computer Science Research at UBILAB, Strategy and Projects; Proceedings of the UBILAB'94 Conference, Zurich, pages 66–92, Universitätsverlag Konstanz, Konstanz, September 1994 (available at http://www.ubilab.org/publications/wei94.html).

Weinand, A., Gamma, E., Marty, R., 1989. Design and Implementation of ET++ – a Seamless Object-Oriented Application Framework. Structured Programming, 10(2), Springer Verlag.

Wirfs-Brock, R.J., Johnson, R.E., 1990. Surveying Current Research in Object-Oriented Design. Communications of the ACM, 33(9).

Index

abstract classes 16, 64, 87–90
abstract coupling 87–8
Abstract Factory pattern, tags for 206–7
abstractions in design process 181–2
aCiRC (abstract Class/interface Responsibility Collaboration) cards 145–8
activation boxes 24
activity diagrams 14
adaptation cases 152, 186–92
adaptation reports 152, 186–7, 193–6
«adapt-dyn» tag 56, 58, 61–2
«adapt-static» tag 54–5, 58–9
aggregation 18
alternatives (in sequence diagrams) 47–8
anonymous inner classes and subclasses 140–1
anonymous objects 20
«anonymous» tag 140
AOCS (Attitude and Orbit Control System) 163–96
architecture of frameworks 7, 113–14
automated tests for Java programs 135–6

Beck, Kent 125, 156

black-box components of frameworks 8–9, 80–1
Bridge pattern, tags for 208
Builder pattern, tags for 209–10

Calculation pattern 106–9
call-back style of programming 6, 67–8
catalog entries, naming of 94
catalog patterns 92–3; *see also* GoF patterns
Chain of Responsibility (COR) pattern 95, 201, 220
class diagrams 14–19, 38–9, 47, 114
class families 151, 157–8, 166, 179–81
class teams 151, 157–8, 169, 179–81
classes, visual representation of 41
cluster cycle model 151–5, 160, 162
collaboration diagrams 14, 24–5
Command pattern, tags for 210–11
comments (in class diagrams) 19
complementary tags 30–1
completeness markers 44–5
completeness tags 40, 198
component diagrams 14–15
'components' and 'component-ware' 5

Composite pattern
  recipe for adaptation of 121–2
  tags for 102–6, 201, 218
composition 18
constraints, concept of 28
control techniques in UML 46–7
Cook S., 4
cookbooks for framework adaptation 10, 113–16
CRC (Class-Responsibility-Collaboration) cards 156, 160, 162
Cunningham, W. 156
CurrencyConverter (case study) 68–74, 77, 79–81, 88, 110–11, 117–18

Decorator pattern, tags for 201, 219
delta (δ) tag 42–4
deployment diagrams 14–15
'design stage' 177
domain experts, role of 162–3, 165, 167
domain-specific tags 106–8, 115
dynamic binding 3
dynamic languages 56

Edwards, J.M. 153
errors as distinct from failures 132
European Space Agency 163
eXtreme Design (XD) 152, 186
eXtreme Programming (XP) 127, 186

Façade pattern 158
Factory Method pattern (case study) 92–3
  tags for, 97–9 204–5
«fixed» tag 54–5, 57–61
framelets 152, 159, 173–83 *passim*
«framework» stereotype 37–8
framework tags 51–63, 95–110, 202
frameworks
  adaptation of 8–9
  building of 6–7
  development costs 10

development process 67, 113, 162
essential construction principles 30, 67–8, 97
flexibility of 160–3
mapping of construction principles 85–6
pros and cons of 9–10
scaling of construction principles 110

Gamma, Erich xi, 65, 92–3, 125, 157–8
generalization 16, 99, 153, 155
  marking of 59–62
  tags for 38
GoF patterns 67, 92–9, 108–10, 140, 167
  tags for 203–20
Goldberg, A. 152
guards (in sequence diagrams) 47
'guided tours' of framework architecture 114

Harel, David 22
Henderson-Sellers, B. 153
hook methods 68–72, 79–80, 91–3, 104, 110–12
«hook» tag 72–7, 200
  definition of 75
horizontal reorganizations 159–60
hot spots 6, 91; *see also* variation points
HTML 148–9
hypertext 115

implementation cases 152, 154, 181–3, 187
  as cookbook recipes 184–5
  for framework specification 183
«implicit» tag 36
information hiding 3
inheritance 3, 6, 16, 112
inheritance indicators 43–4
instantiation of frameworks 187, 190
interface definition and implementation 88–90
Interpreter pattern, tags for 212

Java 3–4, 6, 16, 53, 56, 82, 140
Java interfaces 88–91
Java Swing framework 156–8
Johnson, R.E. 160–1
JUnit testing framework 125–49

lambda (Λ) tag 42–4
lifecycle concept (for software) 153–5
links (to objects) 20–1
«local» stereotype 36

Manager pattern and manageable interfaces 173–7
meta-modeling 31
method adaptation tags 53–6
Meyer, B. 152–5, 165

object-based methodology 3–6, 13, 67–8, 152–3, 178
Object Constraint Language (OCL) 19
object diagrams 15, 19–22
    exemplar nature of 21–2
    UML-F extension of 44–5
Object Management Group (OMG) 4, 11, 13
object-oriented analysis and design (OOAD) 162
object trees 104–6
Observer pattern, tags for 213–14
optional messages (in sequence diagrams) 48

package diagrams 13
«parameter» stereotype 36
Pascal 6
Pasetti, A. 163
Pree, W. 160
prefaces 4
presentation markers (© and '...') 40
presentation tags 30, 38, 42–3, 198–9
product culture 153
profiles, hierarchy of 4–5

project-based culture 153
protocols 87
prototypical objects 19
Protoype pattern, tags for 214–15
public attributes and methods 18

qualitative aspect of framework design 181

recipes for framework adaptations 114–15, 119–22, 133–4, 137–9, 144–6, 184–5
rectangle symbols (for overriding and inheriting of methods) 42–4
referencing (in sequence diagrams) 47–8
repetition (in sequence diagrams) 49
reusable software components 152–3, 155
RoundingPolicy (case study) 79–82, 88, 90, 116–18
Rubin, K. 152

SAP framework 153
satellite systems 164–7, 170–2, 182, 190
Separation principle of framework construction 68, 79–88, 92, 101, 133, 147
    recipe for adaptation of 120–1
    tags for, 83–6, 201
sequence diagrams 14–15, 22–5, 114
    control structures in 46–7
    drawbacks of 45–6
    exemplar nature of 46
    tags for 45–51, 199
    triggered 49
signatures 17, 87–8
State pattern, tags for 216
statechart diagrams 14
stereotypes 28, 31–7
    uses of 32–3
Strategy pattern, tags for 99–102, 217
subsystems (Gamma) 157–8
superclasses 16, 43, 62

tags 27–8, 33–7
    in the context of classes and interfaces 57–8
    in the context of generalization 38, 59–63
    definition of 63–4
    domain-specific 106–8, 115
    for flat and hierarchical representation 41–3
    for framework adaptation 53
    framework-specific 64
    layers of 29–31
    notation for 197–8
    promotion of 62
    purposes of 29
    standard (in UML) 36
    see also complementary tags; completeness tags; framework tags; method adaptation tags; presentation tags; unification tags
telemetry 170–2, 176–9, 190–1, 195
template methods 68–72 passim, 92, 105, 110–12
«template» tag 72–4, 200, 205–6
    definition of 76
test cases (in JUnit framework) 127, 129–30, 134
    definition in one source code file 140–4
    recipe for definition of 137–9
test results (in JUnit framework) 128
    reporting of 147–8
test suites (in JUnit framework) 128, 130–1, 134
    adaptation of 146–8
    recipe for composition of 144–6
top-down system development 153
trigger (in sequence diagrams) 49
«type» tag 37

UML
    extensions to 4
    notation of 13–15
UML-F 4–5, 27–8
    extensions of object diagram notation 44–5
    goals of 11
    mechanism for introducing new tags 63–5
    outlook for 196
    properties of profile 28–31
    support for development and adaptation 10
    unifying stereotypes and tagged values 31–4
UML-RT 4
underspecification principle 28–9
Unification principle of framework construction 68–78, 80, 84, 92, 98
    recipe for adaptation of 119–20
    tags for, 77–8, 210
Unified Process 152
use case diagrams 15
use cases 182–3
«utility» tag 52

variation point cards 160–3
variation points 6, 91, 114, 178, 181
    in ACOS framework 166–72
vertical reorganizations 158–9
views (of model) 39–40
visibility markers 18

Weinand, A. 111
white-box components of frameworks 7–8, 68
Wirfs-Brock, R.J. 160–1
wizards 123